THE NEW GROVE®

Twentieth-century American Masters

IVES   THOMSON   SESSIONS
COWELL   GERSHWIN   COPLAND
CARTER   BARBER   CAGE
BERNSTEIN

John Kirkpatrick   Richard Crawford
Richard Jackson   Wayne Schneider
John Harbison   William W. Austin
Andrea Olmstead   Bayan Northcott
Bruce Saylor   Barbara Heyman
William Lichtenwanger   Charles Hamm
                Joan Peyser

W. W. NORTON & COMPANY
NEW YORK   LONDON

First published in
The New Grove® Dictionary of American Music,
edited by H. Wiley Hitchcock and Stanley Sadie, 1986
and
The New Grove Dictionary of Music and Musicians®,
edited by Stanley Sadie, 1980

The New Grove and *The New Grove Dictionary of Music and Musicians*
are registered trademarks of Macmillan Publishers Limited, London

First published in UK in paperback with additions 1988 by
PAPERMAC
a division of Macmillan Publishers Limited
London and Basingstoke

First published in UK in hardback with additions 1988 by
MACMILLAN LONDON LIMITED
4 Little Essex Street London WC2R 3LF
and Basingstoke

British Library Cataloguing in Publication Data

The New Grove twentieth-century American
masters.——(The New Grove biography series)
1. Composers——United States——Biography
I. Kirkpatrick, John, *1905*–
780'.92'2 ML390

ISBN 0-333-45777-3 (hardback)
ISBN 0-333-45778-1 (paperback)

First American edition in book form with additions 1988 by
W. W. NORTON & COMPANY
500 Fifth Avenue, New York NY 10110

ISBN 0-393-30100-1 (hardback)
ISBN 0-393-01696-X (paperback)

Printed in Hong Kong

Contents

List of Illustrations

Illustration acknowledgments

We are grateful to the following for permission to reproduce copyright illustrative material: John Kirkpatrick, New Haven, CT (fig.1); Music Library, Yale University (Charles Ives Archives), New Haven, CT/Associated Music Publishers, Inc., and G. Schirmer, Inc., New York (fig.2); Music Library, Yale University (Charles Ives Archives), New Haven, CT/photo Frank Gerratana (fig.3); photo Christopher Fox (fig.4); Bettmann Archive, Inc., New York (fig.5); Boosey & Hawkes Music Publishers Ltd., London (figs.6,13); Music Library, University of California, Berkeley/Merion Music, Inc., Bryn Mawr, PA (© 1974) (fig.7); Associated Music Publishers, Inc., New York (figs.8,16); Music Division, Library of Congress, Washington, DC/Breitkopf & Härtel, Wiesbaden (fig.9); Music Division, Library of Congress, Washington, DC/Associated Music Publishers, Inc., New York (figs.10, 17,cover); Theatre Collection, Museum of the City of New York, New York (fig.11,cover); Bodleian Library (Harding Collection), Oxford/Chappell Music Ltd., London, and International Music Publications, and Chappell & Co., Inc., New York (fig.12); Music Division, Library of Congress (Elizabeth Sprague Coolidge Foundation Collection), Washington, DC (fig.14); Aaron Copland (© 1968) and Boosey & Hawkes, Inc., New York (fig.15); World Inc., New York/photo *Saturday Review* (fig.18); Music Division, Library of Congress, Washington, DC/G. Schirmer, Inc., New York (fig.19); Peters Edition Ltd., London/photo James Klosty, Millbrook, New York (fig.20); Performing Artservices, Inc., New York/ photo Remy Charlip (fig.21); Henmar Press, Inc., New York (© 1960), reproduced by permission of Peters Edition Ltd., London (fig.22,cover); Music Division, Library of Congress, Washington, DC/Leonard Bernstein and Stephen Sondheim, G. Schirmer, Inc., and Chappell Music, New York (fig.23); Curtis Institute of Music, Philadelphia (fig.24, cover).

Music example acknowledgments

We are grateful to the following music publishers for permission to reproduce copyright material:

Gershwin   *1* © 1937 Gershwin Publishing Corp., renewed, assigned to Chappel & Co., Inc., New York, and Chappell Music Ltd., London; *2* © 1924, renewed, WB Music Corp., Los Angeles, and Chappell Music Ltd., London; *3* © 1924, renewed, WB Music Corp., Los Angeles, and Chappell Music Ltd., London; *4* © 1927, renewed, WB Music Corp., Los Angeles, and Chappell Music Ltd., London; *5* 1935 Gershwin Publishing Corp., renewed, assigned to Chappell & Co., Inc., New York, and Chappell Music Ltd., London.

Copland   *1* Aaron Copland (© 1945) and Boosey & Hawkes, Inc., New York.

Bibliographical Abbreviations

ACAB	*American Composers Alliance Bulletin*
CBY	*Current Biography Yearbook*
CMc	*Current Musicology*
EwenD	D. Ewen: *American Composers: a Biographical Dictionary* (New York, 1982)
HiFi	*High Fidelity*
HiFi/MusAm	*High Fidelity/Musical America*
IMSCR	*International Musicological Society Congress Report*
IRASM	*International Review of the Aesthetics and Sociology of Music*
ISAMm	Institute for Studies in American Music, monograph
ITO	*In Theory Only*
JAMS	*Journal of the American Musicological Society*
MEJ	*Music Educators Journal*
Mf	*Die Musikforschung*
MJ	*Music Journal*
ML	*Music and Letters*
MM	*Modern Music*
MMR	*The Monthly Musical Record*
MO	*Musical Opinion*
MQ	*The Musical Quarterly*
MR	*The Music Review*
MT	*The Musical Times*
MTNAP	*Music Teachers National Association: Proceedings*
MusAm	*Musical America*
NRMI	*Nuova rivista musicale italiana*
NZM	*Neue Zeitschrift für Musik*
PNM	*Perspectives of New Music*
PRMA	*Proceedings of the Royal Musical Association*
ReM	*La revue musicale*

General Abbreviations

A	alto, contralto [voice]	ed.	editor, edited (by)
a	alto [instrument]	edn	edition
ACA	American Composers Alliance	elec	electric, electronic
acc.	accompaniment, accompanied (by)	eng hn	english horn
amp	amplified	ens	ensemble
appx	appendix	fl	flute
arr.	arrangement, arranged (by/for)	Gk.	Greek
ASCAP	American Society of Composers, Authors and Publishers	glock	glockenspiel
aut.	autumn	gui	guitar
B	bass [voice]	Heb.	Hebrew
b	bass [instrument]	hn	horn
Bar	baritone [voice]	hpd	harpsichord
BBC	British Broadcasting Corporation	inc.	incomplete
BMI	Broadcast Music, Inc.	incl.	includes, including
bn	bassoon	inst	instrument, instrumental
c	circa (Lat.: about)	IRCAM	Institut de Recherche et de Coordination Acoustique/Musique (France)
cb	contrabass [instrument]	ISAM	Institute for Studies in American Music
cbn	contrabassoon	ISCM	International Society for Contemporary Music
cel	celesta	Jap.	Japanese
cl	clarinet	kbd	keyboard
collab.	(in) collaboration (with)	mar	marimba
conc.	concerto	Mez	mezzo-soprano
cond.	conductor, conducted (by)	movt	movement
cptr	computer	MS	manuscript
db	double bass	MSS	manuscripts
ded.	dedication, dedicated (to)	NBC	National Broadcasting Company
dir.	director, directed (by)	n.p.	no place (of publication)
diss.	dissertation		

ob	oboe	ser.	series
obbl	obbligato	SO	Symphony Orchestra
op.	opus (Lat.: work)	spr.	spring
opt.	optional	str	string(s)
orch	orchestra, orchestral	sum.	summer
orchd	orchestrated (by)	sym.	symphony, symphonic
org	organ	synth	synthesizer, synthesized
orig.	original(ly)		
ov.	overture	T	tenor [voice]
		t	tenor [instrument]
perc	percussion	timp	timpani
perf.	performance, performed (by)	tpt	trumpet
pf	piano(forte)	Tr	treble [voice]
pfmr	performer	tr	treble [instrument]
pic	piccolo	trad.	traditional
PO	Philharmonic Orchestra	trans.	translation, translated (by)
posth.	posthumous(ly)	transcr.	transcription, transcribed (by/for)
prol.	prologue		
Ps.	Psalm	trbn	trombone
pseud.	pseudonym	U.	University
Pss.	Psalms	UCLA	University of California, Los Angeles
pt	part		
pubd	published (by)	UNESCO	United Nations Educational, Scientific and Cultural Organization
pubn	publication		
qnt	quintet		
qt	quartet	v	voice
		va	viola
R	photographic reprint	vc	(violon)cello
RAI	Radio Audizioni Italiane (Italy)	vib	vibraphone
		vn	violin
RCA	Radio Corporation of America; RCA Corporation	vol.	volume
		vs	vocal score, piano-vocal score
rec	recorder		
red.	reduction, reduced (for)	vv	voices
repr.	reprinted	vv.	verses
rev.	revision, revised (by)		
RO	Radio Orchestra	win.	winter
		ww	woodwind
S	soprano [voice]		
s	soprano [instrument]	xyl	xylophone

Preface

This volume, based on entries in *The New Grove Dictionary of American Music* (edited by H. Wiley Hitchcock and myself; New York and London, 1986), follows up the series of short biographies derived from *The New Grove Dictionary of Music and Musicians* (London, 1980). The texts were written between 1972 and 1982, and finalized in 1985. For this reprint, they have been reread, checked, and where necessary supplemented by their original authors; the bibliographies have also been updated.

The fact that the texts of the books in this series originated as dictionary articles inevitably gives them a character somewhat different from that of books conceived as such. They are designed, first of all, to accommodate a very great deal of information in a manner that makes reference quick and easy. Their main concern is with fact rather than opinion, and this leads to a larger than usual proportion of the texts being devoted to biography than to critical discussion. The nature of a reference work gives it a particular obligation to convey received knowledge and to treat of composers' lives and works in an encyclopedic fashion, with proper acknowledgment of sources and due care to reflect different standpoints, rather than to embody imaginative or speculative writing about a composer's character or his music. It is hoped that the comprehensive work-lists and extended bibliographies, indicative of the origins of the books in a reference work, will be valuable to the reader who is eager for full and accurate reference information and who may not have ready access to the parent publications or who may prefer to have it in this more compact form.

S.S.

CHARLES IVES

John Kirkpatrick

CHAPTER ONE

Charles Ives

1. UP TO 1899. Charles Edward Ives was the son of George E. Ives (1845–94), a versatile bandmaster whose parents were transcendentalists (according to family tradition Emerson was their guest when he lectured at Danbury in 1859), and Mary Elizabeth Parmelee (1849–1929), whose mother was a choir singer of local prominence; he was born in Danbury, Connecticut, on 20 October 1874.

Ives's father, well grounded in Bach and counterpoint by Carl Foeppl, was the youngest bandmaster in the Union Army (General Grant remarked to Lincoln "it's the best band in the army, they tell me"). After the Civil War he taught theory and many instruments, and trained and led choirs, orchestras, and bands in Danbury and other towns. Although not a composer, he had great curiosity and original ideas about ear training, polytonality, microtones, acoustics, and spatial relations in performance. He had a way with children and shared many of the enthusiasms of his boys, "Charlie" and J. Moss (1876–1939, who became a lawyer and judge). Years later Ives recalled:

he thought that man as a rule didn't use the faculties that the Creator had given him hard enough . . . he would have us sing a tune in E♭, but play the accompaniment in C . . . he made us stick to the end, and not stop when it got hard . . . [There was] something about the way Father played hymns . . . the music meant more than when people sang the words . . . At the outdoor Camp Meeting services . . . Father, who led the singing sometimes with his cornet . . . would always encourage the people to sing their own way . . . the fervor would at times throw the key higher . . . Father had a sliding cornet made, so that he could rise with them and not keep them down.

Ives was equally well grounded by his father not only in Bach but in all types of music dear to an American town, outdoors, indoors, or in church – also in free experiment. He adopted and devoured his father's old copybook, filling the still-blank pages with sketches including "fugues in four keys" (two in C–G–D–A and one in C–F–B♭–E♭, the *Song for Harvest Season*), which show the polytonal basis of much of his later dissonance. By the age of 12 he was composing and playing drums in his father's band, and at 14 he was the youngest salaried church organist in the state. While practicing drum rhythms on the piano, he worked out a variety of dissonant chords for what he called "piano-drumming" (described in *Memos*). Talented also in athletics, he captained various baseball and football teams and played a lot of tennis.

As a boy he was already paradoxical, being remembered as irascible or very quiet, a normal athlete or pathologically shy, an Emersonian visionary but a hymn-singing enthusiast for "the old-time religion." And in his music the marches, sentimental songs, and well-behaved anthems jostled with take-offs and with the polytonal interludes in his organ variations on *America*, and with hymn interludes like the one in the Cowells' book (1955, p.35; "manuals *ppp*"). He was so talented that his father hoped he would become a famous pianist, but he was much too shy for a life of solo performing. His earliest known piece, *Slow March*, uses musical quotation, a habit that stayed with him as long as he composed. At first it was the way a march might bring in a well-known tune. Later it was the whole remembered world of his boyhood, a shared vocabulary he could use clearly or subtly, aspiring ideally to be a voicing, as by humanity at large, of the Emersonian "Over-Soul."

With his variety of interests he spread himself thin and was never a brilliant scholar. In 1891 he went from a public school to the newly organized Danbury Academy; he continued as organ-

1. *Charles Ives (left) and Franklin Hobart Miles, battery of the Hopkins Grammar School baseball team, 1894*

3

ist of the Danbury Baptist Church when, early in 1893, he moved to Hopkins Grammar School, New Haven (fig. 1). From 7 May he was organist at St. Thomas Episcopal Church, New Haven, whose English choir director Charles Bonney, who had interesting ideas on naturalness in singing, was a stickler for pointing the psalms. While Ives was at Hopkins, his father came from Danbury for Paderewski's recital, during which he whispered "Why does he have to make Chopin more effeminate than he already is!" On 31 March 1894 Ives saw *Götterdämmerung* in New York (reacting more from than to it), and on 3 April he pitched a game in which Hopkins beat the Yale freshmen (the Hopkins *Critic* reported: "Ives is a little apt to be wild, but he plays coolly and is very quick at catching men napping at bases").

It was probably his experience of chanted psalms that prompted the series of settings (possibly composed during the summer of 1894) that are the major achievement of his early years. They are like Emerson's *Self-Reliance* come to life, or like a clairvoyant vision of Old Testament exaltation seen in the violent context of ancient life and death. In *Memos* he wrote of "psalms that Father let me work over, and some he tried in the choirs but had a hard time – the 150th Psalm was one, part of the 90th, and the 67th (this he thought the best for singing for church) – also 54th, and 24th also?" Each explores different ideas: the 150th, parallel triads in close dissonance and pandiatonic fugato; the 67th, polytonality; the 54th, whole-tone triads and dissonant chordal canon; the 24th, free mirrors radiating from a stable center. The early version of the 90th is lost. The other psalms were later.

All four years at Yale (1894–8) Ives had the same room, roommate, and organist job at Center Church. In 1894 John Cornelius Griggs (Yale, class of 1889) became choirmaster at Center Church and Horatio Parker the new professor of music. Ives probably showed Parker his setting of Psalm lxvii, only to learn that such music would have to go underground. When Ives told his father that Parker wanted him to resolve a certain 9th, he said: "Tell Parker that every dissonance doesn't have to resolve, if it doesn't happen to feel like it, any more than every horse should have to have its tail bobbed just because it's the prevailing fashion."

On 4 November 1894 his father suddenly died (later Ives wrote of "that awful vacuum"). For over ten years they had made a two-man team in musical experiment, so that it has even been said that Charles wrote his father's music. Griggs came closest to filling the void. With his big heart and fine ear (disliking equal temperament), he was always sympathetic to Ives's music and, even when he could hardly understand it, felt and respected its integrity.

Ives so idealized his father that he was somewhat ungrateful to Parker, especially considering that by Yale rules he could take music courses only as an upperclassman, and that Parker was therefore at first giving him extra-curricular time. In *Memos* he recalled repeating the same things in the same textbook, but the manuscripts show that the counterpoints and canons he did for Parker were at a more demanding level than those for his father. There are two routine organ fugues in C minor and in E♭ (which Ives later described as "a stupid fugue and a stupid subject"); two lively ones in B♭ and D for string quartet unfortunately are incomplete. Even though Parker had no ear for Ives's bent, still the First Symphony's controlled mastery, which he owed to Parker, remained a solid foundation of his growth.

At Yale he took no part in competitive athletics – his father had forbidden it, knowing how precarious his grades would be. The track coach said it was a crying shame that Charlie Ives spent so much time on music – he could have been a first-rate sprinter.

One of Parker's habitual assignments was resetting famous song texts. Ives had already done this in various hymn-anthems and in the *Minnelied* (cf Brahms). At Yale he reset 12 German and two French texts, and more in the next few years. Most of them he readjusted later to English texts or words of his own (he had already done this too) – there are 16 such "doubles" and four "triples." In some the music is hardly changed, in others (like *Rough Wind*) quite different. Generally the first words fit the music best. Chadwick thought Ives's *Feldeinsamkeit* "almost as good as Brahms."

Ives continued to experiment with hymn quotation and polytonal dissonance, as in the First String Quartet (whose opening fugue went into the Fourth Symphony), the "fugue in four keys" on *The Shining Shore*, the organ pieces he later combined as *Thanksgiving*, the prelude on *Adeste fideles*, and the *Yale–Princeton Football Game* with its direct picturing of noisy crowds, songs and cheers, end runs, wedge formations, and the referee's whistle.

As at Danbury he kept his freest experiments pretty much to himself, finding that, at Yale as well, most of his contemporaries were musically just as stodgy as the old folks, the main difference being that he no longer had his father to show things to. But with his friendly nature, this appearance of conformity was not entirely insincere. In August 1896 he spent a week in the Adirondacks with the family of his classmate David Twichell. Ives had heard David's father preach, but never dreamed they would become his in-laws. They all liked him. He was always well liked, and was elected to proper student societies. At commencement (June 1898) he was chairman of the Ivy Committee. With all his composing – over 40 songs, various marches, overtures, anthems, and organ pieces, the quartet, and the symphony – his academic average of D+ at Yale is quite understandable. One of his classmates recalled they were surprised when he graduated: "he took his studies lightly." To most of them he was still the composer of *The Bells of Yale*, a pleasant waltz the glee club sang. Fully aware of the gulf between his real musical aims and the general climate, he had weighed the folly of trying music as a livelihood. Providentially his father's cousin, Granville White, was medical examiner for the Mutual Insurance Co., where he was welcomed into the actuarial department. Some Yale men in medical studies had banded together in common lodgings at 317 West 58th Street, New York, which they called "Poverty Flat." It was less exclusively medical by the time Ives and two classmates (and later David Twichell) joined the group.

2. 1899–1910. It was soon clear that Ives was not a born actuary, though he remained grateful for this first-hand experience in the fundamentals of insurance. Early in 1899 he was transferred to Mutual's agency, Charles H. Raymond & Co., his first assignment being to stand in for a young applications clerk named Julian Myrick (1880–1969). When Myrick returned from vacation, Ives was sent to work directly with the agents, developing ways of presenting the idea of insurance. This was a perfect challenge to his creative imagination and transcendentalist humanitarianism. Right from the start he and Myrick worked together, Myrick's common sense and social ease balancing Ives's mercurial inventiveness and frequent shyness. Together they prospered.

At the same time Ives was leading his double life, composing at night and on weekends – what Poverty Flat called "resident disturbances." From 1898 to 1900 he was organist at the First Presbyterian Church, Bloomfield, New Jersey, thereafter at Central Presbyterian Church, New York (then at Broadway and 57th Street). In autumn 1901 Ives and his friends moved half of Poverty Flat up to 65 Central Park West where he finished the Second Symphony, the so-called "Pre-First Violin Sonata," the lost clarinet trio, etc., and *From the Steeples and the Mountains* (perhaps started on New Year's eve 1901 – the sketch has "Ring out, wild bells" and at the end "Amen"). This last work was the most drastic aural challenge he had yet posed, and strains the credibility of his later remark: "I've never written anything I couldn't hear" (probably true).

On 18 April 1902 his seven-movement cantata *The Celestial Country* was given at the church. It was tame Ives, and was reviewed favorably. The next month he resigned, but stayed on until 1 June, when he generously but naively left all his best anthems and organ music in the choir library (when the church moved in 1915 all these manuscripts were thrown out; many of his anthems are now known only from sketches and lack organ parts, and little of his organ music survives).

With his Sundays free, his music became more preponderantly experimental (in *Memos* he told of writing the opening theme of the First Violin Sonata on his first free Sunday). The change was gradual. *Walking* (1900–?02) was based on an old anthem, the Third Symphony and *Thanksgiving* on old organ pieces, and the lost *Orchard House Overture* on hymns (all 1904).

In 1905 he again met Harmony Twichell (1876–1969), known as "the most beautiful girl in Hartford," at that time a registered nurse. Their courtship was long. This love stabilized in him a new self-confidence, exploding a whole world of far-out music: first the *Three-page Sonata* (1905), starting with the motif B–A–C–H), then in 1906 the *Set for Theatre Orchestra*, *Over the Pavements*, *Set no.1*, *Hallowe'en*, two pieces called *Largo risoluto*, *All the Way Around and Back* ("foul ball – and the base runner on 3rd has to go all the way back to 1st"), and his most famous piece, originally titled "I. A Contemplation of a Serious Matter or The Unanswered Perennial Question. II. A Contemplation of Nothing Serious or Central Park in the Dark in the Good Old Summer Time." This two-movement work (perhaps an "anti-symphony") may be his most original brainstorm: two orchestras proceed as if unaware of each other (in the first piece, tonal background, atonal foreground, in the second, atonal background, tunes in the foreground), requiring two conductors who never synchronize (as required later in parts of the Fourth Symphony). Counterbalancing these (as his church music formerly had) was a whole series of songs he hoped Harmony would sing and her family would like, eventually including their collaborations. The first was Harmony's thinly disguised confession *The World's Highway* (the only one she learned to sing).

Late in 1906 Ives's heart began to give concern, and Mutual's medical department suggested a vacation. He and Myrick spent Christmas week at Old Point Comfort, Virginia, and while there they talked about starting their own business. They knew the president of Washington Life, who established them as its agency, called Ives & Co. They started out with such high ideals that fiasco was predicted, but soon they were ahead of all competitors.

In 1907 Ives sketched an *Emerson Overture* or concerto ("the orchestra was the world and people hearing, and the piano was Emerson"). It had "centrifugal cadenzas" (Emerson's essays radiate from a center), but no score was ever finished, and the sketch is now incomplete. The cadenzas became the Studies for piano.

Ives and Harmony Twichell were married by her father at Hartford on 9 June 1908, and spent two weeks hiking in the Berkshires. That autumn Washington Life sold out to Pittsburgh Life which did no business in New York, thereby discontinuing Ives & Co. But their old friends set them up as Mutual's agency, now called Ives & Myrick, as of 1 January 1909. Soon they had started a training school for agents for which Ives wrote various pamphlets, among which *The Amount to Carry* is still used. In volume of business they led the whole country.

In April 1909 Harmony was ill and in the hospital. Her mother wrote in May about "Charley with his great loving heart" and "the revelations of tenderness in him through the great trial that has come to you." That year he finished *Washington's Birthday* and the First Piano Sonata (he once told of "the boy" off on his own in the ragtimes, "the old folks" anxious at home in the middle movement). All this time he had had no performances since his years as church organist. A friend arranged for Walter Damrosch to try an informal reading of the First Symphony in March 1910. He started the second movement, charmed, but when it went into two against three it was considered too difficult: the young man should make up his mind. Next month Twichell's old friend Mark Twain died, and the night after his funeral Mrs. Twichell died very unexpectedly (Harmony's *Mists* is an elegy for her mother).

In May 1910 Halley's comet was at its peak. Although it had not been the star of Bethlehem, to a devout imagination it would evoke "that glory-beaming star" of the hymn *Watchman* (already quoted in the First Violin Sonata of 1902–8). This was probably the origin of the Fourth Symphony, begun in August.

3. 1911–20. In 1911 the Iveses moved out of New York to Hartsdale, where he started *The Fourth of July*. That August he had the idea of a *Concord Sonata* for piano – recomposing the *Emerson Overture* into a sonata movement (glorifying the adventurer into the unknown), some *Hawthorne* sketches into an extravagant fantasy (a visionary blur of the real and unreal), the *Orchard House Overture* into a family group of *The Alcotts* (like an exalted daguerreotype), and some *Thoreau* sketches into "an autumn day of Indian summer at Walden Pond" (a strangely inner intensity) – the whole recomposition being "one person's impression of the spirit of transcendentalism." He played it all for a friend in 1912, still improvising a few details. Also in 1912 he finished the *Robert Browning Overture* (later he disliked it because the old devices of inversion etc. were too obvious), and virtually finished the *First Orchestral Set: Three Places in New England*, one of his most endearing works (a meditation on Foster's *Old Black Joe*, a martial dream of jaunty tunes, an impression of hearing a hymn

10

from a church across the river), also *Decoration Day* (first composed for violin and piano – but it is uncertain just when Ives was imagining the *Holidays* as a "third piano sonata" or a "fifth violin sonata"). During one of the Hartsdale summers he heard a sermon contrasting Christian faith and stoic pessimism, and composed *Two Slants* that afternoon.

In July 1912 he bought part of a farm in West Redding, Connecticut, with a beautiful view of the hills towards Danbury. He and his wife designed the house themselves; the cellar was "almost finished in December." The red barn was built like the old ones. In May they spent a week in Danbury, going to Redding every day to plant potatoes. They finally settled in for the whole of September and he finished *The Fourth of July* and the Second String Quartet, subtitled: "S.Q. for 4 men – who converse, discuss, argue, fight, shake hands, shut up – then walk up the mountainside to view the firmament," to a final burst of *Bethany* ("Nearer, my God, to thee") and the *Westminster Chimes* (which became the nucleus of the end of the Fourth Symphony).

The January 1914 issue of *The Independent* reviewed Vachel Lindsay's *General Booth . . . and other Poems*, reprinting 32 lines; these made a perfect song text which Ives used for his greatest song. That autumn, wanting to finish his Third Violin Sonata, but not before he had tried the first one with a reputable violinist, he invited Franz Milcke (Seidl's former concertmaster), whom Harmony had met in Hartford, to Redding. The mutual frustration of the encounter is described in *Memos*; one result was that the sonata was tamed down. Ives thought it "a weak sister," but actually its plain vocabulary reveals his musical character all the more clearly.

Outraged at the German invasion of Belgium, he sketched a short unison chorus, *Sneak Thief*. In two other choruses, *Majority* (1914–15) and *On the Antipodes* (1915–23), he set poems of his own that were in a form derived from antiphonal psalmody. In

11

November 1914 the Iveses moved back to New York, where they spent the rest of their winters, going to Redding usually in May and staying into November. The sinking of the *Lusitania* off Ireland on 7 May 1915 was responsible for a curious incident in New York: late in the day an organ-grinder under a downtown "elevated" station was playing *In the Sweet Bye and Bye*, and everyone on the station platform above sang it; this sparked off the third movement of the *Second Orchestral Set* (as told in *Memos*).

The Iveses were so happy at Redding that in 1915 they started (through the Fresh Air Fund) to invite families for a month in the little cottage by the road. When the second family left, their baby seemed to need more country air, so the Iveses kept her and eventually adopted her as Edith Osborne Ives (1914–56); she was a great joy to them. That autumn in the Adirondacks Ives imagined a spatial composition for two or more orchestras to be called *The Earth and the Firmament* or *Universe Symphony*. It was to be in three movements:

a striving to present – to contemplate in tones rather than in music as such . . . to paint the creation, the mysterious beginnings of all things, known through God to man, to trace with tonal imprints the vastness, the evolution of all life . . . from the great roots of life to the spiritual eternities, from the great inknown to the great unknown.

He worked at it off and on until 1928, but never finished it; half the sketches are now missing.

In 1916 Ives finished the Fourth Symphony (fig. 2), a roundly integrated synthesis of his music, ideas, and aims. In a prelude the Star poses the question (of existence? of the Incarnation?) and humanity asks the Watchman. Three answers are heard: comic (chaotically mundane and busily picturesque), traditionally religious (an orderly fugue), and universally religious (a meditation on *Bethany* and other hymns). It combines elements from 14 earlier works. In autumn 1916 he finished from sketches of 1905–6 a violin sonata (his fourth) with an easy violin part for

12

his nephew Moss White Ives. The first movement incorporates a student fugue by his father.

The USA finally declared war against Germany on Good Friday 6 April 1917. It may have been during Easter weekend that Ives set *In Flanders Fields* by John McCrae (late medical examiner for Mutual in Canada) for a convention of insurance men around 15 April. It was followed by *He is there!* in May and by *Tom Sails Away* in September. On 22 May David Talmadge (Moss White's violin teacher) and Stuart Ross played the Third Violin Sonata for an invited audience at Carnegie Chamber Music Hall.

Ives was getting more deeply involved in the Red Cross and Liberty Loan drives. In 1918 he tried to enlist as an ambulance driver. At the end of September, in a meeting discussing Liberty Bonds, Ives argued for small bonds to permit support from people at large. The chairman thought them too trivial to bother with. Ives gained his point ("Baby Bonds" were the result), but that night had a severe heart attack and was out of business for a year. His health collapsed and his future uncertain, he started as soon as he could to put some of his hastily sketched music in order. The Iveses spent two winter months at Asheville, North Carolina, where he made clear ink copies of *Concord* and finished the *Essays Before a Sonata* (both privately printed in 1920), and started a *Third Orchestral Set* (unfinished). Then he put his songs and potential songs in order (adding almost 20 new ones, 1919–21) in the book of *114 Songs* (privately printed, 1922). These printings he sent free to many musicians who he hoped would be interested. Reactions varied all the way from wastebaskets to the lectures and articles of Henry Bellamann, who in 1921 recognized *Concord* as "an essay of lofty thought and feeling . . . elevating and greatly beautiful" (later Ives set two poems of Bellamann). The most valuable critique of the *Essays* (which with the "Postface" to the book of songs and other essays was reprinted in 1962 as *Essays Before a Sonata and Other Writings,* ed. H. Boatwright) is by Griggs (*Memos*).

13

2. Excerpt from the autograph MS of the fourth movement (1911–16) of Ives's Fourth Symphony

4. 1920–54. The 1920 election made Ives feel that the majority voter had rejected Wilson's idealism and the horizon of world peace offered by the League of Nations. He must have sketched *An Election* in the heat of anger. In autumn 1923 the French pianist E. Robert Schmitz came to Ives & Myrick in search of insurance and made a lifelong musical friend, perhaps encouraging Ives to finish his quarter-tone pieces (1923–4). At this time Ives started to reconstruct the lost setting of Psalm xc, but one can see from the two pages of the way it was coming back to him that he must have thought it unworthy of the sublime text, so he recomposed it using the same themes, but exploring the alternation of a few contrasting harmonic idioms. Mrs. Ives recalled his saying that it was the only one of his works that he was satisfied with. The Iveses spent six weeks in England during summer 1924.

The few pieces he started after that gave him little confidence, the last being the song with violin obbligato *Sunrise* (August 1926). That autumn he bought a house at 164 East 74th Street in New York, but shortly after they moved in (as Mrs. Ives told later) "he came downstairs one day with tears in his eyes and said he couldn't seem to compose any more – nothing went well – nothing sounded right." His creative flair was exhausted from his double life, and never recovered. From this time on his musical activities consisted of revising and finishing earlier works, and indulging his habitual generosity, whose extent will never be known.

By then Ives's music was beginning to awaken enthusiasm and receive performance. His old friend Clifton Furness was teaching at Horace Mann School in New York and brought him one of the students, Elliott Carter. Schmitz engineered performances of the quarter-tone pieces in 1925 and of parts of the Fourth Symphony in 1927 (with program notes by Bellamann; the second movement was printed in Henry Cowell's *New Music* in

1929). Furness and Oscar Ziegler were playing *The Alcotts*, Anton Rovinsky *The Celestial Railroad*, Keith Corelli *Emerson*. Ives's health was having its ups and downs, and he finally retired from business on 1 January 1930.

Cowell urged Nicolas Slonimsky to do some Ives with his Boston Chamber Orchestra. He performed *Three Places in New England* in the USA, Havana, and Paris in 1931, and *The Fourth of July* in Paris, Berlin, and Budapest in 1932. In answer to many inquiries Ives wrote and dictated *Memos* from March to May 1932 (ed. J. Kirkpatrick, 1972), then spent over a year in Europe. Between sightseeing, their longer stops were at London, Edinburgh, Berlin (with Cowell, Adolph Weiss, and Mary Bell), Paris, Interlaken, winter at Taormina (where he copied the full score of *Thanksgiving*), Rome, Florence, Venice, and London again; they returned home in July 1933.

The performance by Hubert Linscott and Aaron Copland of seven songs at the first Yaddo festival (1 May 1932) had opened the ears of all present, and sparked off many other performances. A whole group of young composers made Ives their patron saint. The Iveses returned to England and Scotland briefly in 1934 and 1938. Cataracts were successfully removed from his eyes in 1937. Lawrence Gilman's review of John Kirkpatrick's performance of *Concord* in 1939 ("the greatest music by an American") made Ives respectable even for theses and dissertations. The Pulitzer Prize in 1947 (after Lou Harrison's performance of the Third Symphony in 1946) further strengthened his reputation, and the Cowells started their biography. Edith's happy marriage to George Tyler had given them a grandson.

From 1948 Carl and Charlotte Ruggles spent each winter in New York, and found much joy in seeing the Iveses; Carl told how once Ives took the *Robert Browning Overture* and threw it across the room – "no damn good." Another time, in a burst of enthusiasm for David Wallace Reeves's *Second Connecticut March*

3. Charles Ives

(the one that ends *Decoration Day*), they started shouting the tune and marching around the dining-room table (Charlotte later recalled "those two *boys* – and there sat Harmony, perfectly serene, just as if nothing was going on!").

By long habit Ives never attended performances of his own music. Mrs. Ives remembered how, years before, they used to sit apart: "we'd suffer by ourselves – Charlotte always sat with Carl – she was braver than I was." Each year he grew a little weaker, but stronger in the certainty that his work was proven by ever widening appreciation and devotion.

In May 1954 he was recovering perfectly from a minor operation, but suddenly suffered a stroke and died in New York on 19 May. Edith told afterwards how the three of them held hands quietly – that it was a time of the kind of luminous serenity that animates his greatest music; he seemed as if transfigured. It was an intimate communion of unspoken awareness she could never have imagined, a serenity resolving all the tensions of his life that somehow persisted intact after he had quietly stopped breathing.

5. STYLES. Ives's death was in a way a birth of textual clarification of his music. For many years he had been reticent about his manuscripts. To any offer to sort and list he would evasively reply, "When I feel better, I'll get around to it." Any publication of his music while he lived was from only one source, often with textual uncertainties – and although he could be a meticulous proofreader his eyes seldom permitted long scrutiny. In 1956 Mrs. Ives gave his manuscripts to the Library of the Yale School of Music, and now in spite of tragic lacunae one can see how most of his music grew.

Elliott Carter used to see him alter sketches, adding dissonant touches, and wondered how far back his "modernity" really went. But most of his dissonance is structural, not isolated. Despite his paradoxical datings (often too early, often by revisions), one can believe that the trial reading of the *Song for Harvest Season* was (as he wrote) "about when the new Baptist Church in Danbury was opened" (dedicated on 16 April 1893), and that "Father let me work over" certain psalms which therefore must date from 1894. Most of the pieces grouped above as "1906" bear on their sketches an address good only up to 1907.

So much attention has been given to the surprisingly early dates of his innovations in polytonality, polyrhythm, and poly-texture that one is apt to forget that, like Ruggles, he was primarily a melodist, with a genius for melodic variation and eloquence. Though his quotation of tunes is often meant to be recognizable, and can be magically evocative (as in *Decoration Day* where *Bethany* accompanies *Taps*), equally often the tune is only a hidden springboard towards some transformation with old empathy glowing through a fresh disguise. Over 150 tunes he quoted have been identified, and there are surely many more.

Where Ives used tunes together, they are often related melodically. For instance, in describing the First Piano Sonata he mentioned *Where is my wandering boy tonight?*, which he hardly used, preferring *Lebanon* ("I was a wand'ring sheep"); they start as each other's inversions. In *Concord, Martyn* ("Jesus, lover of my soul") is a variant of the opening theme of Beethoven's Fifth Symphony. He even used these correspondences for musical puns like the verbal puns so fashionable in his youth. At the end of the First Violin Sonata the echoes of *Work, for the night is coming* turn slyly into "The union forever" (chorus of *The Battle Cry of Freedom*). Early in *The Saint-Gaudens* the chorus of *Old Black Joe* ("I'm coming") turns into "Yes, Jesus loves me." This is not tongue-in-cheek, but an ability, perhaps not exclusively American, to get some fun out of the things one regards most reverently.

Any attempt to find in Ives a consistent development of musi-

19

cal style would have encountered his scorn for the whole idea of "manner." He regarded the cultivation of a personal idiom as a limitation, a retreat from freely pursued ideals, a lowering of standards. Right through from 1893 (*Song for Harvest Season* and *There is a certain garden*) to 1925 (*Johnny Poe* and the harmonization of Edith's *Christmas Carol*), he used the whole spectrum of complex-to-simple, serving the statement at hand as if improvising freshly each time. It was more a consistent development of inner vision, the end of the Fourth Symphony being something towards which he must have been aspiring ever since *Thanksgiving*.

The question of the lasting worth of his music has been tossed back and forth, perhaps prematurely. Much has been made of his lack of audience contact in his most productive years, and of the limited time he had, often precluding the fine, single-pointed focus of communicative intensity which his aims imply. This very looseness he put to good effect, suggesting either a warmly human diversity of life, a spontaneous naturalness, a caustic wit, or a visionary amazement. Probably there is still much to be found out about the conscious art by which he achieved these things, an exploration which may even open up horizons of transcendent exaltation. These heights and depths and jigs and jokes are so convincing and treasurable to his performers, and to many of his listeners, that they constitute a kind of mystery, posing many questions still unanswered. However, it has been shown, chiefly by J. Peter Burkholder, that, whereas Ives's experimental pieces have an extravagance all their own, his sonatas and symphonies (perhaps even the Fourth) are part of the European-American mainstream and are addressed to the same audience; the more one tries to disentangle earlier and later states of Ives's manuscripts, the more they reveal that the music did indeed fit into the mainstream at the time of composition, before Ives later stepped up the level of dissonance.

20

WORKS

Fragments, exercises, and most lost or incomplete works omitted; unless otherwise stated, printed works published in New York; MSS at CtY-Mus; numbers from Kirkpatrick's unpublished revision of his 1960 catalogue

unf. – unfinished   rej. – rejected   > – derived into   < – developed from

Index: v – orchestral and band; w – chamber music; x – keyboard; y – choral and partsongs; z – songs

Principal publishers: Associated, Mercury: Merion, Peer, Peters, Presser

V – ORCHESTRAL AND BAND
(for full orchestra, with multiple wind, unless otherwise stated)

No.	Title and instrumentation	Date	First performance	Remarks and publication
1	Holiday Quickstep, pic, 2 cornets, 2 vn, pf	Dec 1887	Danbury, CT, 16 Jan 1888	<lost band arr.; ed. J. Sinclair (1975)
2	March no.2, with A Son of a Gambolier	1892		>x4, <z29; ed. K. Singleton (1977)
3	March no.3, with My Old Kentucky Home	1892		>lost pf version; ed. K. Singleton (1975)
4	March "Intercollegiate," with Annie Lisle, band	1892		>x6; (?Philadelphia, 1896); ed. K. Brion (1973)
5	Postlude, F	1895		>lost org postlude, 1892
6	Overture, g	?1895		inc., ?unf., ?intended for lost ovs. In These United States
7	March, F and C, with Omega Lambda Chi, band	1896		>x5; ed. K. Brion (1974)
8	First Symphony	1895–8	Washington, DC, 26 April 1953, cond. R. Bales	(1971)
	1 Allegro			
	2 Adagio molto	1895		>early sketch of z51a
	3 Scherzo: Vivace			
	4 Allegro molto	1897–8		

21

No.	Title and instrumentation	Date	First performance	Remarks and publication
9	Fugue in 4 keys, on The Shining Shore, fl, cornet, str	1897		ed. J. Kirkpatrick (1975)
10	Yale–Princeton Football Game	?1898		
11	Second Symphony		New York, 22 Feb 1951, New York PO, cond. L. Bernstein	(1951); ed. M. Goldstein (in preparation)
	1 Andante moderato	1900–01		>lost org sonata, lost Down East Ov.
	2 Allegro	1900–01		>lost ovs. In These United States
	3 Adagio cantabile	1902		>lost org prelude, 1896, rej. 2 of v8
	4 Lento maestoso	?1901		>lost Town, Gown and State Ov., 1896
	5 Allegro molto vivace	1902		>lost ov. The American Woods, 1889
12	Ragtime Dances nos. 1–4, small orch	1902–4		inc., <x17, > and <x13, <v22:2, v37:2; ed. J. Sinclair (1984)
13	Overture and March "1776," small orch	1903		<v30:2, v34; ed. J. Sinclair (1976)
14	Country Band March, small orch	1903		<x19:2, v30:2, v39:2, x23; ed. J. Sinclair (1976)
15	Third Symphony "The Camp Meeting," small orch	1904	New York, 5 April 1946, New York Little SO, cond. L. Harrison	(1947); ed. P. Echols and K. Singleton (in preparation)
	1 Andante "Old Folks Gatherin'"			>lost org prelude, 1901
	2 Allegro "Children's Day"			>lost org postlude, 1901
	3 Largo "Communion"			>lost org communion, 1901, <z88 unf.
16	The General Slocum	July 1904		
17	Thanksgiving and/or Forefathers' Day	Aug 1904	New York, 9 April 1954, Minneapolis SO, cond. A. Dorati	>lost org prelude and postlude, Nov 1897
18	Autumn Landscapes from Pine Mountains, small orch	1904		lost
19	Runaway Horse on Main Street, band	?c1905		inc., <z81, z119
20	Over the Pavements, small orch	1906–13		>w10; (1954)
21	The Pond, small orch	May 1906		<z122; ed. J. Monod (1973)

No.	Work	Date	Première	Publication / Notes
22	Set for Theatre or Chamber Orch		Danbury, CT, Feb 1932	(San Francisco, 1932)
	1 In the Cage	July 1906		>/<z75
	2 In the Inn	1906–11		>v12, >x17:2b
	3 In the Night	June 1906		>w2, lost hymn–anthem, 1902
23	[Two Contemplations], small orch		New York, 11 May 1946, cond. T. Bloomfield	
	1 The Unanswered Question	1906		(1953); ed. P. Echols and N. Zahler (1985)
24	2 Central Park in the Dark	July–Dec 1906		ed. J. Monod (1973)
	Cartoons (Take-offs), small orch	c1898–1916		?incl. w10
	7 Mike Donlin – Johnny Evers	sum. 1907		inc.
	8 Willy Keeler at the Bat	sum. 1907		inc.
25	Emerson Overture/Concerto, pf, orch	1907		unf., inc., <x16:2, 9, x19:1, x20
26	Washington's Birthday, small orch	1909	San Francisco, 3 Sept 1931, cond. N. Slonimsky	(San Francisco, 1937); ed. J. Sinclair (in preparation)
27	Set no.1, small orch	1910–11		ed. D. Porter (in preparation)
	1 The See'r	?sum. 1908		>lost Beecher Ov., ?1904, <z92, x22:2
	2 A Lecture	1907–8		<z82
	3 The Ruined River	1911		<y30, z91
	4 Like a Sick Eagle	1909		<z94
	5 Calcium Light Night	sum. 1911		
	6 When the moon, or Allegretto sombreoso	1907–8		<z123; (1958)
	6¼ [v10]			
28	The Gong on the Hook and Ladder (Firemen's Parade on Main Street), small orch	?1911	New York, 21 Jan 1967, New York PO, cond. Bernstein	added later in a list; orig. pubd H. Cowell in New Music, xxiv/4 (1953) as Calcium Light; 1st authorized pubn (1960); ed. J. Sinclair (1979)
29	Robert Browning Overture	1908–12	New York, Oct 1963, cond. L. Stokowski	<z136; (1959); ed. J. Elkus (in preparation)

No.	Title and instrumentation	Date	First performance	Remarks and publication
30	First Orchestral Set (A New England Symphony; Three Places in New England)		New York, 10 Jan 1931, Boston Chamber Orchestra, cond. Slonimsky	rev. 1929 for small orch (1935); ed. J. Sinclair for full orch (1976)
	1 The Saint-Gaudens in Boston Common	1911–12		
	2 Putnam's Camp, Redding, Connecticut	1912		>v13, v14
	3 The Housatonic at Stockbridge	1908–214		<z125
31	Decoration Day	1912	Havana, Cuba, 27 Dec 1931, Havana SO, cond. A. Roldán	>w18; ed. J. Sinclair (in preparation)
32	Set no.2, small orch	?1912		
	1 Largo "The Indians"	1912		<z126
	2 "Gyp the Blood" or Hearst!? Which is Worst?!	Oct ?1912		unf.; ed. K. Singleton (1978)
	3 Andante "The Last Reader"	4 June 1911		<z124
33	Matthew Arnold Overture	9–15 Dec 1912		inc., <z127
34	The Fourth of July	1911–13	Paris, France, 21 Feb 1932, Paris SO, cond. Slonimsky	>v13; (San Francisco, 1932)
—	Holidays		Minneapolis, 9 April 1954, Minneapolis SO, cond. A. Dorati	assembled from v26, v31, v34, v17, each pubd separately
35	The Rainbow (So May It Be!), small orch	1914		<z130; (1959)
36	Quarter-tone Chorale, str	1913–14		lost, <x22:3; ed. A. Stout (1976)
37	Second Orchestral Set			ed. J. Sinclair (in preparation)
	1 An Elegy to our Forefathers	1909		orig. title: Elegy to Stephen Foster
	2 The Rockstrewn Hills Join in the People's Outdoor Meeting	1909		>v12
	3 From Hanover Square North, at the End of a Tragic Day, the Voice of the People Again Arose	1915		

38	Tone Roads et al, small orch		
	1 Fast "All Roads Lead to the Center"	?1915 / 1911	(1949); ed. R. Swift and J. Kirkpatrick (in preparation)
	2 Slow	1911–19	lost
	3 Slow and fast "Rondo rapid transit"	1915	(1952); ed. R. Swift (in preparation)
39	Fourth Symphony		New York, 26 April 1965, American SO, cond. Stokowski	(1965)
	1 Prelude: Maestoso	1910–11	>w16:3
	2 Allegretto	1911–16	>v14, x19:2, <x23
	3 Andante moderato	1909–11	>w1:1
	4 Largo, SATB ad lib	1911–16	>lost Memorial Slow March, org, 1901
40	Set no.3, small orch	?1918	
	1 Adagio sostenuto "At Sea"	?1902/?1912	<z120; (1969)
	2 Luck and Work	Oct 1916	>z95
	3 Premonitions	Jan 1918	<z132
41	Chromâtimelôdtune, small orch	?1919	New York, 6 Dec 1962, cond. Schuller	>w23; arr. G. Schuller (1963)
42	Third Orchestral Set, small orch	1919–26	New York, 6 Dec 1962, cond. Schuller [Schuller arr.]	3 unf. movts: hymn-tune movt, comedy of Danbury reminiscence, hymn-tune movt
43	Universe Symphony	1911–28	
	1 Section A "Past: Formation of the waters and mountains"		
	2 Section B "Present: Earth, evolution in nature and humanity"		
	3 Section C "Future: Heaven, the rise of all to the Spiritual"		unf., inc.

Ives planned 8 other sets, with some new orchestrations: [Set no.4]: z32:3, v27:1, v23:1; [Set no.5]: v27:4, v40:2, v32:1; [Set no.6]: v27:3, v32:1, z137; Three Poets and Human Nature: z136, y34, z127; The Other Side of Pioneering (Side Lights on American Enterprise): v27:3, v32:1, z119, z137; From the Side Hill: z86, v35, z111, z144; Water Colors: v40:1, z100, v21, z150; Three Outdoor Scenes, ?1949: w11, v21, v23:2. Orchestral realizations of songs, ed. K. Singleton: z84, 1v/fl, theater orch (1976), z119, z144, both chamber orch, opt. 1v (1983)

No.	Title and instrumentation	Date	First performance	Remarks and publication
			W – CHAMBER MUSIC	
1	First String Quartet "From the Salvation Army"	May 1896	New York, 24 April 1957, Kohon String Quartet	(1961)
	1 Chorale			>lost org fugue, <v39:3
	2 Prelude			?>lost org prelude
	3 Offertory			?>lost org prelude/offertory
	4 Postlude			>lost org postlude, 1896
—	Intermezzo, str qt			see Y23:4
2	Prelude, trbn, 2 vn, org	?1898		<lost hymn–anthem, 1902, v22:3
3	From the Steeples and the Mountains, tpt, trbn, 4 sets of bells	1901–?2		(1965)
4	Pre-First Violin Sonata			
	1 Allegretto moderato	1899–1901		<w17:2
	2a rej. Largo, G	1901		<w5; ed. P. Zukofsky (1967)
	2 Largo, D	1902–?3		<w16:2
	3a rej. Scherzo	1902		unf., <w17:2
	3 Adagio–Allegro	1902		<w17:1
5	Largo, vn, cl, pf	?1902		>w4:2a, ?part of w6; (1953)
6	Trio, vn, cl, pf	1902–?3	Berea, OH, 24 May 1948, Baldwin-Wallace College Faculty Trio	lost, ?incl. w5
7	An Old Song Deranged, cl/eng hn, harp, str qt	?1903		>z26; ed. K. Singleton (in preparation)
8	Pre-Second String Quartet	1904–5		unf, lost, <w15:1, z146, z151
9	Trio, vn, vc, pf	1904–11		(1955); ed. J. Kirkpatrick (1985)
	1 Andante moderato			
	2 TSIAJ [this scherzo is a joke] (Medley on the Campus Fence)			
	3 Moderato con moto			

No.	Title, scoring	Date	Première	Notes
10	Take-off no.3 "Rube trying to walk 2 to 3!!," cl, bn, tpt, pf	1906		<v20, z135, see also v24
11	Hallowe'en, str qt, pf	1 April 1906	San Francisco, 28 May 1934	(1949)
12	Largo risoluto no.1 "as to the Law of Diminishing Returns," str qt, pf	1906	New York, 19 Feb 1965, Kohon String Quartet	(1961)
13	Largo risoluto no.3 "a shadow made – a silhouette," str qt, pf	1906		(1961); no.2 lost
14	All the Way Around and Back, cl, bugle, vn, bells, pf 4 hands	1906		(1971)
15	A Set of 3 Short Pieces	?1908		
	1 Largo cantabile "Hymn," str qt, db	Aug 1904		>w8, <z121; (1966)
	2 Scherzo "Holding Your Own," str qt	1903–14	New York, 19 Feb 1965, Kohon String Quartet	(1958)
	3 Adagio cantabile "The Innate," str qt, db, pf	24 Nov 1908		<z102; (1967)
16	First Violin Sonata		New York, 31 March 1946, J. Field, R. Lev	(1953)
	1 Andante–Allegro	1902–26		>w4 : 2
	2 Largo cantabile	1908		>lost sacred song Watchman, <v39 : 1, z90
	3 Allegro	1906–28		(1951)
17	Second Violin Sonata		New York, 18 March 1924, J. Goldstein, R. Tillson	
	1 Autumn	Oct 1907		>w4 : 3, <z89
	2 In the Barn	Nov 1907		>w4 : 1, W4 : 3a
	3 The Revival	1909–10		>w22 : 3a
18	Decoration Day, vn, pf	1912		<v31; ed. J. Kirkpatrick (in preparation)
19	Second String Quartet		Saratoga Springs, NY, 15 Sept 1946, Walden String Quartet	(1954, repr. 1970)

No.	Title and instrumentation	Date	First performance	Remarks and publication
	1 Discussions	1911–13		
	2 Arguments	1907–11		
	3 The Call of the Mountains	1911–13		
20	In re con moto et al, str qt, pf	1913		(1968)
21	Third Violin Sonata	1913–?14	Los Angeles, 16 March 1942, S. Babitz, I. Dahl	ed. S. Babitz and I. Dahl (San Francisco, 1951)
	1 Adagio			>lost org prelude, 1901
	2 Allegro			>lost ragtime piece, 1902–3
	3 Adagio cantabile			>lost org prelude, 1901
22	Fourth Violin Sonata "Children's Day at the Camp Meeting"		New York, 14 Jan 1940, E. Shapiro, I. Jacobi	(1942)
	1 Allegro	1914–?16		>G. Ives's Fugue in B♭, 1862, and lost sonata, tpt, org, 1901
	2 Largo	1906–?16		>sketch, 1905, <z101
	3 Allegro	1914–?16		<w17 : 3
	3a rej. Adagio–Faster	1906		<v41
23	Chromâtimelôdtune, brass qt, pf	?1919		
Realization of z122 for chamber ens, opt. lv, ed. K. Singleton (1977)				

x – KEYBOARD
(*pf unless otherwise stated*)

1	Variations on Jerusalem the Golden, org	?1888		<lost band arr.
2	March no. 1, with The Year of Jubilee	?1890		<lost band arr., lost orch arr.
3	Variations on America, org	?1891	Brewster, NY, 4 July 1891, Ives	(1949)
4	March [no.2], with The Son of a Gambolier	?1892		inc., <v2, z29

No.	Title	Date	Notes
5	March no.3, with Omega Lambda Chi	?1892	<v7
6	March no.5, with Annie Lisle	1892	<v4
7	March no.6, with Here's to Good Old Yale	1892–?7	3 versions, <lost band/orch arr.
8	[Canzonetta], F, org	?1893	
9	March, G and C, with See the conquering hero comes	spr. 1893	
10	March "The Circus Band"	?1894	<z.20
11	[Invention], D	?1896	
12	Prelude on Adeste fideles, org	?Dec 1897	(1949)
13	Ragtime Dances	1902–4	> and <v12, <x17:2a, x17:2b; ed. H. Cowell (1949); rev. ed. J. Kirkpatrick (1975)
14	Three-page Sonata	Sept 1905	ed. J. Kirkpatrick (1985)
15	[Set of Five Take-offs]	1906–1 Jan 1907	
	1 The Seen and Unseen		
	2 Rough and Ready et al and/or The Jumping Frog		
	3 Song Without (Good) Words (Melody in F and F♭)		
	4 Scene Episode		
	5 Bad Resolutions and Good One	1 Jan ?1907	>/<x17:5
16	Studies	1907–?8	
	1 [?Allegro]		inc.
	2 Andante moderato – Allegro molto		inc.
	3		>cadenza for v25
	4 [?Allegro moderato]		lost
	5 Moderato [con] anima		inc.
	6 Andante		ed. A. Mandel (in preparation)
	7 Andante cantabile		renumbered no.14
	8 Trio: Allegro moderato – Presto		renumbered no.15

29

No.	Title and instrumentation	Date	First performance	Remarks and publication
9	The Anti-abolitionist Riots	1908	New York, 3 April 1950, J. Cox	>cadenza for v25; ed. H. Cowell (1949)
10–18	Unidentified ?3-movt piece:			?lost
–	[Allegro moderato]			renumbered no.15
–	Andante cantabile			inc., renumbered no.16
19	untitled, amorphous sketch			
20	[March:] Slow allegro or Fast andante			ed. J. Kirkpatrick (1981)
21	Some Southpaw Pitching	?1909	New York, 3 April 1950, Cox	ed. H. Cowell (1949); rev. ed. J. Kirkpatrick (1975)
22	Andante maestoso – Allegro vivace	?1909		ed. H. Cowell (1947); rev. ed. J. Kirkpatrick (1973)
?23	Allegro	?1909		ed. J. Kirkpatrick (1984)
17	First Piano Sonata		New York, 17 Feb 1949, W. Masselos	>v12; (1954); ed. P. Echols, L. Harrison, W. Masselos (1980)
	1 Adagio con moto	1901–9		
	2a 1st verse and chorus	1902–?8		>x13
	2b 2nd verse and chorus	1902–?8		>x13, <v22:2
	3 Largo – Allegro	1902–9		
	4a 3rd verse and chorus	?1909		
	4b 4th verse and chorus	1902–?8		>x13
	5 Andante maestoso	1905–8		>/<x15:4
18	Waltz-Rondo	1911		ed. J. Kirkpatrick and J. Cox (1978)
19	Second Piano Sonata "Concord, Mass., 1840–60"		New York, 20 Jan 1939, J. Kirkpatrick	(Redding, CT, 1920, rev. edn 1947); ed. J. Kirkpatrick (in preparation)
	1 Emerson	1911–12		>v25, <x20
	2 Hawthorne	1911		>v14, v39:2, x23
	3 The Alcotts	1912–14		>lost Orchard House Ov., 1904
	4 Thoreau, incl. ?obbl fl	1910–15		<z99

20	Four Transcriptions from Emerson		New York, 12 March 1948, W. Aitken	>v25, x19:1
	1 Slowly	?1917		
	2 Moderato	?1922		
	3 Largo	?1922		
	4 Allegro agitato – Broadly	?1922		
21	Varied Air and Variations	?1923		inc. edn as 3 Protests (San Francisco, 1947); ed. J. Kirkpatrick and G. Clarke (1972)
22	Three Quarter-tone Pieces, 2 pf	1923–4		ed. G. Pappastavrou (1968)
	1 Largo			
	2 Allegro		New York, 14 Feb 1924, H. Barth, S. Kelin	>v27:1
	3 Chorale		New York, 14 Feb 1924, H. Barth, S. Kelin	>v36
23	The Celestial Railroad	?1924–?5		>v14, x19:2, v39:2
–	Three Improvisations		recorded ?11 May 1938	ed. G. and J. Dapogny (1984)

Y – CHORAL AND PARTSONGS

No.	Title	First line	Forces	Author	Date	Remarks and publication
1	Psalm xlii	As pants the hart	SATB, org		?1888	
2	The year's at the spring		SATB	Browning	?1889	
3	I think of Thee, my God		SATB	Monsell	?1889	<z11
4	Benedictus in E	Blessed be the Lord God of Israel	SATB, org		?1890	ed. J. Kirkpatrick (in preparation)
5	Turn Ye, Turn Ye		SATB, org	J. Hopkins	?1890	org pt lost; (1952); ed. J. Kirkpatrick (1973)
6	Crossing the Bar	Sunset and evening star	SATB, org	Tennyson	?1890	org pt lost; ed. J. Kirkpatrick (1974)
7	Communion Service		SATB, org		1891	org pt lost
8	Serenade	Stars of the summer night	SATB	Longfellow	?1891	ed. J. Kirkpatrick (1984)
9	Bread of the World		unison female vv, org	Heber	?1891	unf.
10	I Come to Thee	God of my life	SATB, org	C. Elliott	?1892	ed. J. Kirkpatrick (1983)
11	Easter Carol	Wake, wake, earth	S, A, T, B, SATB, org		1892–1901	ed. J. Kirkpatrick (1973)
12	Lord God, Thy sea is Mighty		SATB, org		?1893 or 1894	org pt lost; ed. J. Kirkpatrick (1983)
13	Psalm cl	Praise ye the Lord	SSAATTBB, boys' TrTrAA, org		sum. ?1894	ed. J. Kirkpatrick and G. Smith (1972)
14	Psalm lxvii	God be merciful unto us	SSAATTBB		sum. ?1894	(1939)
15	Psalm liv	Save me, O God	SAATBB		sum. ?1894	ed. J. Kirkpatrick and G. Smith (1973)
16	Psalm xxiv	The earth is the Lord's	SSAATTBB		sum. ?1894	(1955)
	Psalm xc, see no. 40					
17	The Light that is Felt		1v, SATB, org	Whittier	?1895	<z74
18	For You and Me!		TTBB		?1895/6	(1896), (1973)
19	A Song of Mory's		TTBB	Merrill	1896	in the Yale Courant (Feb 1896); ed. K. Singleton (in preparation)

No.	Title	First line	Author	Scoring	Date	Notes
20	The Bells of Yale, or Chapel Chimes		Mason	Bar, TTBB, vc/pf	1897–?8	3 versions, 1 in *Yale Melodies* (1903); ed. K. Singleton (in preparation)
21	O Maiden fair			1v, TTBB, pf	1897–?8	
22	All-forgiving, look on me		Palmer	SATB, ?org	?1898	?org pt lost; ed. J. Kirkpatrick (in preparation)
23	The Celestial Country		Alford	S, S, A, A, T, T, B, B, SATB, str qt, tpt, euphonium, timp, org	1898–9	org pt lost; full score ed. J. Kirkpatrick (in preparation); 2 in A, H, L, 6 in A, F, L [see z – "Songs"]
	1 Far o'er yon horizon, prelude, trio and chorus					
	2 Naught that country needeth					
	3 Seek the things before us					
	4 Intermezzo					
	5 Glories on glories					
	6 Forward, flock of Jesus					
	7 To the eternal Father, chorale and finale					
24	Psalm c	Make a joyful noise		SSAATTBB, boys' TrTrAA, bells ad lib	1898–?9	ed. J. Kirkpatrick and G. Smith (1975)
25	Psalm xiv	The fool hath said		SATB, SATB, org	?1899	org pt lost
26	Psalm xxv	Unto thee O God		SSAATTBB, org	1899–?1901	ed. J. Kirkpatrick and G. Smith (1979)
27	Psalm cxxxv (Anthem–Processional)	Praise ye the Lord		SSAATTBB, tpt, trbn, timp, org	?1900	ed. J. Kirkpatrick (1980)
28	Three Harvest Home Chorales			SATB, 4 tpt, 3 trbn, tuba, org		(1949); ed. P. Echols (in preparation)
	1 Harvest Home	The harvest dawn is near	Burgess		?1898	
	2 Lord of the Harvest		Gurney		?1901	
	3 Harvest Home	Come, ye thankful people	Alford		?1901	
29	Processional	Let there be light	Ellerton	TTBB/SATB, org/brass	1901	(1955)
30	The New River	Down the river	Ives	unison vv, orch	June 1911	>v27: 3; (1971)

33

No.	Title	First line	Forces	Author	Date	Remarks and publication
31	Lincoln, the Great Commoner	And so he came	unison vv, orch	Markham	1912	<z96; (San Francisco, 1932)
32	December		unison vv, brass, wind	Rossetti, after Folgore	1912–13	<z93; ed. N. Slonimsky (1963)
33	Two Slants (Christian and Pagan)				sum. 19?11/ ?12/?13	<z128
	1 Duty	So nigh is grandeur	unison vv, orch	Emerson		
	2 Vita	Nascentes morimur	unison vv, org	Manlius		
34	Walt Whitman	Who goes there?	unison vv, orch	Whitman	1913	<z129
35	General Booth	Booth led boldly	unison vv, orch	Lindsay	1914	>z98, unf.
36	Sneak Thief	People of the world	unison vv, tpt, pf 4 hands	Ives	12 Oct 1914	
37	Majority (The Masses)	Fifteen years ago today	unison vv, orch	Ives	1914–15	<z131
38a	He is there!	There's a time	unison vv, orch	Ives	1917	>z104a
38b	They are there!	It strikes me		Ives	1942	>z104b; ed. L. Harrison (1961)
39	An Election		unison vv, orch	Ives	Nov 1920	<z133
40	Psalm xc	Lord, thou hast been	SSAATTBB, bells, org		1894, rev. 1924	ed. J. Kirkpatrick and G. Smith (1970)
41	Johnny Poe	When fell the gloom	TTBB, orch	Low	1925	unf.; ed. J. Kirkpatrick (1978)

z – SONGS

(revisions and adaptations to new words listed together)

Editions: *114 Songs* (Redding, CT, 1922) [A]
    50 Songs (1923, from plates of A) [A*]
    7 Songs (1932) [B]
    34 Songs (San Francisco, 1933) [C]
    19 Songs (San Francisco, 1935), also as *18* [sic] *Songs* [D]

    14 Songs (1955) [H]
    9 Songs (1956) [J]
    13 Songs (1958) [K]
    [12] *Sacred Songs* (1961) [L]

4 Songs (1950) [E]
10 Songs (1953) [F]
12 Songs (1954) [G]

11 Songs and 2 Harmonizations, ed. J. Kirkpatrick (1968) [M]
3 Songs (1968) [N]
40 Earlier Songs, ed. J. Kirkpatrick (in preparation) [P]

No.	Title	First line	Forces	Author	Date	Remarks and publication
1	Slow March	One evening just at sunset		Brewster, Ives family	?1887	rev. 1921; A, F
2a	Hear my Prayer, O Lord	O have mercy, Lord, on me		Tate, Brady	?1888	A, H
2b	When the waves softly sigh			?Ives	?1892	A, H
2c	A Song for Anything	Yale farewell! we must part		Ives	?1898	A, H
3	At Parting	The sweetest flow'r that blows		F. Peterson	?1889	C
4	Abide with me			Lyte	?1890	new acc. later; K, L
5	Far from my heav'nly home			Lyte	?1890	M
6a	Country Celestial	For thee, o dear, dear country		Neale, after Bernard of Cluny	?1891	P
6b	Du bist wie eine Blume			Heine	?1897	P
6c	When stars are in the quiet skies			Bulwer-Lytton	?1898	A*, C
7	Rock of Ages	Rock of ages, cleft for me		Toplady	?1891	org acc.; M
8	My Lou Jeninne	Has she need of monarch's swaying wand			?1891	P
9	In Autumn	The skies seemed true above thee			?1892	P
10	A Perfect Day	Bland air and leagues of immemorial blue			?1892	P
11	Through Night and Day	I dream of thee, my love		?Ives	?1892	>y3, P
12a	Minnelied	Holder klingt der Vogelsang		Hölty	?1892	P
12b	Nature's Way	When the distant evening bell		Ives	1908	A*, H
13	[Friendship]	All love that has not friendship for its base			sum. 1892	P
14a	Her Eyes	Her eyes are like unfathomable lakes			?1892	P

No.	Title	First line	Forces	Author	Date	Remarks and publication
14b	Mirage	The hope I dreamed of		C. Rossetti	1902	A*, F
15a	Canon	Not only in my lady's eyes			Jan 1893	P
15b	Canon	Oh the days are gone		Moore	?1894	A, D
16	There is a certain garden				1893	M
17	Song for Harvest Season	Summer ended		Phillimore	1893	org acc. or tpt, trbn, tuba; C
18	Song	She is not fair to outward view		H. Coleridge	?1893	P
19	Waltz	Round and round the old dance ground		Ives	?1894	A, G
20	The Circus Band	All summer long we boys		Ives	?1894	>x10; A*, F
21	The Old Mother	Oh dearest mother		Corder, after Vinje	?1894	1st setting; see also z66a
22a	Far in the wood				?1894	P
22b	A Night Song	The young May moon		Moore	1895	A, (1952), K
23	A Christmas Carol	Little star of Bethlehem		Ives	Dec 1894	A*, D
24a	Rosamunde	Der Vollmond strahlt		W. von Chézy	?1895	P
24b	Rosamunde	J'attends, hélas, dans la douleur		Bélanger	1898	A, H
25a	Ein Ton	Mir klingt ein Ton		Cornelius	?1895	P
25b	Night of Frost in May			Meredith	1899	A*, D
26	Songs my mother taught me			Macfarren, after Heyduk	1895	<w7; A*, H
27a	In April-tide	Be ye in love with April-tide		C. Scollard	?1895	P
27b	Amphion	The mountain stirred its bushy crown		Tennyson	1896	A*, F
28	My Native Land, or Un rêve			after Heine	?1895	1st setting; see also z69; A, G
29	A Son of a Gambolier				1895	>x4; A, J
30	Kären, or Little Kären	Do'st remember, child		Kappey, after Ploug	?1895	A*, G
31a	Gruss	Leise zieht durch mein Gemüth		Heine	?1895	P

No.	Title	First line	Text source	Date	Code
31b	The World's Wanderers	Tell me, star	Shelley	?1895	A*, F
32a	Die Lotosblume		Heine	?1895	rev. ?1899; A*, C
32b	The South Wind	When gently blows	H. Twichell	April 1908	A*, C
33a	In my Beloved's Eyes	I looked into the midnight deep	Chauvenet	?1895	P
33b	A Night Thought	How oft a cloud	Moore	?1903	A*, C
34	The All-enduring	Man passes		1896	>/<TTBB version, lost; P
35a	Marie	Marie, am Fenster sitzest du	Gottschall	1896	P
35b	Marie	Marie, I see thee, fairest one	Rücker, Ives	1896	A*, H
36	An Old Flame, or A Retrospect	When dreams enfold me	Ives	1896	A, K
37	In the Alley	On my way to work	Ives	1896	A, K
38	William Will	What we want is honest money	S. Hill	1896	(1896), P
39	A Scotch Lullaby	Blaw! skirlin' win'	Merrill	1896	Yale Courant (1896), P
40a	Frühlingslied	Die blaue Frühlingsaugen	Heine	8 Nov 1896	P
40b	I travelled among unknown men		Wordsworth	1901	A*, F
41	God Bless and Keep Thee	I know not if thy love be as a flower		?1897	M
42	Dreams	When twilight comes	after Baroness Porteous	1897	A, J
43	Qu'il m'irait bien		?after M. Delano	?1897	A, G
44	Her gown was of vermilion silk			July 1897	P
45	Memories, A, Very Pleasant, B, Rather Sad	We're sitting	Ives	1897	A, F
46a	Widmung	O danke nicht für diese Lieder	Müller	?1897	P
46b	There is a lane		Ives	1902	A*, J
47a	Feldeinsamkeit	Ich ruhe still	Almers	1897	A*, D
47b	In Summer Fields	Quite still I lie	Chapman	1897	A*, D
48a	No More	They walked beside the summer sea	Winter	Dec 1897	M
48b	Hymn of Trust	[O] Love divine	O. W. Holmes	?1898	P

No.	Title	First line	Forces	Author	Date	Remarks and publication
49a	Ich grolle nicht			Heine	1898	A, C
49b	I'll not complain			J. S. Dwight	1898	C
50	Chanson de Florian	Ah s'il est dans votre village		Florian	?1898	A, (1950)
51a	On Judges' Walk	That night on Judges' Walk		Symons	1893–?8	<v8 : 1; P
51b	Rough Wind			Shelley	1902	A, C
52a	The Only Son	The lark will make her hymn to God		Kipling	?1898	P
52b	Harpalus	Oh Harpalus! thus would he say		Percy: Reliques	1902	A, C
53a	Wie Melodien zieht es mir			Groth	?1898	P
53b	Evidence	There comes o'er the valley a shadow		Ives	1910	A, J
54	The Love Song of Har Dyal	Alone upon the housetops		Kipling	?1898	P
55a	Tarrant Moss	I closed and drew for my love's sake		Kipling	?1898	A
55b	Slugging a Vampire	I closed and drew, but not a gun		Ives	1902	D
56a	[?The Song of the Dead]	Hear now the song of the dead		Kipling	?1898	P
56b	The Ending Year	Frail autumn lights		Ives	1902	P
56c	The Waiting Soul	Breathe from the gentle south		Cowper	1908	A*, G, L
57	Because of you	What have you done for me, dear one			Sept 1898	P
58	I knew and loved a maid				?1898	P
59	Flag Song	Accept you these emblems		Durand	Nov 1898	>lost song; (1968)
60	Because thou art	My life has grown so dear to me			?1899	P
61a	Grace	Sweetheart, sweetheart			?1899	P
61b	Where the eagle	Phantoms of the future		M. Turnbull	1906	A, (1935), K, L, N
62	Omens and Oracles				Aug 1899	A, F
63a	Sehnsucht	Ich konnte heute nicht schlafen		Lobedanz, after Winther	?1899	P

63b	Rosenzweige	Wohl manchen Rosenzweig brach' ich	Stieler	?1899	P
63c	Allegro	By morning's brightest beams	Ives	1900	A, K
64	[Romanzo di Central Park]	Grove, rove, night, delight	L. Hunt	1900	A, H
65a	Wiegenlied	Guten Abend, gute Nacht	Des Knaben Wunderhorn	?1900	P
65b	Berceuse	O'er the mountain towards the west	Ives	?1903	A*, K
66a	The Old Mother	Du alte Mutter	Lobedanz, after Vinje	1900	2nd setting; see also z21; A, K
66b	My dear old mother	Between the dark and the daylight	Corder, after Vinje	1900	A, K
67	The Children's Hour		Longfellow	1901	A*, C
68	Elégie	O doux printemps d'autrefois	Gallet	1901	A*, J
69	My Native Land		after Heine	?1901	2nd setting; see also z28; P
70	Ilmenau	Über allen Gipfeln ist Ruh'	Goethe	1901	A*, (1952)
71	Weil' auf mir		Lenau	?1901	A, H
72	Walking	A big October morning	Ives	1900–?02	>lost anthem, 1898; A*, B
73a	The Sea of Sleep	Good night, my care and my sorrow		4 Jan 1903	P
73b	Those Evening Bells		Moore	1907	A, H
74	The light that is felt		Whittier	Nov 1903	>y17; A; (1950)
75	The Cage	A leopard went	Ives	1906	>/<v22 : 1; A, (San Francisco, 1932), H
76	Pictures	The ripe corn bends low	M. Turnbull	1906	M
77	The World's Highway	For long I wandered happily	H. Twichell	1906	A, K
78	Spring Song	Across the hill	H. Twichell	14 Aug 1907	>lost song; A*, G
79	Soliloquy	When a man is sitting before the fire	Ives	1907	C

39

No.	Title	First line	Forces	Author	Date	Remarks and publication
80	Autumn	Earth rests		H. Twichell	Nov 1907	>lost song, ?1902; A, J
81	Runaway Horse on Main Street	So long, Harris		Ives	?1909	inc., >v19, <z119
82	Tolerance	How can I turn from any fire		Kipling	?1909	>v27:2; A, C
83	A Farewell to Land	Adieu, adieu! my native shore		Byron	Dec 1909	D
84	Mists	Low lie the mists		[Mrs.] H. T. Ives	1910	A*, C, orch realization ed. K. Singleton (1976)
85	Religion	There is no unbelief		L. Y. Case	?1910	>lost anthem, 1902; A*, G, L
86	Requiem	Under the wide and starry sky		Stevenson	Nov 1911	D
87	Vote for Names			Ives	Nov 1912	unf., (1968)
88	The Camp Meeting	For the grandeur		Ives, after C. Elliott	1912	>v15:3; A, K, L
89	His Exaltation			Robinson	1913	>w17:1; A, J, L
90	Watchman			Bowring	1913	>w16:3; A*, H, L
91	The New River	Down the river comes a noise		Ives	July 1913	>v27:3; A*, C
92	The See'r	An old man with a straw in his mouth		Ives	?1913	>v27:1; A, B
93	December	Last for December		Rossetti, after Folgore	?1913	>v32; A, C
94	Like a Sick Eagle	The spirit is too weak		Keats	?1913	>v27:4; A*, C
95	Luck and Work	While one will search		Johnson	?1913	>v40:2; A, C, E
96	Lincoln, the Great Commoner	And so he came from the prairie cabin		Markham	?1913	>v31; A, (1952)
97	Old Home Day	Go, my songs		Ives, after Virgil	?1913	with fife/vn/fl obbl; A*, K
98	General William Booth Enters into Heaven	Booth led boldly with his big bass drum		Lindsay	1914	<y35; D
99	Thoreau	He grew in those seasons		Ives, after Thoreau	1915	>x19:4; A, C
100	Swimmers	Then the swift plunge		Untermeyer	1915	rev. 1921; A, C

101	At the River	Shall we gather	Lowry	?1916	>w22:3; A, C
102	The Innate	Voices live in every finite being	Ives	1916	>w15:3; A, D
103	In Flanders Fields		McCrae	April 1917	A, H
104a	He is there!	Fifteen years ago today	Ives	30 May 1917	<v38a; A, P
104b	They are there!	There's a time in every life	Ives	1942	<v38b; J
105	The Things our Fathers Loved	I think there must be a place in the soul	Ives	1917	A, H
106	Tom Sails Away	Scenes from my childhood	Ives	Sept 1917	A, D
107	To Edith	So like a flower	H. T. Ives	Jan 1919	>lost song, 1892; A*, F
108	Down East	Songs! visions	Ives	1919	?>lost Down East Ov..; A, K, L
109	Serenity	O Sabbath rest of Galilee	Whittier	1919	>lost earlier version; A, B
110	Cradle Song	Hush thee, dear child	A. Ives, 1846	1919	A*, D
111	Afterglow	At the quiet close of day	J. F. Cooper, Jr.	1919	A, C
112	The Collection	Now help us Lord	Kingsley	1920	?>lost early anthem; A, K, L
113	Grantchester		R. Brooke	1920	A*, J
114	La fede		Ariosto	1920	A*, D
115	August	For August	Rossetti, after Folgore	1920	A, G
116	September	And in September	Rossetti, after Folgore	1920	A, C
117	On the Counter	Tunes we heard in "ninety-two"	Ives	1920	A, H
118	Maple Leaves	October turned my maple's leaves to gold	Aldrich	1920	A, B
119	Charlie Rutlage	Another good cow-puncher	D. J. O'Malley	1920/21	>v19, z81; A*, B, orch realization ed. K. Singleton (1983)
120	At Sea	Some things are undivined except by love	Johnson	1921	>v40:1; A*, C

No.	Title	First line	Forces	Author	Date	Remarks and publication
121	Hymn	Thou hidden love of God		Wesley, after Tersteegen	1921	>w15:1; A*, C
122	Remembrance	A sound of a distant horn		Ives	1921	>v21; A*, G, chamber realization ed. K. Singleton (1977)
123	Incantation	When the moon is on the wave		Byron: Manfred	1921	>v27:6; A, C
124	The Last Reader	I sometimes sit beneath a tree		Holmes	1921	>v32:3; A*, C
125	The Housatonic at Stockbridge	Contented river		Johnson	1921	>v30:3; A, G
126	The Indians	Alas for them, their day is o'er		Sprague	1921	>v32:1; A*, C
127	West London	Crouch'd on the pavement		M. Arnold	1921	>v33; A*, C
128	Two Slants, or Christian and Pagan				1921	>v33; A*, C, E
	1 Duty	So nigh is grandeur to our dust		Emerson		
	2 Vita	Nascentes morimur finisque ab origine pendet		Manlius		
129	Walt Whitman	Who goes there?		Whitman	1921	>y34; A*, C
130	The Rainbow	My heart leaps up		Wordsworth	1921	>y35; A, C
131	Majority	The masses have toiled		Ives	1921	>y37; A, D
132	Premonitions	There's a shadow on the grass		Johnson	1921	>v40:3; A, C
133	Nov 2, 1920	It strikes me that		Ives	1921	>y39; A, D
134	The Side-show	Is that Mister Riley		Ives, after P. Rooney	1921	>lost sketch, 1896; A, G
135	1, 2, 3	Why doesn't one, two, three		Ives	1921	>w10; A, E
136	Paracelsus	For God is glorified in man		Browning	1921	>v29; A*, D
137	Ann Street	Quaint name, Ann Street		Morris	Jan 1921	A, C
138	Immortality	Who dares to say the spring is dead		Ives	?March 1921	A*, C
139	Two Little Flowers	On sunny days		Ives, H. T. Ives	?April 1921	A*, D, (1940), N

No.	Title	First line	Text	Date	Notes
140	The Greatest Man	My teacher said	A. Collins	?June 1921	A*, C, (1942), N
141	Resolution	Walking stronger under distant skies	Ives	1921	A*, D
142	Disclosure	Thoughts which deeply rest at evening	Ives	1921	A*, G, L
143	The White Gulls		Morris, after the Russian	?Aug 1921	A*, C
144	Evening	Now came still evening on	Milton	1921	A*, B, orch realization ed. K. Singleton (1983)
145	On the Antipodes	Nature's relentless, nature is kind	Ives	1915–23	D
146	Aeschylus and Sophocles	We also have our pest	Landor	1922	>w8; D
147	The One Way	Here are things you've heard before	Ives	?May 1923	M
148	Peaks	Quiet faces that look in faith	Bellamann	?Sept 1923	M
149	Yellow Leaves	Heart-shaped yellow leaves	Bellamann	?Oct 1923	M
150	A Sea Dirge	Full fathom five thy father lies	Shakespeare	Jan 1925	M
151	Sunrise	A light low in the east	Ives	Aug 1926	with inst (vn) obbl, >w8; ed. J. Kirkpatrick (1977)

INDEX TO THE SONGS

48b; Ich grolle nicht, 49a; Ich konnte heute nicht schlafen, 63a; Ich ruhe still, 47a; I closed and drew, 55; I dream of thee, my love, 11; I knew and loved a maid, 58; I know not if thy love be as a flower, 41

I'll not complain, 49b; Ilmenau, 70; I looked into the midnight deep, 33a; Immortality, 138; In April-tide, 27a; In Autumn, 9; Incantation, 123; In Flanders Fields, 103; In my Beloved's Eyes, 33a; In Summer Fields, 47b; In the Alley, 37; I sometimes sit beneath a tree, 124; Is that Mister Riley, 134; I think there must be a place, 105; I travelled among unknown men, 40b; It strikes me that, 133; J'attends, hélas, dans la douleur, 24b; Judges' Walk, see On Judges' Walk; Kären, 30; La fede, 114; Last for December, 93

Leise zieht durch mein Gemüth, 31a; Like a Sick Eagle, 94; Lincoln, the Great Commoner, 96; Little Kären, 30; Little star of Bethlehem, 23; Love Divine, 48b; Low lie the mists, 84; Luck and Work, 95; Majority, 131; Man passes, 34; Maple Leaves, 118; Marie, 35; Memories, A, Very Pleasant, B, Rather Sad, 45; Minnelied, 12a; Mirage, 14b; Mir klingt ein Ton so wunderbar, 25a; Mists, 84; My dear old mother, 66b; My heart leaps up, 130; My life has grown so dear to me, 60

My Lou Jeninne, 8; My Native Land, 28, 69; My teacher said, 140; Nascentes morimur finisque ab origine pendet, 128; Nature's relentless, nature is kind, 145; Nature's Way, 12b; Night of Frost in May, 25b; No More, 48a; Not only in my lady's eyes, 15a; Nov 2, 1920, 133; Now came still evening on, 144; Now help us Lord, 112; October turned my maple's leaves to gold, 118; O danke nicht für diese Lieder, 46a; O doux printemps d'autrefois, 68; O'er the mountain towards the west, 65b

O have mercy, Lord, on me, 2a; Oh dearest mother, 21; Oh Harpalus! thus would he say, 52; Oh the days are gone, 15b; Old Home Day, 97; Omens and Oracles, 62; One evening just at sunset, 1; 1, 2, 3, 135; On Judges' Walk, 51a; On my way to work, 37; On sunny days, 139; On the Antipodes, 145; On the Counter, 117; O Sabbath rest of Galilee, 109; Paracelsus, 136; Peaks, 148; Phantoms of the future, 62; Pictures, 76; Premonitions, 132; Quaint name, Ann Street, 137

Quiet faces that look in faith, 148; Qu'il m'irait bien, 43; Quite still I lie, 47b; Religion, 85; Remembrance, 122; Requiem, 86; Resolution, 141; Rock of Ages, 7; [Romanzo di Central Park], 64; Rosamunde, 24; Rosenzweige, 63b; Rough Wind, 51b; Round and round the old dance ground, 19; Runaway Horse on Main Street, 81; Scenes from my childhood, 106; Sehnsucht, 63a; September, 116; Serenity, 109; Shall we gather, 101; She is not fair to outward view, 18; Slow March, 1; Slugging a Vampire, 55b

So like a flower, 107; Soliloquy, 79; So long, Harris, 81; Some things are undivined except by love, 120; Song, 18; Song for Harvest Season, 17; Songs

Bibliography

ARRANGEMENTS

Beethoven: Adagio from Pf Sonata, op.2 no.1, for str qt, ?1889

Schubert: March, D, op.51 no.1, for orch, ?1891; Impromptu, c, op.90 no.1, for orch, 1892, inc.

Schumann: Préambule and Valse noble from Carnaval, op.6, for orch, 1892/?3

E. Ives: Christmas Carol, 1924, for unison female vv, pf/org, bells, Nov 1925, in 11 Songs and 2 Harmonizations (1968)

Give me Jesus [Negro spiritual], for 1v, pf, 1929, in 11 Songs and 2 Harmonizations (1968)

Search me, O God (response), and Love does not die, S, T, pf, are probably not by Ives

BIBLIOGRAPHY

CATALOGUES AND BIBLIOGRAPHIES

J. Kirkpatrick: *A Temporary Mimeographed Catalogue of the Music Manuscripts and Related Materials of Charles Edward Ives 1874–1954* (New Haven, 1960/R1973)

D. Hall: "Charles Ives: a Discography," *HiFi*, xiii (1964), no.4, p.142; no.5, p.102; no.6, p.92

D.-R. De Lerma: *Charles Ives, 1874–1954: a Bibliography of his Music* (Kent, OH, 1970)

R. Warren: *Charles E. Ives: Discography* (New Haven, 1972)

H. Gleason and W. Becker: "Charles Ives," *20th-century American Composers*, Music Literature Outlines, ser. iv (Bloomington, IN, rev. 2/1981), 105 [incl. further bibliography]

H. Henck: "Literatur zur Charles Ives," *Neuland*, iii (1983–4), 243

F. Freedman and J. Burk: *A Charles Ives Bibliography* (in preparation)

LIFE AND WORKS

"Business Man who Composes," *Christian Science Monitor* (24 March 1924)

H. Cowell: "Charles Ives," *MM*, x (1932–3), 24

H. Bellamann: "Charles Ives: the Man and his Music," *MQ*, xix (1933), 45

H. Cowell: "Charles E. Ives," *American Composers on American Music* (Stanford, CA, 1933/R1962), 128

C. Seeger: "Charles Ives and Carl Ruggles," *Magazine of Art*, xxxii (1939), 396

E. Carter: "Ives Today: his Vision and Challenge," *MM*, xxi (1943–4), 199

P. Moor: "On Horseback to Heaven," *Harper's*, cxcvii (1948), Sept, 65

H. Taubman: "Posterity Catches up with Charles Ives," *New York Times Magazine* (23 Oct 1949)

G. Chase: "Composer from Connecticut," *America's Music* (New York, 1955), 653

H. Cowell and S. Cowell: *Charles Ives and his Music* (New York, 1955, rev. 2/1969)

L. Schrade: "Charles E. Ives: 1874–1954," *Yale Review*, xliv (1955), 535

P. Yates: "Charles Ives," *Arts & Architecture*, lxxviii (1961), no.2, p.6; no.3, p.4; no.5, p.6

P. Dickinson: "Charles Ives: 1874–1954," *MT*, cv (1964), 347

J. Cage: "Two Statements on Ives," *A Year from Monday* (Middletown, CT, 1967), 36

J. Bernlef and R. de Leeuw: *Charles Ives* (Amsterdam, 1969)

W. W. Austin: "Ives and Histories," *Bericht über den Internationalen Musikwissenschaftlichen Kongress Bonn 1970* (Kassel, 1971), 299

A. F. Rosa: "Charles Ives: Music, Transcendentalism, and Politics," *New England Quarterly*, xliv (1971), 433

L. Wallach: *The New England Education of Charles Ives* (diss., Columbia U., 1973)

P. Garland, ed.: *Ives, Ruggles, Varèse* (n.p., 1974) [articles on Ives by L. Harrison, P. Corner, J. Tenney, M. Goldstein]

V. Perlis: *Charles Ives Remembered: an Oral History* (New Haven, 1974)

R. S. Perry: *Charles Ives and the American Mind* (Kent, OH, 1974)

G. Vinay: *L'America musicale di Charles Ives* (Turin, Italy, 1974)

D. Wooldridge: *From the Steeples and Mountains: a Study of Charles Ives* (New York, 1974)

CMc, no.18 (1974) [articles on Ives by H. Perison, J. Tick, C. W. Ward]

CMc, no.19 (1975) [articles on Ives by H. Helms, L. Wallach]

Parnassus, iii/2 (1975) [articles on Ives by E. Carter, L. Harrison, A. Koppenhaver, D. Walker, P. Yates]

P. Perrin: "The Composer as Historian," *Artscanada* (1975), nos.198–9, p.58

F. Rossiter: *Charles Ives and his America* (New York, 1975)

R. Taruskin: [Letter in reply to H. Helms, 1975], *CMc*, no.20 (1975), 33

Student Musicologists at Minnesota, vi (1975–6) [articles on Ives by D. Argento, H. Helms, J. Kirkpatrick, A. Mandel, J. Riedel, and others]

S. Blum: "Ives's Position in Social and Musical History," *MQ*, lxiii (1977), 459

H. W. Hitchcock and V. Perlis, eds.: *An Ives Celebration* (Urbana, IL, 1977)

S. Feder: "Decoration Day: a Boyhood Memory of Charles Ives," *MQ*, lxvi (1980), 234

R. H. Mead: "Cowell, Ives, and *New Music*," *MQ*, lxvi (1980), 538

R. DiYanni: "In the American Grain: Charles Ives and the Transcendentalists," *Journal of American Culture*, iv/4 (1981), 139

S. Feder: "Charles and George Ives: the Veneration of Boyhood," *Annual of Psychoanalysis*, ix (1981), 265

48

——: "The Nostalgia of Charles Ives: an Essay in Affects and Music," *Annual of Psychoanalysis*, x (1982), 301

J. P. Burkholder: *Charles Ives: the Ideas behind the Music* (New Haven, CT, 1985)

GENERAL STUDIES OF WORKS

H. Bellamann: "The Music of Charles Ives," *Pro-Musica Quarterly*, v/1 (1927), 16

P. Rosenfeld: "Charles E. Ives, Pioneer Atonalist," *New Republic*, lxxi (20 July 1932), 262

P. Rosenfeld: "Ives," *Discoveries of a Music Critic* (New York, 1936), 315

E. Carter: "The Case of Mr. Ives," *MM*, xvi (1938–9), 172

——: "An American Destiny," *Listen*, ix/1 (1946), 4

L. Harrison: "On Quotation," *MM*, xxiii (1946), 166

——: "The Music of Charles Ives," *Listen*, ix/1 (1946), 7

R. J. Moore, Jr.: *The Background and the Symbol: Charles Ives* (thesis, Yale U., 1954)

E. Carter: "Shop Talk by an American Composer," *MQ*, xlvi (1960), 189; repr. in *Problems of Modern Music*, ed. P. H. Lang (New York, 1962), 51

C. Ives: *Essays Before a Sonata and Other Writings*, ed. H. Boatwright (New York, 1962)

D. Marshall: "Charles Ives's Quotations: Manner or Substance?," *PNM*, vi/2 (1968), 45

C. W. Henderson: *Quotation as a Style Element in the Music of Charles Ives* (diss., Washington U., St. Louis, 1969)

C. Ward: *Hymn Tunes as "Substance and Manner" in Charles Ives* (thesis, U. of Texas, 1969)

A. Davidson: "Transcendental Unity in the Works of Charles Ives," *American Quarterly*, xxii (1970), 35

D. Dujmic: "The Musical Transcendentalism of Charles Ives," *IRASM*, ii (1971), 89

V. Thomson: "The Ives Case," *American Music Since 1910* (New York, 1971), 22; repr. in *A Virgil Thomson Reader* (Boston, 1981), 460

P. Corner: "Thoreau, Charles Ives, and Contemporary Music," *Henry David Thoreau: Studies and Commentaries*, eds. W. Harding, G. Brenner, P. A. Doyle (Rutherford/Madison/Teaneck, NJ, 1972), 53

C. W. Henderson: "Structural Importance of Borrowed Music in the Works of Charles Ives: a Preliminary Assessment," *IMSCR*, xi, *Copenhagen 1972*, 437

C. Ives: *Memos*, ed. J. Kirkpatrick (New York, 1972) [dictated 1932; commentaries by Ives with annotations and appendixes]

H. Isham: "The Musical Thinking of Charles Ives," *Journal of Aesthetics and Art Criticism*, xxxi (1972–3), 395

R. P. Morgan: "Rewriting Music History: Second Thoughts on Ives and Varèse," *Musical Newsletter*, iii (1973), no.1, p.3; no.2, p.15

P. Dickinson: "A New Perspective for Ives," *MT*, cxv (1974), 836

R. Middleton: "Ives and Schoenberg: an English View," *Saturday Review/World*, ii (21 Sept 1974), 39

C. Ward: *Charles Ives: the Relationship between Aesthetic Theories and Compositional Processes* (diss., U. of Texas, 1974)

D. Eiseman: "George Ives as Theorist: Some Unpublished Documents," *PNM*, xiv/1 (1975), 139

H. W. Hitchcock: *Ives* (London, 1977/*R*1983 with addenda)

L. Starr: "Charles Ives: the Next Hundred Years – Towards a Method of Analyzing the Music," *MR*, xxxviii (1977), 101

N. S. Josephson: "Intervallische Permutationen im Spätwerk von Charles Ives," *Zeitschrift für Musiktheorie*, ix/2 (1978), 27

R. P. Morgan: "Ives and Mahler: Mutual Responses at the End of an Era," *19th Century Music*, ii (1978–9), 72

C. Ballantine: "Charles Ives and the Meaning of Quotation in Music," *MQ*, lxv (1979), 167

N. Schoffman: "Serialism in the Works of Charles Ives," *Tempo*, no.138 (1981), 21

J. P. Burkholder: *The Evolution of Charles Ives's Music: Aesthetics, Quotation, Technique* (diss., U. of Chicago, 1983)

L. Starr: "The Early Styles of Charles Ives," *19th Century Music*, vii (1983–4), 71

J. P. Burkholder: " 'Quotation' and Emulation: Charles Ives's Uses of his Models," *MQ*, lxxi (1985), 1

W. Crutchfield: "Why our Greatest Composer Needs Serious Attention," *New York Times* (10 May 1987), §II, 19

STUDIES OF INDIVIDUAL WORKS

(chamber)

L. Perkins: *The Violin Sonatas by Charles Ives* (diss., Eastman School, 1961)

U. Maske: *Charles Ives in seiner Kammermusik für drei bis sechs Instrumente* (Regensburg, Germany, 1971)

Y. Bader: "The Chamber Music of Charles Edward Ives," *MR*, xxxiii (1972), 292

H. Enke: "Charles Ives' 'The Unanswered Question'," *Zur musikalischen Analyse*, ed. G. Schumacher (Darmstadt, Germany, 1974), 232

(piano)

C. Ives: *Essays Before a Sonata* (Redding, CT, 1920); repr. in *Essays Before a Sonata and Other Writings*, ed. H. Boatwright (New York, 1962)

H. Bellamann: "Concord, Mass., 1840–60," *Double Dealer*, ii/10 (1921), 166

C. Ives: "Some 'Quarter-tone' Impressions," *Franco-American Musical Society Bulletin* (March 1925), 24; repr. in *Essays Before a Sonata and Other Writings*, ed. H. Boatwright (New York, 1962)

P. Rosenfeld: "Ives' Concord Sonata," *MM*, xvi (1938–9), 109

L. Gilman: "A Masterpiece of American Music," *New York Herald-Tribune* (21 Jan 1939) [review of *Concord Sonata*]

H. Boatwright: "Ives' Quarter-tone Impressions," *PNM*, iii/2 (1965), 22

M. A. Joyce: *"The Three Page Sonata" of Charles Ives: an Analysis and a Corrected Version* (diss., Washington U , St Louis, 1970)

T. R. Albert: *The Harmonic Language of Charles Ives' "Concord Sonata"* (diss., U. of Illinois, Urbana-Champaign, 1974)

S. R. Clark: "The Element of Choice in Ives's *Concord Sonata*," *MQ*, lx (1974), 167

M. J. Babcock: "Ives' 'Thoreau': a Point of Order," *American Society of University Composers: Proceedings*, ix–x (1974–5), 89

R. Newman: "Ragtime Influences on the Music of Charles Ives," *Proceedings of NAJE Research*, v (1985), 110 [on Pf Sonata no. 1]

M. J. Alexander: "Bad Resolutions or Good? Ives's Piano 'Take-Offs'," *Tempo*, no. 158 (1986), 8

(orchestral and band)

B. Herrmann: "Four Symphonies by Charles Ives," *MM*, xxii (1944–5), 215

S. R. Charles: "The Use of Borrowed Materials in Ives' Second Symphony," *MR*, xxviii (1967), 102

J. Burk: "The Wind Music of Charles Ives," *The Instrumentalist*, xxiv/3 (1969), 36

G. Cyr: "Intervallic Structural Elements in Ives's Fourth Symphony," *PNM*, ix/2–x/1 (1971), 291

C. Sterne: "The Quotations in Charles Ives's Second Symphony," *ML*, lii (1971), 39

J. Elkus: *Charles Ives and the American Band Tradition: a Centennial Tribute* (Exeter, NH, 1974)

N. S. Josephson: "Zur formalen Struktur einiger später Orchesterwerke von Charles Ives," *Mf*, xxvii (1974), 57

W. Brooks: "Unity and Diversity in Charles Ives's Fourth Symphony [First mov't]," *Yearbook for Inter-American Musical Research*, x (1974), 5

W. Zimmermann: *Desert Plants: Conversations with 23 American Musicians* (Vancouver, BC, 1976), 207 [on *Universe Sym.*]

J. V. Badolato: *The Four Symphonies of Charles Ives: a Critical, Analytical Study of the Musical Style of Charles Ives* (diss., Catholic U. of America, 1978)

A. Maisel: "The Fourth of July by Charles Ives: Mixed Harmonic Criteria in a Twentieth-century Classic," *Theory and Practice*, vi/1 (1981), 3

W. Brooks: "A Drummer-boy Looks Back: Percussion in Ives's Fourth Symphony," *Percussive Notes*, xxii/6 (1984), 4–45

L. A. Lipkis: *Aspects of Temporality in Debussy's 'Jeux' and Ives's 'Symphony No. 4,' Fourth Movement* (diss., .U. of California, Santa Barbara, 1984)

M. D. Nelson: "Beyond Mimesis: Transcendentalism and Processes of Analogy in Charles Ives's *The Fourth of July*," *PNM*, xxii/1–2 (1983–4), 353

W. Rathert: "Charles Ives, 'Symphonie Nr. 4,' 1911–1916," *Neuland*, iii (1983–4), 226

L. Austin: "Charles Ives's *Life Pulse Prelude for Percussion Orchestra*: a Realization for Modern Performance from Sketches for his *Universe Symphony*," *Percussionist*, xxiii/6 (1985), 58

R. Pozzi: "Polemica antiurbana ed isolamento ideologico in *Central Park in the Dark* di Charles Ives," *NRMI*, xix (1985), 471

(vocal)

C. Ives: "Postface," *114 Songs* (Redding, CT, 1922); repr. in *Essays Before a Sonata and Other Writings*, ed. H. Boatwright (New York, 1962)

A. Copland: "One Hundred and Fourteen Songs," *MM*, xi (1933–4), 59; repr. in *Our New Music* (New York, 1941)

H. G. Sear: "Charles Ives, Song Writer," *MMR*, lxxxi (1951), 34

B. Layton: *An Introduction to the 114 Songs* (diss., Harvard U., 1963)

P. E. Newman: *The Songs of Charles Ives* (diss., U. of Iowa, 1967)

W. C. Kumlien: *The Sacred Choral Music of Charles Ives: a Study in Style Development* (diss., U. of Illinois, Urbana-Champaign, 1969)

H. W. Hitchcock: "Charles Ives's Book of *114 Songs*," *A Musical Offering: Essays in Honor of Martin Bernstein*, ed. E. H. Clinkscale and C. Brook (New York, 1977), 127

N. Schoffman: "Charles Ives's Song 'Vote for Names'," *CMc*, no.23 (1977), 56
——: *The Songs of Charles Ives* (diss., Hebrew U. of Jerusalem, 1977)

L. Starr: "Style and Substance: 'Ann Street' by Charles Ives," *PNM*, xv/2 (1977), 23

D. M. Green: "A Chord Motive in Ives's 'Serenity'," *ITO*, iv/5 (1978), 20

J. Kirkpatrick: "*Sunrise*: Charles Ives' Last Composition," *Peters Notes*, i/2 (1978), 7

D. Grantham: "A Harmonic 'Leitmotif' System in Ives's Psalm 90," *ITO*, v/2 (1979), 3

VIRGIL THOMSON

Richard Jackson

CHAPTER TWO

Virgil Thomson

1. CAREER. Virgil Garnett Thomson was born in Kansas City, Missouri, on 25 November 1896; he learned to play the piano at the age of five and began lessons with local teachers when he was 12. He studied organ from 1909 until 1917 and again in 1919; from the beginning of this period he also worked as organist in the family church (Calvary Baptist) and other churches in Kansas City. Thomson attended Central High School (1908–13) and a local junior college (1915–17, 1919). During the American involvement in World War I he enlisted in the army and was in a field artillery unit; he was also trained in radio telephony at Columbia University and in aviation at a pilots' ground school in Texas. He was set for embarkation to France when the war ended.

In autumn 1919 Thomson entered Harvard University, where he was decisively influenced from the start by three men: the French-trained composer Edward Burlingame Hill, with whom he studied orchestration and modern French music among other subjects; Archibald T. Davison (also French-trained), the conductor of the Harvard Glee Club, for whom he was accompanist for three years; and S. Foster Damon, a Blake scholar, poet, and composer, who introduced him to the works of Satie and to *Tender Buttons*, Gertrude Stein's early and most obscure collection of writings. Thomson began to compose at Harvard in 1920. In the summer of 1921 the Glee Club toured Europe, with Thomson

4. Virgil Thomson, 1983

56

occasionally conducting, and he stayed on for a year in Paris under a John Knowles Paine Traveling Fellowship. He chose to study organ at the Ecole Normale with Boulanger, and he also studied counterpoint with her privately. During the year he met Jean Cocteau and Les Six and was introduced to Satie. He composed, and wrote his first published critical work, music reviews for the *Boston Evening Transcript*. Back in the USA he returned to Harvard and was made organist and choirmaster at King's Chapel, Boston. He gave the first American performance of Satie's *Socrate* with the Harvard Musical Club and graduated from the university in 1923. In New York, with a grant from the Juilliard Graduate School, he studied conducting with Chalmers Clifton and counterpoint with Rosario Scalero.

Thomson returned in autumn 1925 to Paris, where he lived, apart from visits to the USA, until 1940. His first composition from this period was the *Sonata da chiesa*, a neoclassical chamber work for five instruments completed in February 1926 and consisting of a Chorale, Tango, and Fugue. The conception of the piece – chic, ironic, and deliberately outrageous – derived from Stravinsky's recent works. Thomson later called it his "graduation piece in the dissonant style of the time"; he consulted with Boulanger for the last time while the work was in progress. He also composed four organ pieces based on American Protestant hymns (the *Variations on Sunday School Tunes*) and the *Symphony on a Hymn Tune*, his first symphony.

Thomson met Gertrude Stein in autumn 1926, and the two expatriates began to lay plans for an opera that would concern Spanish saints and the Spanish landscape. Meanwhile, Thomson composed settings of two texts by Stein: the song *Preciosilla* and *Capital Capitals*, an unorthodox cantata-like piece for four male voices and piano. (He had set Stein's *Susie Asado* before their meeting.) Stein completed the libretto for the opera, *Four Saints in Three Acts*, in June 1927, and Thomson finished the piano

57

equivalents of Stein's word pictures of the same name. Thomson was rambling, plotless, and hermetic, with no clearcut division into scenes and acts and with little indication of which character was speaking at any given moment. Stein's saints, led by Teresa of Avila and Ignatius Loyola, are devoid of any real character; they are preoccupied with asking questions ("How many saints are there in it?," "How many acts are there in it?"), counting, and repeating children's rhymes. The text does contain religious symbolism and private references to events in the writer's life, but these serve only as material for word games and random remarks. Thomson imposed order on the material, eventually deleting about a third of it, and fashioned a work consisting of a prologue and four acts. In the absence of a plot, Thomson's painter friend Maurice Grosser devised a scenario, or series of tableaux and processions, for staging the work. The score consists of elements that were to be characteristic of much of Thomson's subsequent work: simple diatonic harmony (with occasional bichordal clashes), short tunes in Protestant-hymn style, extended parlando and chant passages reminiscent of Anglican liturgy, quotations of familiar airs (e.g., *God Save the King* or *My Country, 'tis of thee*), popular dance rhythms (especially the waltz and the tango), and careful, highly polished prosody. When *Four Saints* received its initial performances in Hartford (fig.5), New York, and Chicago (with Stein present), it was widely publicized and became something of a *succès de scandale*. Though it never took a permanent place in the repertory, it is the composer's most famous work.

For a period of about seven years after the opera Thomson worked at expanding his technical facility, especially in writing for string instruments. Almost all of his works featuring strings – the Violin Sonata, the two string quartets, etc. – date from this period. He also composed the Symphony no.2 (adapted from the First Piano Sonata) and a series of "portraits," the musical

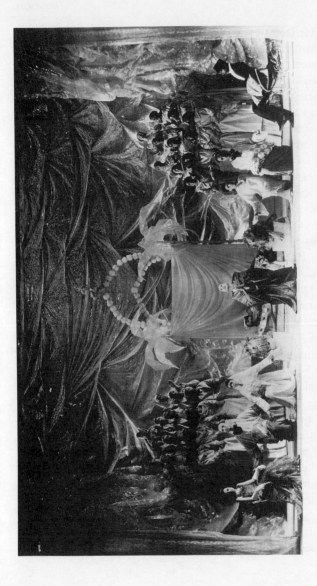

5. Thomson's "Four Saints in Three Acts": Prologue from the first production, Hartford, 8 February 1934

59

score a year later (it was orchestrated in 1933). The original text eventually composed over 100 of these pieces, some of which he orchestrated and used as sections of larger works. None of the works of this period contains allusions to hymn-tune style or traditional material (though Thomson's waltz strain is still prominent); they are concerned, rather, with problems of "pure" music-making. Thomson returned to the nationalistic vein in earnest, however, with two film scores and a ballet in the later 1930s. For *The Plow that Broke the Plains* and *The River*, widely acclaimed documentary films directed by Pare Lorentz and sponsored by an American government agency, he used cowboy songs, traditional southern spirituals, old popular tunes, and (for *The River*) the finale of the *Symphony on a Hymn Tune*. The dance score *Filling Station* was commissioned by Kirstein for Ballet Caravan and was called (by Balanchine) "the very oldest classic ballet with a specifically native American theme in the extant repertory." It has waltzes, tangos (one reworked from the *Sonata da chiesa*), and suggestions of a Salvation Army band.

In October 1940 Thomson was appointed music critic of the *New York Herald-Tribune*. During 14 years at this post he established himself as one of the major critical writers of the era. His newspaper pieces – all stylish, bright, deliberately provocative, and unshakably opinionated – furnished material for four anthologies: *The Musical Scene*, *The Art of Judging Music*, *Music Right and Left*, and *Music Reviewed, 1940–1954*. At a time when music critics tended to be wordy, to make ostentatious displays of their musical knowledge, and to use technical jargon, Thomson was plain and concise. For example, of *Porgy and Bess* he wrote "Its faults are numberless; but its inspiration is authentic, its expressive quotient high." At a time, too, when critics tended to accept as given the artistic value of works in the standard repertory and to concentrate on performances, Thomson wrote about the quality of the music, usually treating performances secondarily. He clashed with other critics who venerated certain performers; he became famous for his lack of enthusiasm for Toscanini when the conductor was generally regarded as one of the greatest living musicians, and he once characterized Heifetz's performance style as producing only "silk-underwear music."

While working as a critic, Thomson also continued to compose, most notably a second opera on a Stein text, *The Mother of us all* (commissioned by the Alice M. Ditson Fund), and the score for another documentary film, *Louisiana Story*, directed by Robert Flaherty. Stein's libretto, begun in 1945 and completed by March 1946 (four months before her death), was less abstract than her *Four Saints*, though still unconventional; it again required a scenario by Maurice Grosser for staging. The theme of the piece is the women's suffrage movement as typified by Susan B. Anthony, and it is played against a tapestry of 19th-century Americana. With its homespun hymn tunes, waltzes, and marches, Thomson's setting is similar in many respects to that of *Four Saints*, but he provided a richer palette and moments of greater sentiment and seriousness. The score for *Louisiana Story* is an adroit mixture of folk material and descriptive music cast in formal sections (Pastorale, Chorale, Fugue, and Passacaglia). Thomson subsequently fashioned from it two widely performed suites, *Acadian Songs and Dances* and *Louisiana Story*. The film score itself won the 1948 Pulitzer Prize for music.

Throughout the 1950s and 1960s Thomson traveled widely, lecturing at universities and participating in conferences, writing articles, conducting in the USA and Europe (he conducted the first Paris performance of *Four Saints* in 1952), and continuing to compose. His numerous awards included appointment to the Légion d'honneur (1947), election to the National Institute of Arts and Letters (1948) and to the American Academy of Arts and Letters (1959), the National Book Critics Circle Award for *A Virgil Thomson Reader*, and a Kennedy Center Honor (1983).

2. STYLE. During Thomson's long career as a composer he worked with several different styles. Cage, in his study (with Kathleen Hoover) of Thomson's music, referred to "the great variety and all but intangible nature of [his] work." He often took up a style (such as that of Gregorian chant and modal polyphony in the early choral pieces with Latin texts), and then dropped it or blended it with other elements. Baptist hymns were perhaps the major preoccupation, revealed initially in the ambivalent Sunday-school pieces, in which the gentle home-grown source material is disposed in a tortuous patchwork of variations and the organ is treated like a giant calliope. In many later works, however, such as the *Symphony on a Hymn Tune* and the Cello Concerto, the tunes are treated with affection and humor.

Thomson also made prominent use of the popular music of the 19th century, sometimes simply quoting the melodies, sometimes creating his own new settings of them, and sometimes (as in *The Mayor LaGuardia Waltzes*) using the older genres as models for new composition. He used the waltz in numerous works, including both of his string quartets (somewhat covertly in the first, more openly in the second) and the *Double Glissando* from his Ten Etudes for Piano. In such works as *The Squeeze-box* (from the film score *Louisiana Story*) and the third movement of the Third Piano Sonata, he set the waltz rhythm against a melody that alternates phrases of four beats and three. The tango rhythm appears in the *Sonata da chiesa* and the *Tango Lullaby: a Portrait of Mlle* [Flavie] *Alvarez de Toledo*, ragtime in one of the Ten Etudes, and even the early English song *Drink to me only with thine eyes* in *Tenor Lead (Madrigal)*, another of the Ten Etudes.

Open 4ths, 5ths, and octaves are common in Thomson's music, as are fanfare-like flourishes (all three operas begin with rolls on the snare drum, for instance). The harmonic language is often conventionally tonal, as in the second song of *La belle en dormant*, the triumphant C♯-major ending of *The Plow that Broke the Plains*, the *Four Songs to Poems of Thomas Campion*, and at least four of the *Five Songs from William Blake*. But frequently the music is better described simply as adopting a wandering, nonfunctional diatonicism that may come to rest where one expects it to or on a chord that sounds remote. There are diatonic clashes, as in the curious overlapping lines and chords of the *Missa pro defunctis*, and many surprises; at the end of *Guitar and Mandolin*, the last of the Nine Etudes for Piano, the pianist is instructed to "reach into the piano and strike strings with flat of hand, pedal down," and the Kyrie of the *Missa pro defunctis* begins and ends with a perfect, but seemingly incongruous, 12-tone row.

Another kind of diatonic dissonance is also common in Thomson's music: that which is brought about when one element (i.e., a simple and repetitive bass or accompaniment figure) is set against another (i.e., a melody), each proceeding innocently, but persistently, on its own way. Such incidents seem often intended to create a deadpan comic effect, and they invariably upset the tonal equilibrium. Two good examples among many are the *Variations on Sunday School Tunes* and the first song in *La belle en dormant*.

Thomson's curious "portraits" follow in a variety of styles. Paul Bowles described a group of them in 1942 as giving "the impression of having come from nowhere, [moving] airily in and out of the focus of consonance like breezes through a pagoda." A kind of serial technique is used in *A Solemn Music*, which develops from a series of 12 chords, and three "pictures" for orchestra (*The Seine at Night*, *Wheat Field at Noon*, *Sea Piece with Birds*) are painted in a nostalgic latterday impressionism.

The greatest influence on Thomson was the music of Satie, and Satie's ideals of clarity, simplicity, irony, and humor underlie the diversity of his work. The words used by Thomson to define

Satie's aesthetic could be used to describe his own:

It has eschewed the impressive, the heroic, the oratorical, everything that is aimed at moving mass audiences . . . it has directed its communication to the individual. It has valued in consequence, quietude, precision, acuteness of auditory observation, gentleness, sincerity, and directness of statement.

The work which comes closest to drawing together the various stylistic facets into a cohesive and congenial unity is Thomson's third opera, *Lord Byron*. He and his librettist, Jack Larson, worked on the opera for seven years, and it is undoubtedly his most ambitious project. The Thomson wit and playfulness are here, as is the meticulous (if occasionally monotonous) prosody — a hallmark of his vocal writing. Yet there is a seriousness of tone, a comparative richness of texture, and a lyrical expansiveness seldom encountered in his earlier works. There are the expected liturgical elements and the use of quotations (*Auld Lang Syne*, for instance, is worked into an impressive septet), but the style, in general, is not greatly dependent on the Baptist hymnbook. Thomson's "classical" string-writing period is represented in an important ballet sequence (deleted from the score after the opera's première) which uses material from the String Quartet no.2. What finally sets *Lord Byron* apart from Thomson's previous work, however, is its emotional content: the opera rises to moments of real passion. This suggests a new dimension for a composer who frequently demonstrates his ability to entertain but whose expressive voice is always carefully muted.

WORKS

Collections: *Portraits for Piano Solo: Album 1* (New York, 1948) [P1]
    Portraits for Piano Solo: Album 2 (New York, 1949) [P2]
    Portraits for Piano Solo: Album 3 (New York, 1950) [P3]
    Portraits for Piano Solo: Album 4 (New York, 1953) [P4]
    Nine Portraits for Piano Solo (New York, 1974) [P5]
    Thirteen Portraits for Piano Solo (New York, 1981) [P6]
    Nineteen Portraits for Piano Solo (New York, 1983) [P7]

Arrangements have been included only when by Thomson; dates of alternative versions and of arrangements are the same as those of original versions unless otherwise stated. Portraits of which the full titles are "[title]: a Portrait of [subject]" are listed below in the form "[title] . . . [subject]." All works are published unless otherwise stated.

OPERAS

Four Saints in Three Acts (G. Stein), 1927–8, orchd 1933, unpubd; Hartford, CT, 8 Feb 1934, cond. Smallens; arr. with pf acc.; Saints' Procession arr. SATB, pf, arr. TTBB, pf, unpubd; Pigeons on the Grass Alas arr. Bar, pf, 1934, arr. Bar, orch, 1934, unpubd

The Mother of us all (Stein), 1947, unpubd; New York, 7 May 1947, cond. Luening; arr. with pf acc., arr. orch suite

Lord Byron (J. Larson), 1961–8, unpubd; New York, 20 April 1972, cond. G. Samuel; arr. with pf acc. [ballet from Act 3 pubd as Sym. no.3]

BALLETS

Filling Station (L. Christensen), 1937, unpubd; New York, 18 Feb 1938, cond. E. Schenkman; arr. pf, Hartford, CT, 6 Jan 1938; arr. orch suite

The Harvest According (De Mille), 1952, unpubd; New York, 1 Oct 1952, cond. Thomson [arr. from Sym. on a Hymn Tune, Vc Conc., and Suite from The Mother of us all]

Parson Weems and the Cherry Tree (E. Hawkins), 1975; Amherst, MA, 1 Nov 1975; arr. pf

ORCHESTRAL AND BAND

Two Sentimental Tangos, 1923, unpubd [arr. of pf piece]

Symphony on a Hymn Tune, 1928; New York, 22 Feb 1945, Philharmonic Symphony Society, cond. Thomson

Symphony no.2, 1931, rev. 1941 [arr. of Pf Sonata no.1]; Seattle, WA, 17 Nov 1941, Seattle SO, cond. Beecham; arr. pf 4 hands, 1932, unpubd; choreographed by E. Hawkins as Hurrah!, 1975

The Plow that Broke the Plains, suite [from the film score], 1936; Philadelphia, 2 Jan 1943, Philadelphia Orchestra, cond. Thomson; arr. pf

The River, suite [from the film score], 1937; Brooklyn, NY, 12 Jan 1943, Brooklyn SO, cond. Beecham

Filling Station, suite [from the ballet], 1937, unpubd; New York, WNYC radio, 2 Feb 1941; concert perf. New York, 14 Dec 1941, Philadelphia SO, cond. Rodzinski; arr. pf

Fugue and Chorale on Yankee Doodle, suite [from the film score Tuesday in November], 1945; Atlanta, GA, 16 April 1969, Emory Chamber Orchestra, cond. W. Lemonds

The Seine at Night, 1947; Kansas City, MO, 24 Feb 1948, Kansas City PO, cond. E. Kurtz

Acadian Songs and Dances [from the film score Louisiana Story], 1948: Sadness, Papa's Tune, A Narrative, The Alligator and the Coon, Super-sadness, Walking Song, The Squeeze-box; Philadelphia, 11 Jan 1951, Philadelphia Orchestra, cond. Ormandy; choreographed by Balanchine as Bayou, 1952

Louisiana Story, suite [from the film score], 1948; Philadelphia, 26 Nov 1948, Philadelphia Orchestra, cond. Ormandy

Wheat Field at Noon, 1948; Louisville, 7 Dec 1948, Louisville Orchestra, cond. Thomson

At the Beach, concert waltz, tpt, band [arr. of Le bains-bar, vn, pf, 1929], 1949; New York, 21 July 1950, E. White, Goldman Band, cond. R. F. Goldman; version for tpt, pf, New York, 19 Feb 1949, E. White

The Mother of us all, suite [from the opera], 1949, unpubd; Knoxville, TN, 17 Jan 1950, Knoxville SO, cond. Thomson

A Solemn Music, band, 1949; New York, 17 June 1949; arr. orch, 1961, New York, 15 Feb 1962

Cello Concerto, 1950, unpubd; Philadelphia, 24 March 1950, P. Olefsky, Philadelphia Orchestra, cond. Ormandy; arr. vc, pf

Sea Piece with Birds, 1952; Dallas, 10 Dec 1952, Dallas SO, cond. W. Hendl

Eleven Chorale Preludes [arr. from Brahms: op.122], 1956; New Orleans, 25 March 1957, New Orleans Philharmonic SO, cond. Thomson

The Lively Arts Fugue, 1957, unpubd

Fugues and Cantilenas [from the film score Power among Men], 1959; Ann Arbor, MI, 2 May 1959, Philadelphia Orchestra, cond. Thomson

A Joyful Fugue, 1962; New York, 1 Feb 1963; arr. band

Autumn, concertino, harp, str, perc [arr. from the pf pieces Homage to Marya Freund and to the Harp, Pf Sonata no.2], 1964; Madrid, Spain, 19 Oct 1964, N. Zabaleta, Orquesta Municipal de Valencia, cond. E. Jorda

Pilgrims and Pioneers [from the film score Journey to America], 1964; New York, 27 Feb 1971, Mozart Festival Orchestra, cond. B. Hastings; arr. band

Ode to the Wonders of Nature, brass, perc, 1965; Washington, DC, 16 Sept 1965, Smithsonian Tower Musicians

Fantasy in Homage to an Earlier England, 1966; Kansas City, MO, 27 May 1966, Kansas City PO, cond. N. Rescigno

Symphony no.3, 1972; New York, 26 Dec 1976, American SO, cond. K. Akiyama; arr. pf as Ballet from Lord Byron, unpubd [= ballet from Lord

Byron, orch version of Str Qt no.2]
Thoughts for Strings, str orch, 1981

(Portraits. arrangements of pf pieces where noted; unpublished unless otherwise stated)

The John Moser Waltzes, 1935, orchd 1937 [used as no.6 in the ballet Filling Station]

Canons for Dorothy Thompson, 1942; New York, 23 July 1942, New York PO, cond. Kostelanetz

The Mayor LaGuardia Waltzes, 1942; Cincinnati, 14 May 1942, Cincinnati SO, cond. Kostelanetz

Bugles and Birds . . . Pablo Picasso, 1940, orchd 1944; Philadelphia, 17 Nov 1944, Philadelphia Orchestra, cond. Thomson

Cantabile for Strings . . . Nicolas de Chatelain, 1940, orchd 1944, pubd; Philadelphia, 17 Nov 1944, Philadelphia Orchestra, cond. Thomson

Fanfare for France . . . Max Kahn, 1940, arr. ww 1944, pubd; Cincinnati. 15 Jan 1943, Cincinnati SO, cond. Goossens

Fugue . . . Alexander Smallens, 1940, orchd 1944; Philadelphia, 17 Nov 1944, Philadelphia Orchestra, cond. Thomson

Meditation . . . Jere Abbott, 1935, orchd 1944; Vancouver, BC, 21 Nov 1948, Vancouver SO, cond. J. Singer

Aaron Copland, Persistently Pastoral, 1942, orchd as Pastorale, 1944; New York, 15 March 1945, New York City SO, cond. Thomson [used in the film score Tuesday in November]

Percussion Piece . . . Jessie K. Lasell, 1941, orchd 1944; Philadelphia, 17 Nov 1944, Philadelphia Orchestra, cond. Thomson

Tango Lullaby . . . Mlle [Flavie] Alvarez de Toledo, 1940, orchd 1944, pubd; Philadelphia, 17 Nov 1944, Philadelphia Orchestra, cond. Thomson

Concerto . . . Roger Baker, fl, harp, str, perc, 1954; Venice, Italy, 14 Sept 1954, E. Schaffer, N. Zabaleta, Orchestra del Teatro La Fenice, cond. N. Sanzogno; arr. fl, pf

Edges . . . Robert Indiana, 1966, arr. band, 1969; Cambridge, MA, spr. 1973, Harvard University Band

Study Piece: Portrait of a Lady, orig. Insistences . . . Louise Crane, 1941, arr. band, 1969; Cambridge, MA, spr. 1973, Harvard University Band

Metropolitan Museum Fanfare: Portrait of an American Artist, orig. Parades . . . Florine Stettheimer, 1941; arr. brass, perc, 1969; New York, 16 Oct 1969, cond. Thomson

A Love Scene, orig. Dead Pan: Mrs. Betty Freeman, 1981, orchd 1982

Intensely Two: Karen Brown Waltuck, 1981, orchd 1982

Loyal, Steady, and Persistent: Noah Creshevsky, 1981, orchd 1982

67

Something of a Beauty: Anne-Marie Soullière, 1981, orchd 1982
David Dubal in Flight, 1982, orchd 1982

CHORAL

(accompanied)

Fête polonais, TTBB, pf, 1924, unpubd; Boston, 1925, Harvard Glee Club, cond. Thomson [arr. from Chabrier: Le roi malgré lui]

Capital Capitals (Stein), 4 male vv, pf, 1927, rev. 1968; Paris, France, 30 May 1928, P. Steward, O. S. Walker, V. Prahl, E. Foster, E. Pendleton

Mass, 2vv, 1934; New York, 10 April 1935, Adesdi Chorus, cond. M. Dessoff

Seven Choruses from the Medea of Euripides (trans. C. Cullen), SSAA, perc, 1934: 1 O gentle heart, 2 Love, like a leaf, 3 O, happy were our fathers, 4 Weep for the little lambs, 5 Go down, O sun, 6 Behold, O earth, 7 Immortal Zeus controls the fate of man; New York, 16 Dec 1942, St. Cecilia Club, cond. H. Ross

The Bugle Song (Tennyson), unison children's chorus, pf, 1941; arr. 2-part children's chorus, unpubd

Welcome to the New Year (Farjeon), 2-part children's chorus, pf, 1941; arr. SATB, pf, unpubd

Crossing Brooklyn Ferry (Whitman), SSATB, pf, 1958, arr. SATB, orch, 1961, unpubd

Missa pro defunctis (Requiem Mass), double chorus, orch, 1960, vs pubd

Dance in Praise (Gaudeamus igitur, trans. J. Symonds), SATB, 1962, unpubd

Five Auvergnat Folk Songs (trad.), SATB, pf/orch, 1962, 1964: 1 La pastoura als camp, 2 Ballero, 3 Pastourelle, 4 La fiolaire, 5 Passo pel prat [arr. of work by J. Canteloube]

When I survey the bright celestial sphere (W. Habbingdon), unison vv, org/pf, 1964

The Nativity as Sung by the Shepherds (R. Crashaw), A, T, B, SATB, orch, 1966–7, unpubd; Chicago, 7 May 1967, C. Brent, W. Carringer, H. Noel, Rockefeller Chapel Choir, Chicago SO, cond. R. Vikstrom; arr. with pf acc.

Cantata on Poems of Edward Lear, S, 2 Bar, SATB, pf, 1973, rev. 1974: 1 The Owl and the Pussycat, 2 The Jumblies, 3 The Pelican Chorus, 4 Half an Alphabet, 5 The Akond of Swat; arr. with orch, unpubd, Baltimore, 18 Nov 1973, Towson State College Madrigal Singers, Towson State College Community Orchestra, cond. Thomson; nos.2, 4, and 5, and The Courtship of the Yongly Bongly Bo [from no.2] pubd separately

The Peace Place (J. Larson), SATB, pf, 1979; rev. 1983 as Fanfare for Peace, SATB, pf, arr. with brass, unpubd

A Prayer to Venus (J. Fletcher), SATB, pf, 1981

Cantantes eamus (P. V. Maro), TTBB, pf, 1982, arr. with brass

Southern Hymns, SATB, pf, 1984: 1 How bright is the day! (S. B. Sawyer), 2 Mississippi (from Kentucky Harmony, 1820), 3 Death of General Washington (S. Jenks), 4 Convention (from Caldwell: Union Harmony, 1837)

(unaccompanied)

De profundis (Ps. xxx), SATB, 1920, rev. 1951

O my Deir Hart, SATB, 1921, rev. 1978

Sanctus, TTBB, 1921, unpubd

Tribulationes civitatum (Lat.), SATB, 1922; Boston, 1922, Harvard Glee Club, cond. Thomson; arr. TTBB, unpubd

Three Antiphonal Psalms (Pss. cxxiii, cxxxiii, cxxxvi), SA/TB, 1922–4; New York, 1923, University Women's Chorus of New York, cond. G. Reynolds

Agnus Dei, 3 equal vv, 1924, unpubd

Missa brevis, TTBB, 1924, unpubd

Agnus Dei, TTBB, 1925, unpubd

Benedictus, TTBB, 1926, unpubd

Sanctus, TTBB, children's chorus, 1926, unpubd

My shepherd will supply my need (I. Watts, after Ps. xxiii), SATB, 1937, pubd in various choral arrs.; arr. 1v, pf, 1959

Scenes from the Holy Infancy According to St. Matthew, T, Bar, B, SATB, 1937: 1 Joseph and the Angel, 2 The Wise Men, 3 The Flight into Egypt; New York, 12 Dec 1937, Madrigal Singers, cond. L. Engel

Surrey Apple-howler's Song (trad.), round, children's chorus, 1941

Hymns from the Old South, SATB/SSA, 1949: 1 Morning Star (anon.), 2 Green Fields (Newton), 3 Death, 'tis a melancholy day (Watts)

Kyrie Eleison, SATB, 1953, incl. in Missa pro defunctis

Never Another (M. Van Doren), SATB, 1955, pubd as Praise him who makes us happy

Song for the Stable (A. B. Hall), SATB, 1955, pubd as It seems that God bestowed somehow

How will ye have your partridge today (N. Brown), round, 4vv, 1967, unpubd

Hymn for Pratt Institute (R. Fjelde), SATB, 1968, unpubd

SOLO VOCAL
(with orch)

Five Songs from William Blake, Bar, orch, 1951, unpubd: 1 The Divine Image, 2 Tiger! Tiger!, 3 The Land of Dreams, 4 The Little Black Boy, 5 And did those feet; Louisville, 6 Feb 1952, M. Harrell, Louisville Orchestra, cond. Thomson; arr. Bar, pf; no.2 arr. SATB, pf, 1955, unpubd, arr. TTBB, pf, 1955

Collected Poems (K. Koch), S, Bar, orch, 1959, unpubd; arr. with pf acc.

The Feast of Love (from Pervigilium veneris, trans. Thomson), Bar, orch, 1964; Washington, DC, 1 Nov 1964, D. Clatworthy, National SO, cond. W. Hendl; arr. Bar, pf, unpubd

From Byron's Don Juan, T, orch, 1967, unpubd: 1 Shipwreck, 2 Juan and Haidee; New York, 11 April 1968, R. Kness, New York PO, cond. Stokowski
(with insts)

Five Phrases from The Song of Solomon, S, perc, 1926: 1 Thou that dwellest in the gardens, 2 Return, O Shulamite, 3 O, my Dove, 4 I am my beloved's, 5 By Night; Paris, 30 May 1928, M. Marthine, V. Prahl

Stabat mater (M. Jacob), S, str qt, 1931, rev. 1981; Paris, 15 June 1931, M. Leymo, Krettly Quartet; arr. S, str orch, unpubd, arr. 1v, pf, 1960

Four Songs to Poems of Thomas Campion, Mez, cl, va, harp, 1951: 1 Follow your saint, 2 There is a garden in her face, 3 Rose cheek'd Laura, come, 4 Follow thy fair sun; New York, 11 Feb 1952, H. Glaz, N. Germinara, L. Fuchs, C. Salzedo; arr. Mez, pf, arr. SATB, pf, 1955
(with pf)

The Sunflower (Blake), 1920, unpubd; Vernal Equinox (A. Lowell), 1920, unpubd; 3 Sentences from The Song of Solomon, 1924, unpubd: 1 Thou that dwellest in the gardens, 2 Return, O Shulamite, 3 I am my beloved's; Susie Asado (Stein), 1926; The Tiger (Blake), 1926; Preciosilla (Stein), 1927; La valse grégorienne (G. Hugnet), 1927, rev. 1971: 1 Les écrevisses, 2 Grenadine, 3 La rosée, 4 Le wagon immobile; Le berceau de Gertrude Stein, ou Le mystère de la rue de Fleurus (Hugnet), 1928; Commentaire sur St. Jérome (Marquis de Sade), 1928; Les soirées bagnolaises (Hugnet), 1928, unpubd

3 poèmes de la Duchesse de Rohan, 1928: 1 A son Altessa la Princesse Antoinette Murat, unpubd, 2 Jour de chaleur aux bains de mer, 3 La Seine; Portrait of F. B. [Frances Blood] (Stein), 1929; Air de Phèdre (Racine), 1930; Film: 2 soeurs qui ne sont pas soeurs (Stein), 1930; Oraison funèbre de Henriette-Marie de France, Reine de la Grande-Bretagne (J. Bossuet), 1930, rev. 1934, unpubd; Le singe et le léopard (J. de La Fontaine), 1930; La belle en dormant (Hugnet), 1931: 1 Pour chercher sur la carte des mers, 2 La première de toutes, 3 Mon amour est bon à dire, 4 Partis les vaisseaux; Chamber Music (A. Kreymborg), 1931, unpubd; Dirge (J. Webster), 1939

At the Spring (J. Fisher), 1955; The Bell doth Toll (T. Heywood), 1955; Consider, Lord (Donne), 1955; The Holly and the Ivy (anon. 1557), 1955, unpubd, arr. SATB, pf, 1963; If thou a reason dost desire to know (F. Kynaston), 1955, 1958; John Peel (J. W. Graves), 1955; Look, how the floor of heav'n (Shakespeare), 1955; Remember Adam's Fall (anon. 15th century), 1955; Shakespeare Songs, 1956–7: 1 Was this fair face the cause?, 2 Take, O take those lips away, 3 Tell me where is fancy bred, 4 Pardon, goddess of the night, 5 Sigh no more, ladies

3 estampas de Niñez (R. Rivas), 1957: 1 Todas las horas, 2 Son amigos de todos, 3 Nadie lo oye como ellos; Mostly about Love (Songs for Alice Estey) (K. Koch), 1959: 1 Love Song, 2 Down at the Docks, 3 Let's take a walk, 4 A Prayer to St. Catherine; Mass, 1v/unison vv, pf, 1960, orchd 1962, unpubd; Praises and Prayers, 1963: 1 From the Canticle of the Sun (St. Francis of Assisi, trans. M. Arnold), 2 My master hath a garden (anon.), arr. SATB/ SSA, pf, 1963, 3 Sung by the Shepherds, from A Hymn to the Nativity (R. Crashaw), 4 Before Sleeping (anon.), 5 Jerusalem, my happy home, from the Meditations of St. Augustine

2 by Marianne Moore, 1963: 1 English Usage, 2 My Crow Pluto; From Sneden's Landing Variations (F. O'Hara), 1972, unpubd; The Courtship of the Yongly Bongly Bo (E. Lear), 1973–4 [from Cantata on Poems of Edward Lear]; What is it? (T. Campion), 1v, pf/gui, 1979; The Cat (Larson), S, Bar, pf, 1980

(unaccompanied)

Go to Sleep, Alexander Smallens, Jr., 1935, unpubd; Go to Sleep, Pare McTaggett Lorentz, 1937, unpubd; Go to Sleep, Gabriel Liebowitz, 1979, unpubd

CHAMBER AND INSTRUMENTAL

Sonata da chiesa, cl, tpt, hn, trbn, va, 1926, rev. 1973; Paris, 5 May 1926

[8] Portraits for Violin Alone, 1928–1940: 1 Señorita Juanita de Medina accompanied by her Mother, 2 Madame Marthe-Marthine, 3 Georges Hugnet, Poet and Man of Letters, 4 Miss Gertrude Stein as a Young Girl, 5 Cliquet-Pleyel in F, 6 Mrs. C. W. L. [Chester Whitin Lasell], 7 Sauguet, from Life, 8 Ruth Smallens; Paris, 14 Nov 1928, L. Schwartz

Five Portraits for Four Clarinets, 2 cl, a cl, b cl, 1929: 1 Portrait of Ladies: a Conversation, 2 Portrait of a Young Man in Good Health: Maurice Grosser with a Cold, 3 Christian Bérard, Prisoner, 4 Christian Bérard as a Soldier, 5 Christian Bérard in Person; Boston, 1929, Boston Flute Players Club

Le bains-bar, vn, pf, 1929, unpubd, arr. 2 vn, vc, db, pf, unpubd; arr. tpt, pf as At the Beach, 1949, arr. tpt, band

Portraits for Violin and Piano, 1930–40: 1 Alice Toklas, 2 Mary Reynolds, 3 Anne Miracle, 4 Yvonne de Casa Fuerte; pubd with Cynthia Kemper, a Fanfare, as Five Ladies

Violin Sonata, 1930; Paris, 24 Jan 1931, L. Schwartz, Thomson

Serenade for Flute and Violin, 1931; American première, New York, 13 Nov 1935, C. S. Smith, R. Kemper

String Quartet no.1, 1931; Paris, 15 June 1931, Krettly Quartet; rev. 1957

String Quartet no.2, 1932; Hartford, CT, 14 April 1933, Philharmonic Scholarship Quartet; rev. 1957

Sonata for Flute Alone, 1943; 1943, R. Leroy

Barcarolle for Woodwinds (A Portrait of Georges Hugnet), fl, ob, eng hn, cl, b cl, bn, 1944; Pittsburgh, 29 Nov 1946, Pittsburgh SO, cond. Thomson [arr. of pf piece, 1940]

Party Pieces (Sonorous and Exquisite Corpses), *c*1945, 20 pieces by Thomson, Cowell, Cage, and Harrison [arr. fl, cl, bn, hn, pf, by R. Hughes]

Lamentations: Etude for Accordion, 1959

Variations for Koto, 1961, unpubd

Etude for Cello and Piano . . . Frederic James, 1966, unpubd

Family Portrait, 2 tpt, hn, 2 trbn, 1974: 1 A Fanfare: Robin Smith, 2 At 14: Annie Barnard, 3 A Portrait of Howard Rea, 4 Scherzo: Priscilla Rea, 5 Man of Iron, Willy Eisenhart; New York, 24 March 1975, American Brass Quintet [no.5 arr. from pf piece, 1972]

For Lou Harrison and his Jolly Games 16 Measures (count 'em), theme without instrumentation, 1981, unpubd

A Short Fanfare, 2 tpt/3 tpt/(3 tpt, 2 drums), 1981, unpubd

Bell Piece, 2/4 players, 1983

Cynthia Kemper: a Fanfare, 1983, pubd with Portraits for Violin and Piano as Five Ladies

Lili Hasings, vn, pf, 1983, unpubd

A Portrait of Two [Joelle Amar, Benjamin Zifkin], 1984, unpubd

Jay Rosen: Portrait and Fugue, b tuba, pf, 1984–5, unpubd

Stockton Fanfare, 3 tpt, 2 drums, 1985

KEYBOARD
(Portraits, pf)

1929: Travelling in Spain . . . Alice Woodfin Branlière, P6; Alternations . . . Maurice Grosser, P1; Catalan Waltz . . . Ramón Senabre, P2

1930: Madame Dubost chez elle, P5; Pastoral . . . Jean Ozenne, P3; Russell Hitchcock Reading, P5; Clair Leonard's Profile, P6

1935: Meditation . . . Jere Abbott, P2, orchd 1944; Sea Coast . . . Constance Askew, P2; A Portrait of R. Kirk Askew [Jr.], P2; The Hunt . . . A. Everett Austin, Jr., P4; Helen Austin at Home and Abroad, P5; Souvenir . . . Paul Bowles, P3; Connecticut Waltzes . . . Harold Lewis Cook, P6; Hymn . . . Josiah Marvel, P4; Tennis . . . Henry McBride, P4; The John Moser Waltzes [used as no.6 in the ballet Filling Station]; Prelude and Fugue . . . Miss Agnes Rindge, P3; An Old Song . . . Carrie Stettheimer, P1; Ettie Stettheimer, P5; A Day Dream . . . Herbert Whiting

1938: Maurice Bavoux: Young and Alone, P6; Portrait of Claude Biais, unpubd; A French Boy of Ten: Louis Lange, P5

Work-list

1940: Tango Lullaby . . . Mlle [Flavie] Alvarez de Toledo, P1, orchd 1944; With Tpt and Hn . . . Louise Ardant, incl. in 9 Etudes; Poltergeist . . . Hans Arp, P4; Stretching . . . Jamie Campbell, P6; Cantabile . . . Nicolas de Chatelain, P3, arr. str orch, 1944; Duet . . . Clarita, Comtesse de Forceville, P6; In a Bird Cage . . . Lise Deharme, P2; Pf Sonata no.4: Guggenheim jeune [Peggy Guggenheim]; Barcarolle . . . Georges Hugnet, P1, arr. fl, ob, eng hn, cl, b cl, bn, 1944; Aria . . . Germaine Hugnet, P2; Invention: Theodate Johnson Busy and Resting, P6; Fanfare for France . . . Max Kahn, P2, arr. ww, 1944; 5-finger Exercise . . . Léon Kochnitzky, P2; Awake or Asleep . . . Pierre Mabille, P5; The Bard . . . Sherry Mangan, P3; Canons with Cadenza . . . André Ostier, P3; Bugles and Birds . . . Pablo Picasso, P1, arr. vc, pf, 1942, orchd 1944; Dora Maar or the Presence of Pablo Picasso, P6; Lullaby which is also a Spinning Song . . . Howard Putzel, P4; The Dream World of Peter Rose-Pulham, P3; Fugue . . . Alexander Smallens, P1, orchd 1944; Swiss Waltz . . . Sophie Tauber-Arp, P4; Eccentric Dance . . . Madame Kristians Tonny; Pastoral . . . Tristan Tzara, P5; Toccata . . . Mary Widney, P3

1941: Insistences . . . Louise Crane, P4, arr. band as Study Piece, 1969; With Fife and Drums . . . Mina Curtiss, P1; Perc Piece . . . Jessie K. Lasell, unpubd, orchd 1944; Parades . . . Florine Stettheimer, P6, arr. brass, perc, as Metropolitan Museum Fanfare, 1969

1942: James Patrick Cannon, Professional Revolutionary, P6; Aaron Copland, Persistently Pastoral, P6, orchd as Pastorale, 1944; Scottish Memories: Peter Monro Jack, P6; Prisoner of the Mind: Schuyler Watts, P5; Wedding Music . . . Jean [Mrs. Schuyler] Watts, P4

1943: 5-finger Exercise . . . Briggs Buchanan, incl. in 10 Etudes

1945: Solitude . . . Lou Harrison, P1

1951: Chromatic Double Harmonies . . . Sylvia Marlowe, incl. in 9 Etudes

1956: Homage to Marya Freund and to the Harp, P6, arr. harp, orch, as movt 1 of Autumn, 1964

1958: A Study in Stacked-up Thirds, rev. 1969 as For Eugene Ormandy's Birthday, 18 Nov 1969, P5

1966: Edges . . . Robert Indiana, arr. band, 1969

1972: Man of Iron . . . Willy Eisenhart, arr. brass qnt as movt 5 of Family Portrait, 1974

1981, all incl. in P7: Franco Assetto: Drawing V. T.; Gerald Busby: Giving Full Attention; Sam Byers: with Joy; Christopher Cox: Singing a Song; Noah Creshevsky: Loyal, Steady, and Persistent; Barbara Epstein: Untiring; Norma Flender: Waltzing; Richard Flender: Solid not Stolid; Dead Pan: Mrs. Betty Freeman; Morris Golde: Showing Delight; Buffie Johnson: Drawing V. T. in

Charcoal; Bill Katz: Wide Awake; Round and Round: Dominique Nabokov; Craig Rutenberg: Swinging; Anne-Marie Soullière: Something of a Beauty; Karen Brown Waltuck: Intensely Two; Scott Wheeler: Free-wheeling; John Wright: Drawing

1982, unpubd unless otherwise stated: Dennis Russell Davies: in a Hammock; Molly Davies: Terminations; David Dubal: in Flight; Doña Flor: Receiving; Rodney Lister: Music for a Merry-go-round; Dr. Marcel Roche: Making a Decision; Paul Sanfaçon: on the Ice, P7

1983, unpubd: Mark Beard: Never Alone; Power Boothe: with Pencil; Charles Fussell: in Meditation; Glynn Boothe Harte: Reaching; Bennett Lerner: Senza espressione; Peter McWilliams: Firmly Spontaneous; Malitte Matta: in the Executive Style; Phillip Ramey: Thinking Hard; Louis Rispoli: in a Boat; Vassilis Voglin: on the March

1984, unpubd: Brendan Lemon; John Houseman: No Changes, rev. 1985 and orchd as A Double Take; Lines: for and about Ron Henggeler; Boris Baranovic: Whirling; Tony Tommasini: a Study in Chords, orchd as Major Chords

1985, unpubd: Christopher Beach Alone; Danyal Lawson: Playing; Jane Bowles Early and as Remembered; Philip Claflin: dans le temps très noceur; Robin Holloway

(other pf)

Prelude, 1921; 2 [orig. 3] Sentimental Tangos, 1923, unpubd, orchd 1923; Synthetic Waltzes, 2 pf / pf 4 hands, 1925; 5 2-part Inventions, 1926; 10 Easy Pieces and a Coda, 1926; Sonata no.1, 1929, orchd as Sym. no.2, 1931; Sonata no.2, 1929, arr. harp, orch as movts 2–4 of Autumn, 1964; Sonata no.3, 1930

10 Etudes, 1943–4: 1 Repeating Tremolo (Fanfare), 2 Tenor Lead (Madrigal), 3 Fingered Fifths (Canon), 4 Fingered Glissando (Aeolian Harp), 5 Double Glissando (Waltz), 6 For the Weaker Fingers (Music Box Lullaby), 7 Oscillating Arm (Spinning Song), 8 5-finger Exercise . . . Briggs Buchanan, 9 Parallel Chords (Tango), 10 Ragtime Bass; nos. 2 and 10 pubd separately

9 Etudes: 1 With Tpt and Hn . . . Louise Ardant, 1940, 2 Pivoting on the Thumb, 3 Alternating Octaves, 4 Double Sevenths, 5 The Harp, 6 Chromatic Major Seconds (The Wind), 7 Chromatic Double Harmonies . . . Sylvia Marlowe, 8 Broken Arpeggios (The Waltzing Waters), 9 Gui and Mand, 1951

For a Happy Occasion (Happy Birthday for Mrs. Zimbalist), 1951

(org)

Fanfare, 1922; Passacaglia, 1922, rev. 1974; Pastorale on a Christmas Plainsong, 1922; Prelude, 1922; 5 Chorale-preludes, 1924: 1 O sacred head now wounded!, 2–4 The New-born Babe [3 versions], 5 Praise God, ye Christians ev'rywhere; Variations on Sunday School Tunes, 1926–7: 1 Come ye disconsolate, 2 There's not a friend like the lowly Jesus, 3 Will there be any stars in my crown?, 4 Shall we gather at the river?; Church Organ Wedding Music, 1940, rev. 1978; Pange lingua, 1962; Theme for an improvisation by McNeil Robinson, 1981, unpubd; Organ Voluntaries 1, 2, and 3: a Suite, 1985

FILM SCORES
(all unpublished)

The Plow that Broke the Plains (dir. P. Lorentz), 1936; New York, 25 May 1936; arr. orch suite

The River (dir. Lorentz), 1937; New Orleans, 29 Oct 1937; arr. orch suite

The Spanish Earth (dir. Ivens), montage of Sp. folk music, 1937, collab. Blitzstein

Tuesday in November (dir. J. Houseman), 1945, incl. Fugue and Chorale on Yankee Doodle, Pastorale (Portrait of Aaron Copland), and Walking Song; Walking Song arr. pf, 1951, unpubd

Louisiana Story (dir. R. Flaherty), 1948; Edinburgh, Scotland, 22 Aug 1948; arr. orch suite and as Acadian Songs and Dances

The Goddess (dir. P. Chayevsky), 1957; Brussels, Belgium, June 1958

Power Among Men (dir. Dickinson, J. C. Sheers), 1958; New York, 5 March 1959; arr. orch suite as Fugues and Cantilenas

Journey to America (dir. Houseman), 1964; New York, July 1964; arr. orch suite as Pilgrims and Pioneers

INCIDENTAL MUSIC
(unpublished unless otherwise stated)

Le droit de Varech (G. Hugnet), 1930; A Bride for the Unicorn (D. Johnston), 1934; Hamlet (Shakespeare), 1936; Horse Eats Hat (E. Labiche, trans. E. Denby), 1936 [music by P. Bowles, orchd Thomson]; Injunction Granted, a Living Newspaper, 1936; Macbeth (Shakespeare), 1936; Antony and Cleopatra (Shakespeare), 1937; Androcles and the Lion (G. B. Shaw), 1938 [not orchd by Thomson]; The Trojan Women (Euripides), 1940; The Life of a Careful Man (CBS Workshop), 1941; Oidipous Tyrannos (Sophocles), 1941

The Grass Harp (T. Capote), 1952; King Lear (Shakespeare), 1952; Ondine (J. Giraudoux), 1954, pubd; King John (Shakespeare), 1956; Measure for Measure (Shakespeare), 1956, Take, O take those lips away, pubd; The Merchant of Venice (Shakespeare), 1957, Tell me where is fancy bred, pubd; Much Ado about Nothing (Shakespeare), 1957, Pardon, goddess of the night and Sigh, no more, ladies, pubd; Othello (Shakespeare), 1957; Bertha (Koch), 1959

Papers in *CtY-Mus*

Principal publishers: Boosey & Hawkes, Belwin-Mills, C. Fisher, Peters, Presser, G. Schirmer, Southern

WRITINGS

† – *selected writings from the "New York Herald-Tribune"*
The State of Music (New York, 1939/R1974, rev. 2/1961)
†*The Musical Scene* (New York, 1945/R1968)
†*The Art of Judging Music* (New York, 1948/R1969)
†*Music Right and Left* (New York, 1951/R1969)
Virgil Thomson (New York, 1966/R1977)
†*Music Reviewed, 1940–1954* (New York, 1967)
American Music since 1910 (New York, 1971)
A Virgil Thomson Reader (New York, 1981)

BIBLIOGRAPHY

A. Copland: "Our Younger Generation: Ten Years Later," *MM*, xiii/4 (1936), 5

S. Barlow: "American Composers, XVII: Virgil Thomson," *MM*, xviii (1940–41), 242

R. F. Eyer: "Virgil Thomson," *MusAm*, lxiv/7 (1944), 7

C. Smith: "Gertrude S., Virgil T., and Susan B.," *Theatre Arts*, xxxi/7 (1947), 17

P. Glanville-Hicks: "Virgil Thomson," *MQ*, xxxv (1949), 209 [incl. list of works]

F. W. Sternfeld: "Current Chronicle," *MQ*, xxxv (1949), 115

——: "Louisiana Story," *MTNAP*, xliii (1949), 40

B. H. Haggin: "Virgil Thomson as Critic," *The Nation*, clxxiii (22 Sept 1951), 242 [review of *Music Right and Left*]

C. Smith: "Thomson's Four Saints Live again on Broadway," *MusAm*, lxxii/7 (1952), 7

M. G. Field: "Virgil Thomson and the Maturity of American Music," *The Chesterian*, xxviii (1953–4), 111

H. R. Garvin: "Sound and Sense in Four Saints in Three Acts," *Bucknell Review*, v/1 (1954), 1

E. Helm: "Virgil Thomson's Four Saints in Three Acts," *MR*, xv (1954), 127

K. Hoover and J. Cage: *Virgil Thomson: his Life and Music* (New York, 1959)

R. Jackson: *The Operas of Gertrude Stein and Virgil Thomson* (diss., Tulane U., 1962)

E. Cook: "Virgil Thomson: the Composer in Person," *HiFi/Stereo Review*, xiv/5 (1965), 58 [interview]

D. Hall: "A Thomson Discography," *HiFi/Stereo Review*, xiv/5 (1965), 57

H. C. Schonberg: "Virgil Thomson: Parisian from Missouri," *HiFi/Stereo Review*, xiv/5 (1965), 48

Bibliography

R. Craft: "Selective Self-portrait," *Harper's Magazine*, ccxxxiii (1966), 120

"Thomson, Virgil (Garnett)," *CBY 1966*

M. Steinberg: "Musician as Writer," *Commentary*, xliii/5 (1967), 96

D. Henahan: "And Now, Virgil's Odyssey," *New York Times* (21 March 1971), 15

P. J. Smith: "Musician of the Month," *HiFi/MusAm*, xxi/11 (1971), 8

M. Dulman: "Independent Spirit: Virgil Thomson Speaks Out," *Opera News*, xli/1 (1976), 16

J. Rockwell: "Virgil Thomson Vigorous at 80," *New York Times* (25 Nov 1976), 38

"A Tribute to Virgil Thomson on his 81st Birthday," *Parnassus: Poetry in Review*, v/2 (1977), 405–531

G. Freedman: "Everbest, Virgil Thomson," *MJ*, xxv/3 (1977), 8

K. M. Ward: *An Analysis of the Relationship between Text and Musical Shape and an Investigation of the Relationship between Text and Surface Rhythmic Detail in "Four Saints in Three Acts" by Virgil Thomson* (diss., U. of Texas, Austin, 1978)

"Yale Music Library Receives Thomson Papers," *Notes*, xxxvi (1979–80), 78

H. Gleason and W. Becker: "Virgil Thomson," *20th-century American Composers*, Music Literature Outlines, ser. iv (Bloomington, IN, rev. 2/1981), 170 [incl. further bibliography]

H. W. Hitchcock: "Homage to Virgil Thomson at Eighty-five," *ISAM Newsletter*, xi/1 (1981), 1

R. Craft: "A Musical Offering," *New York Review* (4 Feb 1982), 8 [review of *A Virgil Thomson Reader*]

D. J. Soria: "Artist Life: Virgil Thomson," *HiFi/MusAm*, xxxii/2 (1982), 8

M. Meckna: *The Rise of the American Composer-critic: Aaron Copland, Roger Sessions, Virgil Thomson, and Elliott Carter in the Periodical Modern Music, 1924–1946* (diss., U. of California, Santa Barbara, 1984)

A. C. Tommasini: "The Musical Portraits of Virgil Thomson," *MQ*, lxx (1984), 234

——: *The Musical Portraits of Virgil Thomson* (New York, 1985)

"Virgil Thomson . . . Comments on Turning 90 Years Old," *New York Times* (21 Sept 1986), §I, 66

M. Meckna: *Virgil Thomson: a Bio-bibliography* (Westport, CT, 1986)

L. Raver: "Virgil Thomson, AGO Composer of the Year 1986: the Solo Organ Music," *American Organist*, xx/4 (1986), 115

J. Rockwell: "Virgil Thomson's 'Saints' Goes Marching On," *New York Times* (9 Nov 1986), §II, 1

V. Thomson: *Selected Letters*, ed. T. Page and V. W. Page (New York, 1987)

ROGER SESSIONS

John Harbison
Andrea Olmstead

CHAPTER THREE

Roger Sessions

1. LIFE. Roger Huntington Sessions was born in Brooklyn on 28 December 1896 and grew up in Hadley, Massachusetts, his mother's ancestral home, and in New York, where his father practiced law. At the age of 11 he announced his intention to become a composer, and his sense of purpose was unswerving thereafter. He received the BA at Harvard University when he was 18, and went on to study with Horatio Parker at Yale (BMus 1917), where he was awarded the Steinert Prize for his Symphonic Prelude, and finally and most fruitfully with Ernest Bloch in New York (from 1919). He taught theory at Smith College from 1917 to 1921, when he became Bloch's assistant at the Cleveland Institute; he remained there until 1925.

From 1926 to 1933 Sessions lived mostly in Europe (Florence, Rome, and Berlin), supported by two Guggenheim Fellowships (1926, 1927), a Rome Prize (1928), and a grant from the Carnegie Foundation (1931). There he witnessed the advent of fascism, an experience that nourished an abiding interest in world politics and a special sensitivity to their ethical implications, evidenced in many of his writings. Having seen the destructive power of poor leadership, he retained, as an inveterate humanist, a faith in the healing power of progressive leaders, dedicating elegiac movements to Franklin Roosevelt and John Kennedy in his Second Symphony and Third Piano Sonata. During this period Sessions collaborated with Copland, whom he had met in Paris, in presenting the Copland-Sessions Concerts of contemporary music in New York, between 1928 and 1931. He also served as president of the American section of the ISCM (1934–42), of which he later became co-chairman with Copland (from 1953) and an honorary life member (from 1959). His circle of friends at this time included Paul Hindemith, Artur Schnabel, Otto Klemperer, and Alfredo Casella, as well as the leading American musicians of his generation.

On his permanent return to the USA Sessions resumed his teaching career, holding positions briefly at Boston University, the New School for Social Research, Malkin Conservatory, and the Dalcroze School. In 1935 he joined the faculty at Princeton, remaining there until 1944, when he became professor of music at the University of California, Berkeley. In 1953 he returned to Princeton as Conant Professor of Music and in 1959 was appointed a co-director of the Columbia–Princeton Electronic Music Center in New York. Following his retirement from Princeton in 1965, he was Bloch Professor at Berkeley (1966–7), Norton Professor at Harvard (1968–9), and a faculty member of the Juilliard School. He died in Princeton on 16 March 1985. Sessions was elected to the National Institute of Arts and Letters (1938), the American Academy of Arts and Letters (1953), and the American Academy of Arts and Sciences (1961); his many other honors included a Brandeis University Creative Arts Award (1958), the Gold Medal of the American Academy of Arts and Letters (1961), and a MacDowell Medal (1968). He received two Pulitzer Prizes, the first, a career award, in 1974 and the second for his Concerto for Orchestra in 1982. His Second Symphony received a New York Music Critics' Circle Award in 1950.

Possible influences in the formation of Sessions's musical temperament – expressing melancholy without self-indulgence, loneliness without isolation – may be his parents' early decision to live apart and his own divorce from his first wife Barbara (whom he had married in 1920) in 1937 after years of separation, events

6. Roger Sessions, early 1950s

which, given his generation and social background, carried considerable weight. However, no account of Sessions's life is sufficient without mention of the happy family life he enjoyed with his second wife, Elizabeth Franck, and his long friendships with many colleagues, especially that with the Italian composer Luigi Dallapiccola.

2. TEACHING AND WRITINGS. Sessions's effectiveness as a teacher is attested by the great diversity of approaches now taken by his former pupils, among whom are Babbitt, Cone, Davies, Del Tredici, Kirchner, Martino, Nancarrow, and Weisgall. He taught no method, speaking instead of respect for craft, devotion to the art, and suspicion for "style" and fashion. His writings address many difficult contemporary musical issues, from the practical to the philosophical. Sessions was editor of the *Harvard Musical Review* (1915–17) and contributed regularly to *Modern Music* from 1927 until the early 1940s on musical and theoretical works of Schenker, Krenek, Hindemith, and others. The best overview of his thought is provided by *Roger Sessions on Music: the Collected Essays* (1979) while the most universally applicable and aphoristic is *The Musical Experience*, a set of lectures given at Juilliard in 1949. Of his other books *Harmonic Practice* resulted from his teaching experiences at Berkeley in the 1940s, and *Questions about Music*, an exposition of his aesthetics, dates from his time as Norton Professor at Harvard. Though sometimes marred by a penchant for the qualifying phrase, Sessions's writings at their best are much like his teaching was, reinforcing the best impulses in the reader and giving courage for the struggle toward artistic, cultural, and personal maturity.

3. WORKS. Symphonies, piano sonatas, string quartets, cantatas, and operas form the core of Sessions's catalogue, which is notably sparse in minor works and occasional pieces. He showed

no interest in the mixed chamber ensemble that flourished in the years after World War II, nor in concertos for unusual instruments, nor wind or brass quintets. Unlike Britten, Tippett, Carter, Copland, Shostakovich, and Stravinsky, Sessions seemed to have had no penchant for the practical piece. He said that he "relaxed" from the Whitman cantata (*When Lilacs Last in the Dooryard Bloom'd*) by writing the compact, volatile, technically taxing Rhapsody for large orchestra.

This loftiness of purpose was clear from the start. The early works were written at three- or four-year intervals, each forming a definitive achievement but also representing steps towards an ultimate goal – the fluent, rich, highly inflected style, luxuriant with free chromatic counterpoint, that crystallized in the late 1950s. In the decade following his opera *Montezuma* (1963) Sessions suddenly broke loose, writing five symphonies, two grandly conceived choral cantatas, a Double Concerto for violin, cello, and orchestra, three other orchestral works, and remarkable solo works for piano and cello. Together with Messiaen, Dallapiccola, and Tippett, Sessions helped make the often maligned decade of the 1960s one of the richest in the 20th century.

(*i*) *Up to 1947.* Sessions's most frequently performed work is the early orchestral suite derived from his incidental music for *The Black Maskers* (1923); he often called it his *Firebird* or *Verklärte Nacht*, a reference to the high public profile of the piece compared with that of other more characteristic works. (*The Black Maskers* is in fact even less representative of Sessions than *Firebird* and *Verklärte Nacht* are of Stravinsky and Schoenberg.) It is the work of an arresting composer, but one still unresolved in direction, and its place as Sessions's bridge to a wider public could be taken more aptly by the First Symphony (1926–7).

Sessions began as a Stravinskian in his investigation of new uses for tonality, clearly marked motifs and sections, and bright, non-expressionist orchestral colors. But in the First Symphony, especially in the slow movement, the ways in which Sessions would never resemble Stravinsky are already apparent – a fascination with long phrases, and a love of elaborated transitions and dense accompanying polyphonies. His next work, the Piano Sonata no. 1 (1930), moves even further from a Stravinskian idiom, exhibiting less static harmony, less ostinato, and freer lines. However, the piece retained sufficient allegiances to diatonic stability (mainly through fourth chords) and sturdy, even jazzy, rhythms for Copland, recognizing a co-builder of an American style, to call it "a cornerstone upon which to base an American music."

The degree to which Sessions was not to be confined by an American movement became apparent five years later in the Violin Concerto (1935), a work in which his international and individual tendencies are fully revealed. The music is forged in gigantic periods in which diatonic melodic shapes and harmonies serve only as points of departure (and very occasionally of return). Sessions's "grand ligne" is heard in full cry for the first time with all its implications – a firm, melodically clear, intermittently "functional" bass line, active and shapely yet subordinate accompaniments, and an unrestrainable reaching towards distant and satisfying goals. In the extended tonality of the Violin Concerto Sessions seems to achieve both a mastery and a recognition of its limits, an impression confirmed and consolidated by the String Quartet no. 1 (1936).

The three years that passed before *Pages from a Diary* was completed (1940) were by Sessions's own account one of his most difficult creative episodes. In these short pieces he faced the chromatic implications of the Violin Concerto's linear freedom and, in the second piece, started more consistently to use voice-leading as the basis for his harmony. Sessions began to move towards the Schoenbergian pole of attraction, crucial to his later development. The consequences of this searching transitional stage became evident in the Second Symphony, the first piece in which the experience of the previous three or four years comes to fruition. In emotional force this symphony goes beyond the Violin Concerto and, partly due to the freer dissonant counterpoint and partly to the sheer confidence of the discourse, it takes a dramatic stance new to Sessions's music. The juxtaposition, within a single movement, of extremes of violence and lyricism – a stretching of the sonata principle that placed productive stress on his refined art of transition – thereafter became an important trait of his music. Some sense of key remains in the Second Symphony (1944–6) as well as in the Piano Sonata no.2 and the one-act opera *The Trial of Lucullus*, but the real organizing force has become the control of sectional lengths, the weight of the contrasts, and the allusiveness of the motivic connections. Accompaniments move for the most part in steady rhythms, balancing the increasing volatility of the harmony. Their rhythmic release would not take place until after *Montezuma*.

(ii) 1947–63. It is no accident that Sessions began work on his largest piece, the opera *Montezuma*, at the conclusion of his Second Symphony in 1947, and no surprise that he was able to include unaltered some of the music from this time in the final product of 1963; he had found by 1947 the dramatic scope he needed. His adoption of the 12-tone system a few years later was such a natural outgrowth of his thinking on every level that it caused barely a ripple on the stylistic surface.

In the ten years after the Second Symphony Sessions's productivity increased, in spite of his intense activities as a teacher and writer. The music of this decade sometimes takes on too great an import: despite their many beauties, the Sonata for solo violin and the String Quartet no.2 seem like would-be symphonies, strenuous and even didactic, and the Piano Concerto

87

and the Mass contain passages of a similar nature. But no chalk dust clings to the *Idyll of Theocritus* (1954); instead there is a white heat, fired by the text, and a distinct lack of calculation and reserve. With its flexible use of refrain elements, forceful climaxes, broad, declamatory vocal melodies, and rich orchestral colors, the *Idyll* is one of Sessions's most immediate pieces.

The Third Symphony (1957), composed for the 75th anniversary of the Boston SO, is Sessions's last orchestral work to be as long as a half-hour in duration; thereafter economy and aphorism became more and more prized. The Third Symphony, however, is very amply proportioned. It contains a song-like first movement in sonata form followed by two especially propulsive fast movements (with touches of rough-edged humor), and one of Sessions's most profound slow movements. In this work Sessions fully refined his use of the orchestra, preferring to explore myriad mixtures from all the different families, with the percussion an equal partner, rather than employ the brass, wind, and string choirs antiphonally, in the manner of the "American School." Tuttis are notable for their wide registers and clarity of individual elements, and solos are set in accompaniments of great variety and subtlety. Instruments tend to play in their best registers and are seldom driven to impersonation or caricature; first violins often soar startlingly high, and unusual solo instruments such as the xylophone or contrabassoon are apt to appear. For the remainder of his career this orchestra was to be Sessions's chosen medium.

Such an orchestra dominates *Montezuma* (1963), Sessions's largest work. Filled with spectacular orchestral color, the opera requires a Wagnerian orchestra pit to control the balances between orchestra and singers. G. A. Borgese's text provided Sessions with the kind of ethical conflicts and grand historical moments that had engaged him in the earlier opera *The Trial of Lucullus*, but it also supplied some confusing verbal detail. The vocal music in *Mon-*

tezuma, cast in a pliable declamatory arioso that reflects the composer's affection for late Verdi, brings moments of powerful expression. But the most unforgettable moments in the first productions were pantomimes – the meeting of Cortez and Montezuma, and the Sacrifice – in which the eloquence of the orchestra is more than sufficient.

(iii) After 1963. At the time he completed *Montezuma* Sessions was 67, and about to begin his most productive decade. The opera had forged the idiom that remained constant for the rest of his career: contrasts are more sudden, transitions more swift, sections less balanced, and motivic connections less literal. It is a typical late style with one exception: Sessions had always been a composer so abundant with ideas, even for subordinate figures, that a paring-down did not leave his textures lean. The late pieces retain the verdant detail of previous works but it is marshaled within a different pacing.

The Sixth Symphony, with the bright steely surface of its fast movements, is one of Sessions's most extroverted pieces. It is followed by the slow tempos and harsh pessimism of the Seventh, whose downward pull seems beyond consolation. A more balanced character is achieved in the Eighth Symphony, the first of the more flowing orchestral pieces that Sessions was to favor at the end of his career. Having refined his idiom so painstakingly early in his career, Sessions was not concerned as much in these pieces with new ground as with widening the expressive range of his chosen language.

Nowhere is that range more evident than in the cantata *When Lilacs Last in the Dooryard Bloom'd* (1970; fig. 7). Whitman's text is set with such fervor that it would seem that the piece must break apart, yet no work of Sessions has a more natural and inevitable flow. Sessions had always been a Whitmanesque composer, his irregular rhythms seemingly generated by a sponta-

89

neous extra syllable, and his big, asymmetrical phrases springing forward like Whitman's sprawling, irrepressible poetic lines. One of Sessions's great public successes, this cantata could have been the final statement of a remarkable career, but Sessions continued to compose, at a somewhat less dazzling pace, eventually crowning his career with a Concerto for Orchestra (1981) for the Boston SO's 100th anniversary. At 84 he had written a work of physical vigor and elegant proportions, whose final valedictory pages strike a new tone: ceremonial, generous – a comrade beginning a new journey.

4. CONCLUSION. Sessions's reputation was secured early; Koussevitzky and Mitropoulos introduced the first two symphonies, and his contemporaries recognized his leading position. But followup performances were rare, and Sessions's slow pace prevented him from presenting new pieces in successive seasons. Critical response to his music, especially in the *New York Times*, was guarded and dryly respectful, seldom genuinely enthusiastic. Even after his phenomenally productive late period, his work is less frequently heard than his mastery would seem to mandate. In 1964 Stravinsky expressed the hope that *Montezuma* would soon be produced in the USA, adding, "One would not have to 'hope' if he was a German composer living in Munich and published in Mainz." The opera was eventually staged 11 years later by the Boston Opera Company.

The slow pace of public recognition never affected Sessions's sense of purpose. In his compositions and writings he always insisted on the integrity of the musical idea and the capacity of such ideas to find hearers. His faith was amply justified by later performances of *Lilacs*, the Violin Concerto, and *The Trial of Lucullus*. In his final years he began to receive warm critical appraisals, especially in the *New Yorker* magazine and in the English press.

7. Opening of the autograph MS of Sessions's "When Lilacs Last in the Dooryard Bloom'd," 1970

Sessions often quoted his friend Alfredo Casella, who said that his music was "born difficult." The difficulties for performers and listeners are not the result of calculations or intellectual schemes, but of a complex and spontaneous mind. Copland referred to Sessions as a "philosopher" in music. If so, he was a Stoic, but one capable of ecstatic visions. His music reveals a cultivated but far from elitist personality, one able to resolve intricate conflicts into challenging direct communication. Sessions's works often become clearer to the listener some time after they have been heard: when the demanding textures are recalled synoptically, a flash of insight may occur. They are pieces that occupy more than their moments in time.

WORKS
(all published unless otherwise stated)

STAGE

Lancelot and Elaine (opera, Tennyson), 1910, unpubd

The Black Maskers (incidental music, L. Andreyeff), 1923, unpubd, Northampton, MA, June 1923, cond. Sessions; arr. orch suite, 1928, Cincinnati, 5 Dec 1930, cond. F. Reiner

Turandot (incidental music, Volkmüller), 1925, unpubd; Cleveland, 8 May 1925, cond. Sessions

The Trial of Lucullus (opera, 1, B. Brecht), 1947, unpubd; Berkeley, CA, 18 April 1947, cond. Sessions

Montezuma (opera, 3, G. A. Borgese), 1947–63; Berlin, 19 April 1964, cond. H. Hollreiser

Inc., unpubd: The Fall of the House of Usher (opera, Poe, Eliot), 1925; The Emperor's New Clothes (opera, Porter), 1978–84

ORCHESTRAL

Symphony in D, 1917, unpubd

Nocturne for Orchestra, 1921–2, unpubd

Symphony no.1, e, 1926–7; Boston, 22 April 1927, cond. Koussevitzky

Three Dirges, 1933, withdrawn, unpubd

Violin Concerto, 1930–35; Chicago, 8 Jan 1940, R. Gross, cond. I. Solomon

Symphony no.2, 1944–6; San Francisco, 9 Jan 1947, cond. Monteux

Piano Concerto, 1955–6; New York, 10 Feb 1956, B. Webster, cond. Morel

Symphony no.3, 1957; Boston, 6 Dec 1957, cond. Munch

Symphony no.4, 1958; Minneapolis, 2 Jan 1960, cond. Dorati

Divertimento, 1959–60; Honolulu, HI, 9 Jan 1965, Honolulu SO, cond. G. Barati

Symphony no.5, 1964; Philadelphia, 7 Feb 1964, cond. Ormandy

Symphony no.6, 1966; Newark, 19 Nov 1966, cond. K. Schermerhorn

Symphony no.7, 1966–7; Ann Arbor, MI, 1 Oct 1967, Chicago SO, cond. J. Martinon

Symphony no.8, 1968; New York, 2 May 1968, cond. Steinberg

Rhapsody for Orchestra, 1970; Baltimore, March 1970, cond. Comissiona

Concerto for Violin, Cello, and Orchestra, 1970–71; New York, 5 Nov 1971, P. Zukofsky, J. Sessions, cond. Barzin

Concertino for Chamber Orchestra, 1971–2; Chicago, 14 April 1972, cond. R. Shapey

Symphony no.9, 1975–8; Syracuse, 17 Jan 1980, cond. C. Keene

Concerto for Orchestra, 1981; Boston, 23 Oct 1981, cond. Ozawa

Inc., unpubd: Strophes, pf, orch, 1927–9; Orch Suite, 1929; Sym., 1929; Ballata [after Boccaccio: Decameron], 1929–30; Waltzes, 1929–31, lost; Sym., 1934–5

VOCAL

Romualdo's Song (Andreyeff), S, orch, 1923; Northampton, MA, June 1923

On the Beach at Fontana (Joyce), S, pf, 1930; London, England, 1930

Turn, O Libertad (Whitman), mixed chorus, pf 4 hands/2 pf, 1944; New York, April 1944, cond. Sessions

Idyll of Theocritus (Theocritus, trans. R. C. Trevelyan), S, orch, 1954; Louisville, 14 Jan 1956, A. Nossaman, cond. R. Whitney

Mass for Unison Choir, 1955; New York, April 1956, cond. Sessions

Psalm cxl, S, org, 1963, Princeton, NJ, June 1963; version for S, orch, Boston, 11 Feb 1966, A. Elgar, cond. Leinsdorf, orch score unpubd

When Lilacs Last in the Dooryard Bloom'd (Whitman), cantata, S, A, Bar, chorus, orch, 1964–70; Berkeley, CA, 23 May 1971, H. Joseph, S. Friedman, A. Shearer, cond. M. Senturia

Three Choruses on Biblical Texts (Ps. cxxx, Isaiah, Pss. cxlvii, cxlviii, cl), chorus, orch, 1971–2; Amherst, MA, 8 Feb 1975, cond. L. Spratlan

CHAMBER

Piano Trio, 1916, unpubd

Violin Sonata, 1916, unpubd

Pastorale, fl, 1927, lost, unpubd

String Quartet no.1, e, 1936; Washington, DC, April 1937, Coolidge String
  Quartet
Duo, vn, pf, 1942; Princeton, NJ, Jan 1943, J. Antal, R. Sessions
String Quartet no.2, 1950–1; Madison, WI, 28 May 1951, Pro Arte Quartet
Violin Sonata, 1953; San Francisco, 1953, R. Gross
Quintet, 2 vn, 2 va, vc, 1957–8; movts 1 and 2 only, Berkeley, CA, 1958,
  Griller Quartet, F. Molnar; complete, New York, 23 Nov 1959, Lenox Quar-
  tet, J. Fawcett
Six Pieces, vc, 1966; New York, 31 March 1968, J. Sessions
Canons (to the Memory of Igor Stravinsky), str qt, 1971; London, England
  1972
Inc., unpubd: miscellaneous compositions, 1935–44; Studies in Counterpoint,
  1938–41; Duo, vn, vc, 1978; Violin Sonata, 1981

KEYBOARD

Three Chorale Preludes, org, 1924, 1926; New York, Dec 1927, J. Yasser
Piano Sonata no.1, 1927–30; New York, 6 May 1928, J. Duke
Four Pieces for Children, pf: Scherzino, 1935, March, 1935, Waltz, 1936, Little
  Piece 1939
Pages from a Diary (From my Diary), pf, 1937–9; New York, Nov 1939, R.
  Sessions; 2nd movt rev. 1940
Chorale, org, 1938; Princeton, NJ, April 1938, R. Hufstader
Piano Sonata no.2, 1946; New York, March 1947, A. Foldes
Piano Sonata no.3, 1964–5; Berkeley, CA, March 1969, J. Lateiner
Five Pieces, pf, 1974–5; Davis, CA, May 1977, R. Miller
Waltz, pf, 1977–8

MSS in *DLC*, *NjP*, *NN*
Principal publishers: Marks, Presser

WRITINGS

The Musical Experience of Composer, Performer, Listener (Princeton, NJ, 1950/*R* 1962)
Harmonic Practice (New York, 1951)
Reflections on the Music Life in the United States (New York, 1956)
Questions about Music (Cambridge, MA, 1970/*R* 1971)
ed. E. T. Cone: *Roger Sessions on Music: Collected Essays* (Princeton, NJ, 1979)
Many articles for *MM*, *Harvard Musical Review*, and other periodicals

BIBLIOGRAPHY

EwenD

P. Rosenfeld: "Roger Sessions," *Port of New York* (New York, 1924), 145

R. D. Welch: "A Symphony Introduces Roger Sessions," *MM*, iv/4 (1927), 27

A. Copland: "Contemporaries at Oxford, 1931," *MM*, ix/1 (1931), 22

M. Brunswick: "American Composers, X: Roger Huntington Sessions," *MM*, x (1932–3), 182

A. Copland: *Our New Music* (New York, 1941, rev. and enlarged 2/1968 as *The New Music 1900–1960*)

M. A. Schubart: "Roger Sessions: Portrait of an American Composer," *MQ*, xxxii (1946), 196

D. Diamond: "Roger Sessions: Symphony No.2," *Notes*, vii (1949–50), 438

E. T. Cone: "Sessions: Second String Quartet," *MQ*, xliii (1957), 140

A. Imbrie: "Current Chronicle," *MQ*, xliv (1958), 370

E. Carter: "Current Chronicle," *MQ*, xlv (1959), 375

B. Boretz: "Current Chronicle," *MQ*, xlvii (1961), 386

A. Imbrie: "Roger Sessions: in Honor of his 65th Birthday," *PNM*, i/1 (1962), 117; repr. in B. Boretz and E. T. Cone, eds.: *Perspectives on American Composers* (New York, 1971), 59

Pozzi Escot: "Roger Sessions," *Inter-American Music Bulletin*, no.33 (1963), 3

P. M. Davies: "Montezuma," *New York Times* (21 April 1964)

E. C. Laufer: "Roger Sessions: *Montezuma*," *PNM*, iv/1 (1965), 95

E. Schweitzer: *Generation in String Quartets of Carter, Sessions, Kirchner, and Schuller* (diss., Eastman School, 1965)

E. T. Cone: "Conversation with Roger Sessions," *PNM*, iv/2 (1966), 29; repr. in B. Boretz and E. T. Cone, eds.: *Perspectives on American Composers* (New York, 1971), 90

D. Hamilton: "The New Craft of the Contemporary Concerto: Carter and Sessions," *HiFi/MusAm*, xviii/5 (1968), 67

R. Cogan: "Toward a Theory of Timbre: Verbal Timbre and Musical Line in Purcell, Sessions, and Stravinsky," *PNM*, viii/1 (1969), 75

H. Weinberg and P. Petrobelli: "Roger Sessions e la musica americana," *NRMI*, v (1971), 249

E. T. Cone: "In Honor of Roger Sessions," *PNM*, x/2 (1972), 130

A. Imbrie: "The Symphonies of Roger Sessions," *Tempo*, no.103 (1972), 24

R. Henderson: *Tonality in the Pre-serial Instrumental Music of Roger Sessions* (diss., Eastman School, 1974)

E. T. Cone: "Sessions's Concertino," *Tempo*, no.115 (1975), 2

"Sessions, Roger (Huntington)," *CBY 1975*

E. T. Cone: "In Defense of Song: the Contribution of Roger Sessions," *Critical Inquiry*, ii (1975–6), 93

J. Harbison: "Roger Sessions and Montezuma," *New Boston Review*, ii/1 (1976), 5; repr. in *Tempo*, no.121 (1977), 2

A. Porter: "The Matter of Mexico," *New Yorker*, lii (19 April 1976), 115

——: "An American Requiem," *New Yorker*, liii (16 May 1977), 133

A. Olmstead: "Roger Sessions: a Personal Portrait," *Tempo*, no.127 (1978), 10

A. Porter: "Sessions' Passionate and Profound *Lilacs*," *HiFi*, xxviii/2 (1978), 70

P. Rapoport: "Roger Sessions: a Discography," *Tempo*, no.127 (1978), 17

D. R. Duflin: *The Interpretation of Accent Signs in Roger Sessions' Third Piano Sonata* (diss., Ohio State U., 1979)

C. J. Oja: "The Copland-Sessions Concerts," *MQ*, lxv (1979), 212

D. Burge: "Contemporary Piano: Piano Music of Roger Sessions," *Contemporary Keyboard*, vi/10 (1980), 61

A. Olmstead: "Roger Sessions's Ninth Symphony," *Tempo*, no.133 (1980), 79

G. R. Danchenka: *Quantitative Measurement of Information Content via Recurring Associations in Three Movements of Symphony No.2 by Roger Sessions* (diss., U. of Miami, 1981)

H. Gleason and W. Becker: "Roger Sessions," *20th-century American Composers*, Music Literature Outlines, ser. iv (Bloomington, IN, rev, 2/1981), 185 [incl. further bibliography]

M. J. Merryman: *Aspects of Phrasing and Pitch Usage in Roger Sessions's Piano Sonata No.3* (diss., Brandeis U., 1981)

A. Olmstead: "Roger Sessions on Music: Collected Essays," *PNM*, xix/2 (1981), 491 [review]

A. Porter: "Celebration," *New Yorker*, lvii (9 Nov 1981), 164

M. I. Campbell: *The Piano Sonatas of Roger Sessions: Sequel to a Tradition* (diss., Peabody Institute, 1982)

C. Gagne and T. Caras: "Roger Sessions," *Soundpieces: Interviews with American Composers* (Metuchen, NJ, 1982), 355

S. M. Kress: *Roger Sessions, Composer and Teacher: A Comparative Analysis of Roger Sessions's Philosophy of Educating Composers and his Approach to Composition in Symphonies No.2 and 8* (diss., U. of Florida, 1982)

C. N. Mason: *A Comprehensive Analysis of Roger Sessions' Opera Montezuma* (diss., U. of Illinois, Urbana, 1982)

A. Porter: "The Magnificent Epic," *New Yorker*, lviii (8 March 1982), 128

R. M. Meckna: *The Rise of the American Composer-Critic: Aaron Copland, Roger Sessions, Virgil Thomson, and Elliott Carter in the Periodical "Modern Music," 1924–1946* (diss., U. of California, Santa Barbara, 1984)

S. Wheeler: *Harmonic Motion in the Music of Roger Sessions: an Examination of the*

Quintet, First Movement (diss., Brandeis U., 1984)

B. L. Gorelick: *Movement and Shape in the Choral Music of Roger Sessions* (diss., U. of Illinois, Urbana, 1985)

D. Henahan: Obituary, *New York Times* (18 March 1985)

"In Memoriam Roger Sessions (1896–1985)," *PNM*, xxiii/2 (1985), 110

M. Meckna: "Copland, Sessions, and *Modern Music*: the Rise of the Composer-critic in America," *American Music,* iii/2 (1985), 198

A. Olmstead: "The Plum'd Serpent: Antonio Borgese's and Roger Sessions's *Montezuma*," *Tempo*, no.152 (1985)

——: "Roger Sessions and his Influence," *Essays on Modern Music*, ii (1985), 23

——: *Roger Sessions and his Music* (Ann Arbor, MI, 1985) [incl. bibliography, discography, MSS sources, list of works]

——: *Conversations with Roger Sessions* (Boston, MA, 1986)

"An Appreciation: Roger Sessions, 1896–1985," *Kent Quarterly*, v/2 (1986) [entire issue]

E. Cone and F. Rounds: "The Reminiscences of Roger Sessions" (*NNC*, Oral History Collection) [2 vols. of transcripts of interviews]

HENRY COWELL

Bruce Saylor
William Lichtenwanger

CHAPTER FOUR

Henry Cowell

1. LIFE. Cowell's father Harry immigrated from Ireland to British Columbia in order to manage a fruit orchard, which his father, the Dean of Kildare Cathedral, had given him. The venture failed and Harry moved to San Francisco, where he married Clarissa Dixon, who was from an Indiana-Iowa farming family. Their son Henry Dixon Cowell was born on 11 March 1897 in a tiny cottage in Menlo Park among the California foothills which was to be his home until 1936. At the age of five he began violin lessons, and for three years his father encouraged him as a child prodigy, but the strain was too much for his health and lessons were stopped; nevertheless he decided to become a composer. His parents were divorced in 1903 and Cowell and his mother spent the years 1906–10 visiting relatives in Iowa, Kansas, and Oklahoma, while his mother pursued a professional writing career between periods of illness. She was to die in 1916. In 1908 Cowell began his first long piece, a monodic setting of Longfellow's *Golden Legend.* It remained unfinished, and survives only as the second theme of the piano piece *Antinomy* (1917).

Back in California from 1910, Cowell bought his first piano in 1912. He studied with various local piano teachers and composed constantly, unencumbered by systematic training in composition or by any formal schooling: his parents were "philosophical anarchists," and their ideas of complete educational freedom led him to accept readily the many sounds around him as valid musical material. Important and lasting influences were the sounds

101

of nature and the noises of man, his mother's Midwestern folk-tunes, and the rich variety of oriental musical cultures that existed in the San Francisco Bay area. He grew up hearing more Chinese, Japanese, and Indian classical music than he did Western music and never became familiar with the bulk of the European repertory, either as pianist or listener. Cowell owed his lifelong interest in Irish songs and dances not to his father (who was not musical) but to Midwestern relatives of Irish descent and to the poet John Varian, who had become a father figure to him. Varian's versions of Irish legends inspired such characteristic early pieces as *The Tides of Manaunaun* (?1917), a piano work written to accompany a pageant. To portray the immense waves set in motion by the Irish god, Cowell rolled clusters with his hand and forearm in the low register of the piano to evoke the sea; above this is a sweeping modal melody. He had combined atonal clusters with a folklike tune; such an unfettered openness towards the gamut of musical resources and unusual combinations would characterize the breadth of Cowell's output. He played groups of his piano pieces at small concerts in San Francisco as early as 1912 but first received attention in print at his début concert as a composer-pianist (San Francisco, 5 March 1914) when his *Adventures in Harmony* (1913) and its tone clusters drew comment. By then he had written over a hundred pieces in various styles. His basic musical personality, that of the enthusiastic, spontaneous, and fluent trail-blazer, was firmly established.

Cowell's formal training began in 1914 with Charles Seeger, then at the University of California, Berkeley. Seeger arranged for him to acquire a solid technical foundation by studying harmony and counterpoint with E. G. Stricklen, Wallace Sabin, and the organist Uda Waldrop. At the same time he was to pursue free composition. In 1916 he registered at the Institute of Musical Art in New York, but, impatient with its stultifying academicism, he returned to California after one term. He resumed

8. Henry Cowell, 1959

his exchange of ideas with Seeger and studied English composition with Samuel Seward of Stanford University. At Seeger's insistence he worked out a systematic technique for the new materials he had already explored; with Seward he learned how to express his ideas in words. The result was the book *New Musical Resources* (1930/*R*1969), written between 1916 and 1919 and revised before its publication. This remarkable treatise describes, systematizes, and suggests new notations for Cowell's procedures, including clusters, free dissonant counterpoint, polytriadic harmony, counterrhythms, shifting accents, and a method for relating rhythm and pitch according to overtone ratios.

In February 1918 Cowell enlisted in the army, serving until May 1919. For most of this time he played the flute in military bands at army posts in Allentown, Pennsylvania, and Oswego,

9. Notation for tone clusters (lower staff), the superscript ♭ indicating black keys only and the ♮ white keys only (Henry Cowell, "The Tides of Manaunaun," ?1917; New York: Breitkopf & Härtel, 1922); the distinction between void and solid note heads is purely durational

104

New York. About the same time he began to attract considerable attention as a performer of his own works and as a persistent advocate of the avant garde. By the mid-1920s he had extended his innovative piano techniques to include various types of cluster; stopping, strumming, scraping, plucking, and playing harmonics on the strings; and introducing various objects into the harp of the piano to produce percussive sounds. On 29 November 1919 he presented an all-Cowell recital in New York, then acquired professional management and inaugurated a series of five tours of Europe as composer-pianist (1923–33) that made him an international figure. His recitals of 1923 in Germany and in Paris, Budapest, and London were met with both outrage and intense interest, and he came to know well most of the major composers of Europe. Bartók wrote to him for permission to use his "invention" the cluster (the letter is lost), Schoenberg asked him to play for his class, and in 1932 Webern conducted the Scherzo movement of his Sinfonietta for chamber orchestra in Vienna. After his 1923 tour of Europe, Cowell returned to New York, where he made his formal American débuts (Carnegie Hall, 4 February 1924; Town Hall, 17 February 1924). These concerts received sensational reviews in the press and national wire services; he became a national celebrity, and annual concert-lecture tours of the USA followed, as well as, later, more appearances in Europe and, after 1956, Asia. In 1929 Cowell became the first American composer invited to the USSR. His sensational performances alarmed the authorities but excited his audiences, and the state publishing house printed two piano pieces, *Lilt of the Reel* (1928) and *Tiger* (1930).

From the early 1920s Cowell wrote and acted extensively on behalf of modern music, and he contributed several essays to the volume *American Composers on American Music* (1933/R1962), which he edited. In 1925 he founded the New Music Society in Los Angeles, moving it to San Francisco the following year. The

Society gave concerts of European and American "ultramodern-ist" works until 1936. In 1927 he single-handedly launched *New Music*, "a quarterly of modern compositions" in which contemporary works appeared. The inaugural issue contained Ruggles's *Men and Mountains*. North and South American com-positions predominated, but *New Music* also published music by Europeans, including Schoenberg (op.33b), Webern (op. 17 no.2), and Varèse (*Density 21.5*). Music by Ives, whom Cowell had met in 1927, appeared regularly; indeed, such important works as *The Fourth of July*, *Washington's Birthday*, the second movement of the Fourth Symphony, and many songs were first published in *New Music*. Cowell became Ives's most important link with the larger musical world. In addition to aiding *New Music* (from 1947 *New Music Edition*) and New Music Quarterly Recordings, which Cowell founded in 1934, Ives supported the concerts of American orchestral music that Cowell organized in major Euro-pean cities in his role as director of the North American section of the Pan American Association of Composers (founded by Varèse, Salzedo, Chávez, and Cowell in 1928). Cowell took every oppor-tunity to discuss Ives's work in lecture-concerts and in print throughout his life, and *Charles Ives and his Music* (1955), which he wrote with his wife, remains an important study.

Cowell turned in the mid-1920s to the serious study of non-European musics. In 1931–2 he worked with the comparative musicologist Erich von Hornbostel, with Professor Sambamoor-thy of Madras, and with Raden Mas Jodjhana of Java, all in Berlin, under a Guggenheim Foundation grant. His preoccu-pation with new sounds continued with an unending quest for new ethnic contagions. Cowell began a deliberate attempt to synthesize "ultramodern" materials with the many possibilities offered him by other musical cultures. During these years, how-ever, he embraced conservative idioms for certain commissions, teaching pieces, and music for amateurs. His writings of this

106

period indicate a desire to compose "useful music" in a "neo-primitive" vein. Music could assist in the education of children as well, and could serve other arts such as film and dance, without dominating them. This led Cowell to what may be his most explosive notion, "elastic form." In a series of articles on dance (1934–41) he suggested that performers themselves choose the order of various segments of music provided by the composer: the music was to adapt to the dancers' forms. This implied at least a partial relinquishing by the composer of the total control over the finished product which had been basic to Western musical thought. Two books of this period, *Rhythm* (?1935) and *The Nature of Melody* (?1938), remain unpublished.

In both musical and personal matters Cowell was kind, trusting, and almost childlike. This perhaps explains why he initially deemed the presence of a defense attorney unnecessary when he was brought to court on a morals charge in 1936. Sentenced to imprisonment, he was sent to San Quentin penitentiary until pressure from many different sources, including fellow composers, led to his parole in 1940. He moved to New York, spent a year as secretary to Percy Grainger, and in 1941 married Sidney Hawkins Robertson, a writer, folksong collector, and photographer. In 1942 the governor of California pardoned Cowell at the request of the judge and the prosecuting attorney, who had come to the conclusion that the composer was innocent.

During the war Cowell served as senior music editor of the overseas division of the Office of War Information, having been engaged for his wide knowledge of the traditional musics of several continents. In 1941 he had resumed his teaching career at the New School for Social Research, New York, where in 1930 he had initiated "Composers Forum," a program, still in existence, that presents two composers and their music in discussion with the audience. Also at the New School he lectured about music of the world's peoples and was in charge of musical activities until he resigned in 1963. Cowell also held posts at the Peabody Conservatory (1951–6) and at Columbia University (1949–65), and he lectured at over 50 conservatories and universities throughout the USA, Europe, and Asia. Cage and Harrison were among his pupils, as were, more briefly, George Gershwin and Burt Bacharach. Cowell received many awards, grants, and honorary degrees; he was elected to the National Institute of Arts and Letters in 1951 and served as president of the ACA from 1951 to 1955. His last years were extraordinarily productive: from 1946 until his death he wrote over 100 compositions and published over 100 essays on music. Especially important among the latter is his series of 40 reviews of contemporary music for the *Musical Quarterly* (1947–58). A culmination of his constant search for fresh musical experiences was his world tour during 1956–7; the sponsorship of the Rockefeller Foundation and the US State Department enabled him to listen first-hand to the music of many cultures in their natural surroundings. A widely acknowledged international musical statesman, he represented the USA at the International Music Conference in Teheran and at the East-West Music Encounter in Tokyo (1961). He continued to compose throughout a series of debilitating illnesses from 1957 until his death on 10 December 1965 in Shady, New York.

2. WORKS. Cowell was an indefatigable musical explorer, discoverer, and inventor; his vast output might be characterized by an enthusiastic statement he made in 1955: "I want to live in the *whole world* of music!" His work reflects a bold but ingenuous openness towards many sound materials, novel compositional procedures, and a wide array of non-European and folk influences. He has been described (by Weisgall) as temperamentally incapable of excluding from his work any idea which interested him, and his ecumenical, if uncritical, approach helped provide the "open sesame" for new music in America, to quote Cage. Cowell

seems not to have been interested in style *per se*, nor in the gradual evolution of a single, personal, idiomatic stamp. An idea that interested him for compositional development had, for Cowell, to determine the ultimate language and form of the resultant work. Composition was for him sometimes the result of long and deliberate consideration but more often was a spontaneous response to some recent musical experience. Three general periods of Cowell's work can be discerned, each reflecting an overall focus of attention, not a separate stylistic direction. The first (1912–35) is characterized chiefly by experiment and innovation, the second (1935–50) by various kinds of traditional or folklike models, and the third (1950–65) by an attempt to integrate them all.

Many of Cowell's early innovations were derived from the latent possibilities of the grand piano. He coined the word "tone-clusters" from their look on the printed page (see fig.9). They could be played with fingers, fists, or forearms, and were used at first chiefly for programmatic effect (Cowell always considered these sounds as "chords" and employed them usually to reinforce melodic lines). *Advertisement* (1917) uses both diatonic and semitonal clusters; *Tiger* integrates a greater variety of clusters with free dissonance and more pronounced melodic writing. Clusters appear in Cowell's orchestral music as early as about 1924 (in *Some More Music*) and are exploited to the hilt in the Piano Concerto (1928). Another early invention was what he termed the "string piano." In *The Aeolian Harp* (*c*1923; see fig. 10), the piano strings are to be strummed inside the piano while chords on the keys are depressed silently, and some strings are to be plucked; in *Sinister Resonance* (1930) strings are stopped and harmonics produced; and *The Banshee* (1925) is to be played entirely on the strings while an assistant holds down the damper pedal. Cowell also originated the idea of introducing various objects inside the piano to produce new timbres, an innovation developed by Cage into the prepared piano.

Besides discovering unusual piano sounds, Cowell explored exotic instruments and percussion. Three southwest American Indian thundersticks (bullroarers) originally accompanied two movements of *Ensemble* for string quintet (1924). Cowell used graphic notation for dynamics at the beginning of the thunderstick parts, then gave instructions for the performers to improvise through to the end. In 1931 he collaborated with Lev Termen to develop the Rhythmicon, an electronic machine that could play complicated polyrhythms. For it he wrote the concerto *Rhythmicana* (1931) for a performance in Paris, which, however, did not take place. (In 1971 Leland Smith realized the solo part on a computer, and Sandor Salgo with the Stanford Orchestra gave the first performance under the title "Concerto for Rhythmicon and Orchestra.") As early as the 1920s Cowell composed, but did not always notate, percussion music for dance using found objects, and is generally considered the founder of the "West Coast School" of percussion (with Cage, Harrison, and Strang). His *Ostinato pianissimo* (1934) with its delicate gamelan-like sound remains a standard repertory piece for percussion ensemble. Certain symphonic works make elaborate use of percussion (Symphony no. 11, 1953). The Percussion Concerto (1958) combines the metrically even rhythms of *Ostinato* with melodic writing in clusters, modality, and an orchestral counterpoint.

Among Cowell's most forward-looking ideas was his "rhythm—harmony" system, in which interval ratios from the overtone series are translated into corresponding rhythms. In the *Quartet Romantic* (1917) and the *Quartet Euphometric* (1919) the rhythms of four independent melodic strands are derived from a simple four-part substructure that Cowell called the "theme." Though harmonic resting points taken from the theme provide some sense of harmonic direction, the pitches in the quartets are chosen freely. The attractiveness of the sounds attests to the sensitivity

10. *Opening of the autograph MS of Cowell's "The Aeolian Harp," c1923*

of Cowell's ear. Long considered unplayable, the two quartets have recently been published, performed, and recorded. The indeterminacy implicit in the free thunderstick parts and original open-ended instrumentation of *Ensemble* became explicit in the *Mosaic Quartet* (String Quartet no.3, 1935). Cowell's note in the score instructs that "The Mosaic Quartet is to be played, alternating the movements at the desire of the performers, treating each movement as a unit to build the mosaic pattern of the form." The teaching piece *Amerind Suite* for piano (1939), which permits students at various levels of proficiency to play simultaneously, leaves similar choices to the performers. *Ritournelle* for piano (from the incidental music *Les mariés de la Tour Eiffel*, 1939) perhaps most closely realizes Cowell's theory of "elastic form," and in one of his last pieces, *26 Simultaneous Mosaics* for five players (1963), musical sections of totally different character may be played at random. The principle, its original relation to dance, and the composer's oriental concerns point directly to the work of Cage.

At the time when he formulated his concept of indeterminacy, Cowell's tonal materials were becoming simpler, more oriented around a tonal center. Of the two important quartets from these years, the *Mosaic Quartet* simplifies the internal structure within its short movements. Separate strands of material tend towards diatonicism, while the composite sound alternates between "wrong-note" harmony and free dissonance. The String Quartet no.4 (the "United," 1936) is one of Cowell's earliest attempts at a "more universal music style," as he put it in a kind of apologia prefacing the original edition of the work. The drones, modal scales, unchanging harmonic areas, and frequent stretches of pizzicato most strongly recall eastern European folk music.

From 1936 onwards Cowell more often wrote tonally, and his rhythms became increasingly regular, with an ever stronger basis in traditional folk idioms. During the 1940s Eastern exoticism

112

waned. The Irish jig, which he had always favored, was to provide a "scherzo" in many works, and the rugged diatonicism of early American hymnody, which he knew from William Walker's tunebook *The Southern Harmony* (1835), led to the series of 18 hymns and fuguing tunes for various instrumental combinations (1944–64). Their bisectional form, which Cowell described as "something slow followed by something fast," offered him a concise, down-to-earth form which suited his prolific and expeditious compositional habits. The streamlined style of this "American music," of his functional music for brass ensembles and for band, and of his SATB arrangements for the United Nations illustrated his eagerness to write music for a great variety of performers. He was later to explain the pervasive tonality in his works by pointing out that tonality, not atonality, was common to most musical cultures.

The music from the last two decades of Cowell's life is marked by a partial return to dissonant counterpoint and the amalgamation of previous innovative materials, especially clusters, with his fresh experiences with traditional musics from India (the "Madras" Symphony no. 13, 1956–8), Indonesia (Percussion Concerto and Symphony no. 19, 1965), Iran (*Persian Set* for orchestra, 1957, and *Homage to Iran* for violin and piano, 1957), and Japan (*Ongaku* for orchestra, 1957, and the two koto concertos, 1961–2, 1965). In the Percussion Concerto and Symphony no. 11 ("Seven Rituals of Music," 1953), clusters act as melodic conglomerates within a modal context; the symphony is something like a compendium of his mature practice, each movement being in a different style. Cowell would continue to refashion previous works into new ones: an example is Symphony no. 15 ("Thesis," 1960), in which he used music from his second and third quartets. His long concern with the manipulation of small melodic cells is represented by two fine late works, the Variations for Orchestra (1956) and the Trio for violin, cello, and piano (1965).

113

WORKS

Catalogue: W. Lichtenwanger: *The Music of Henry Cowell: a Descriptive Catalog*, ISAMm (Brooklyn, NY, 1986)

Fragments, sketches, composition exercises, and most lost and incomplete works are omitted. Numbers are from Lichtenwanger; letter suffixes denote arrangements, and numbers following a diagonal indicate a movement or part of a larger work. To facilitate cross-references between sections letter prefixes have been added. Titles follow the forms found on Cowell's MSS or printed editions, except for those in brackets, which are from Lichtenwanger. Cowell's MSS and sketches are in *DLC*; his papers and some MSS are held on deposit at *NN*.

AP   – anniversary piece (Cowell composed 85 short pieces for his wife Sidney Robertson Cowell for various anniversaries beginning in 1941)

pf-str – piano strings (an indication that the part should be played directly on the strings of the piano)

Index: A – orchestral and band; B – concertante; C – choral; D – solo vocal; E – chamber (5 or more insts); F – chamber (3–4 insts); G – chamber (2 insts); H – chamber (solo inst); I – keyboard; J – music for dance and drama; K – arrangements

< – arranged as/developed into   > – arranged from/developed from
* – published work

A: ORCHESTRAL AND BAND
(for orch unless otherwise stated)

147	The Birth of Motion, c1914, inc. [part <A:221a]
213/2a	What's This?, 1920 [>I:213/2]
221a	Some Music, 1922 [>lost pf piece and A:147]
245	Symphony [no.1], b, 1918, rev. 1940
246	Camp March, small orch, 1918–19, lost
253	March, 1918–19
254	[Waltz], band, 1918–19, lost
289	A Symphonic Communication, 1919
305a	Vestiges, 1922 [>I:305]
387a	Manaunaun's Birthing, 1944, lost [>D:387]
404	Some More Music, ?c1924, inc.
415a	Slow Jig, 1933 [>I:415]
439	Three Pieces for Chamber Orchestra, 1928, lost [? = A:443]
443	*Sinfonietta, chamber orch, 1928; as Marked Passages, Boston, 28 April 1928, cond. N. Slonimsky [? = A:439; movts 1 and 2 >movts 1 and 2 of E:380; movt 3 >I:429]

463/1a	Reel (Lilt of the Reel), small orch, 1932; New York, 17 May 1933, cond. B. Herrmann [>no.1 of ɪ:463]
463/1b	Reel for CBS Orchestra, 1942 [>no.1 of ɪ:463]
464	*Synchrony of Dance, Music, Light, retitled Orchesterstück: Synchrony, 1930; Paris, 6 June 1931, cond. Slonimsky
475	[untitled], ?1920–30
484	Two Appositions: One Movement for Orchestra, 1932, lost; Paris, 21 Feb 1932, cond. Slonimsky [arr. str, 484a; <ɪ:484b]
486	Four Continuations for String Orchestra, 1932; Brooklyn, NY, 10 Dec 1933, cond. J. Edward Powers
493	Horn Pipe, 1933; Havana, 22 Oct 1933, cond. A. Roldán
498	Symphonic Episode, ?orch, ?1923–33, inc.
499	Suite for Small Orchestra, 1934; New York, 21 May 1934, cond. C. Vrionides
506	Reel no.2, small orch, 1934; Minneapolis, 9 Jan 1941, cond.·J. Becker [arr. large orch, 506a]
523	How they Take It: Prison Moods, band, 1936, lost [arr. theater orch, 523a, ?1937, lost]
527	Jig in Four, 1936
528	Oriental Dance, concert band, 1936, lost
531	In the Style of a Popular Song, theater orch, 1937, lost
535	Reel Irish, military band, 1937, lost
541	Symphony no.2 "Anthropos," 1938: 1 Repose, 2 Activity, 3 Repression, 4 Liberation; Brooklyn, NY, 9 March 1941, cond. Cowell
543	*Celtic Set, concert band, 1938: 1 Interlochen Camp Reel, 2 Caoine, 3 Hornpipe; Selinsgrove, PA, 6 May 1938, cond. Grainger [arr. orch, 543a, 1944; <ɪ:543b, <ɢ:543c]
545	Air, band, 1938
547a	*Symphonic Set, op.17, 1938; Chicago, 1 April 1940, cond. I. Solomon [>ꜰ:547]
550a	Herman's Wedding March, band, 1938, lost [>ɪ:550]
567	*Old American Country Set, 1939: 1 Blarneying Lilt, 2 Meetinghouse Chorale, 3 Comallye, 4 Charivari, 5 Cornhusking Hornpipe; Indianapolis, 28 Feb 1940, cond. F. Sevitzky [no.1 arr. small orch, 567/1a, 1940, lost, arr. band, 567/1b, 1941]
571	*Shoonthree (The Music of Sleep), band, 1939; Mansfield, PA, 3 May 1940, cond. R. F. Goldman
573	Crystal Set, 1939, lost
574	Quaint Minuet, band, 1939, lost [arr., 574a, lost]

576	Vox humana, 1939 [arr. band, 576a, lost]
577	Andante, orch ens, 1939, lost
578	Chorale, orch ens, 1939, lost
579	The Exuberant Mexican: Danza latina, band, 1939
580	Hornpipe, orch ens, 1939, lost
581	Menuet, orch ens, 1939, lost
582	Orientale, orch ens, 1939, lost
584	Spanish Waltz, orch ens, 1939, lost
587	*Pastoral and Fiddler's Delight, 1940; New York, 26 July 1940, cond. Stokowski
594	American Melting Pot, chamber orch, 1940: 1 Chorale (Teutonic-American), 2 Air (Afro-American), 3 Satire (Franco-American), withdrawn, 4 Alapna (Oriental-American), 5 Slavic Dance (Slavic-American), 6 Rhumba with added 8th (Latin-American), 7 Square Dance (Celtic-American), withdrawn; New York, 3 May 1943, cond. F. Petrides
595	58 for Percy, band, 1940 [<F:595a]
597	*Ancient Desert Drone, 1940; South Bend, IN, 12 Jan 1941, cond. Grainger [<G:597a; arr. small orch, 597b]
598	Purdue, 1940; West Lafayette, IN, 19 Dec 1940, cond. Sevitzky
599	A Bit o' Blarney (This One is a Wise-cracker), band, 1940, inc.
602	Reel, 1940, lost
610	Indiana University Overture, 1941
617	*Shipshape Overture, band, 1941; State College, PA, 31 July 1941, cond. R. F. Goldman
625	Festive Occasion, band, 1942; New York, 3 July 1942, cond. Cowell
634	*Fanfare to the Forces of our Latin-American Allies, brass, perc, 1942; Cincinnati, 30 Oct 1942, cond. E. Goossens
636	Gaelic Symphony (Symphony no.3), band, str, 1942; movt 1, West Saugerties, NY, 24 July 1942, cond. E. Williams
645	American Pipers, 1943; New Orleans, 12 Jan 1949, cond. P. Henrotte
647	*Philippine Return: Rondo on Philippine Folk Songs, orch, 1943: 1 Introduction, 2 Iluli si nonoy [Iloilo cradle song], 3 An mananguete [Leyte coconut gatherer's song], 4 Pispis ining pikoy [Visayan game song], 5 Kalusan [Bataues rowing song]
648	United Music, 1943; Detroit, 23 Jan 1944, cond. K. Krueger
651a	Hymn and Fuguing Tune [no.1], sym. band, 1944; New York, 14 June 1944, cond. E. F. Goldman [>I:651]

652	Improvisation on a Persian Mode for Orchestra, 1943
656	Symphonic Sketch, *c*1943, inc.
657	Hymn and Fuguing Tune no.2, str orch, 1944; WEAF radio, New York, 23 March 1944, cond. H. Nosco
659	*Animal Magic of the Alaskan Esquimo, band, 1944
660	*Hymn and Fuguing Tune no.3, 1944; Los Angeles, 14 April 1951, cond. I. Dahl [<I:660a]
673a	Hymn and Fuguing Tune no.5, str orch, ?1946; Saratoga Springs, NY, 15 Sept 1946, cond. F. C. Adler [>c:673, <movts 1 and 2 of A:788]
679	Big Sing, 1945: 1 Fanfare, 2 Hymn, 3 Testimonials, 4 Great Rejoicing; Fresno, CA, 27 May 1946, cond. ?Cowell
686	Air, band, ?1940–45, inc.
687	Band Piece, ?1940–45
688	Hymn for Strings, str orch, 1946; Denton, TX, 22 March 1946, cond. Cowell
689	*Grandma's Rhumba, band, 1946
692	Festival Overture for Two Orchestras, 1946; Interlochen, MI, 11 Aug 1946, cond. W. E. Knuth
693	Congratulations! To Mr. and Mrs. Howard Hanson, str orch, 1946
697	*Symphony no.4 (Short Symphony), 1946: 1 Hymn, 2 Ballad, 3 Dance, 4 Introduction and Fuguing Tune; Boston, 24 Oct 1947, cond. R. Burgin [movt 4 >fuguing tune of I:696]
705/3a	*Ballad, str orch, 1954; Tucson, AZ, 27 Nov 1956, cond. F. Balazs [>movt 3 of G:705, <E:705/3b]
719	*Saturday Night at the Firehouse, 1948
722	*Symphony no.5, 1948; Washington, DC, 5 Jan 1949, cond. H. Kindler
732	*A Curse and a Blessing, sym. band, 1949; Brooklyn, NY, 21 July 1949, cond. R. F. Goldman
744	*Overture for Large Orchestra, 1949; Santa Rosa, CA, 1 Dec 1968, cond. C. Brown
746	Commencement Parade, band, ?*c*1949, inc.
757	Andante and Allegro, 1950, inc.
767	Air of the Glen/Song of the Glen, band, ?*c*1950–51: 1 Andante – Trio, 2 Schottische; movt 1 arr. as Air for String Orchestra, 767/1b, 1953, inc. [movt 1 <B:767/1a]
769	Fantasie (Enigma Variations) on a Theme by Ferdinand Kücken, band, 1952; West Point, NY, 30 May 1952, cond. F. Resta
770	Symphony no.6, 1952; Houston, 14 Nov 1955, cond. Stokowski

774	Rondo for Orchestra, 1952; Indianapolis, 6 Dec 1953, cond. Sevitzky
776	Symphony no.7, small orch, 1952; Baltimore, 25 Nov 1952, cond. R. Stewart
778	Symphony no.8, opt. A, chorus, orch, 1952; Wilmington, OH, 1 March 1953, cond. T. Johnson
787	Symphony no.9, 1953; Green Bay, WI, 14 March 1954, cond. R. Holder [movt 1 >hymn of G:758]
788	Symphony no.10, 1953; New York, 24 Feb 1957, cond. F. Bibo [movts 1 and 2 >A:673a, movts 5 and 6 >F:713]
790	*Symphony no.11 "Seven Rituals of Music," 1953; Louisville, 29 May 1954; cond. R. Whitney
797	*Singing Band, concert band, 1953
801/1	In Memory of a Great Man, 1954, inc., = no.1 of [6] Memorial Pieces [for nos.2–4, 6, see I:801/2, C:801/3, I:801/4, G:801/6; 801/5, frag.]
807	Toward a Bright Day, 1954: 1 Reel, 2 Vivace
810	Air, 1955, inc.
816	Dalton Suite, school orch, 1955; New York, 16 April 1956
821	Suite, str, ?1950–60
830	*Symphony no.12, 1955–6; Houston, 28 March 1960, cond. Stokowski
833	Variations for Orchestra, 1956, rev. 1959; Cincinnati, 23 Nov 1956, cond. Johnson
838	*Persian Set, chamber orch, 1957; Teheran, Iran, 17 Sept 1957, cond. A. Dorati
839	Teheran Movement, chamber orch, 1957
842	Music for Orchestra, 1957; Athens, Greece, 3 Sept 1957, cond. Dorati
846	Ongaku, 1957; Louisville, 26 March 1958, cond. Whitney
848	*Symphony no.13 "Madras," 1956–8; Madras, India, 3 March 1959, cond. T. Scherman
865	Antiphony for Divided Orchestra, 1959; Kansas City, MO, 14 Nov 1959, cond. H. Schwieger
867	Mela/Fair, 1959, inc.: 1 Thanksgiving, 2 Sowing after Rain, 3 Harvest; broadcast New Delhi, India, 13 Dec 1959
869	Characters, 1959: 1 Cowboy, 2 The Mysterious Oriental, 3 The Profound One, 4 Deep Thinker, 5 The Frightened Scurrier, 6 The Celestial Soul, 7 The Jaunty Irishman
874	Symphony no.14, 1959–60; Washington, DC, 27 April 1961,

	cond. H. Hanson
887	*Symphony no.15 "Thesis," 1960; Murray, KY, 7 Oct 1961, cond. Whitney [movts 1–4 >F:518, movt 6 >F:450]
892	Chiaroscuro, 1961; Guatemala City, 13 Oct 1961, cond. J. M. F. Gil
904	Andante, 1962
909/2a	*Carol, 1965; Tulsa, OK, 16 Nov 1968, cond. F. Autori [>movt 2 of B:909]
912	Symphony no.16 "Icelandic," 1962; Réykjavík, Iceland, 21 March 1963, cond. W. Strickland
916	Symphony no.17, 1963
921a	Hymn and Fuguing Tune no.16, 1964; New York, 6 Oct 1966, cond. Bernstein [>G:921]
930	*Symphony no.18, 1964
932	The Tender and the Wild: Song and Dance, 1964
942	Twilight in Texas, 1965; New York, 20 June 1968, cond. A. Kostelanetz
943	Symphony no.19, 1965; Nashville, TN, 18 Oct 1965, cond. W. Page
945	Symphony no.20, 1965, inc., movt 4 completed and orchd L. Harrison
946	Symphony no.21, 1965, sketches

B: CONCERTANTE

96	[concerto], ?A♭, pf, orch, 1914, lost
440	*Concerto for Piano and Orchestra, 1928; movts 1 and 2, New York, 26 April 1930, Cowell (pf); complete, Havana, 28 Dec 1930, Cowell, cond. P. Sanjuan [movt 1 >movt 1 of E:406]
452	Irish Suite, conc., pf-str, chamber orch, 1928–9: 1 The Banshee, 2 The Leprechaun, 3 The Fairy Bells; Boston, 11 March 1929, Cowell, cond. Slonimsky [movt 1 >I:405, movt 2 >I:448, movt 3 >I:447]
481	Concerto for Rhythmicon and Orchestra, 1931, orig. entitled Rhythmicana; realized cptr, orch, Palo Alto, CA, 3 Dec 1971, L. Smith, cond. S. Salgo
605	Four Irish Tales, pf, orch, 1940: 1 The Tides of Manaunaun, 2 Exultation, 3 The Harp of Life, 4 The Lilt of the Reel; New York, 24 Nov 1940, Cowell, cond. F. Mahler [no.1 >I:219/1, no.2 >I:328, no.3 >I:384, no.4 >no.1 of I:463]

119

620	Suite for Piano and String Orchestra, 1941, pf pt inc., reconstructed D. Tudor; Boston, 11 Jan 1942, Cowell, cond. J. Wolffers; movts 3–5 arr. as Little Concerto, pf, band, 620a, 1941, West Point, NY, 25 Jan 1942, Cowell, cond. F. Resta; movts 3–5 also arr. as Little Concerto, pf, orch, 620b, 1945
767/1a	Air, vn, str orch, 1952 [>movt 1 of A:767]
771	*Flirtatious Jig (Fiddler's Jig), vn, str orch, 1952
813	Hymn and Fuguing Tune no.10, ob, str orch, 1955 [not = H:798]
861	*Concerto for Percussion and Orchestra, 1958; Kansas City, MO, 7 Jan 1961, cond. Schwieger
878	*Concerto brevis for Accordion and Orchestra, 1960
882	Variations on 3rds for Two Violas and String Orchestra, 1960; New York, 10 Feb 1961, cond. D. Antoun
894	Duo concertante, fl, harp, orch, 1961; Springfield, OH, 21 Oct 1961, J. Baker, G. Agostini, cond. J. Wiley
897	*Air and Scherzo for Alto Saxophone and Small Orchestra, 1963 [>G:897]
908	Concerto for Harmonica, 1962
909	Concerto for Koto and Orchestra [no.1], 1961–2; Philadelphia, 18 Dec 1964, K. Eto, cond. Stokowski [movt 2 <A:909/2a]
917	Concerto grosso, fl, ob, cl, vc, harp, str orch, 1963; Miami Beach, FL, 12 Jan 1964, cond. Sevitzky
940	Concerto no.2 for Koto and Orchestra in the Form of a Symphony, 1965; Hanover, NH, 8 May 1965, S. Yuize, cond. M. di Bonaventura
947	Concerto for Harp and Orchestra, 1965

C: CHORAL

53	O salutaris (liturgical), SATB, pf, 1913
95	Maker of Day, Mez, A, Bar, chorus, timp, pf, 1914
148	[untitled choral sketch], 4vv, c1914
154	The Wave of D. . ., 3vv, pf, ?c1914
218	The Light of Peace, chorus, pf, 1917
236	The Sun Shines: Chorale, 9vv, c1917
276a	*Psalm cxxi, chorus, 1953 [>D:276]
533a	*The Road Leads into Tomorrow (D. Hagemeyer), 8vv, pf ad lib, 1947 [arr. from lost song]
536	*The Morning Cometh (T. Chalmers Furness), chorus, 1937
546	*The Coming of Light (Hagemeyer), 4-pt female vv/4 solo vv, 1938
562	*Spring at Summer's End (Hagemeyer), SSA, ?c1938

586	Easter Music, chorus, band, 1940, lost: 1 The Passion, 2 The Vigil at the Cross, 3 The Resurrection
640	*Fire and Ice (R. Frost), male vv, band, 1943
641	*American Muse (S. V. Benét), 2-pt female vv, pf, 1943: 1 American Muse, 2 Swift Runner, 3 Immensity of Wheel
655	Hail, Mills! (L. Seltzer), SSA, pf, c1943
673	Hymn and Fuguing Tune no.5, 5vv, 1945 [arr. as A:673a]
675	*The Irishman Lilts (Henry Cowell), female vv, pf, 1945
690	*Air Held her Breath (A. Lincoln), canon, SATB, 1946
691	*To America (Hagemeyer), SSAATTBB, 1946
707	Union of Voices, 6-pt female vv, ?1945–6
712	*Day, Evening, Night, Morning (P. L. Dunbar), 6-pt male vv, 1947
715	*The Lily's Lament (E. Harald [Lomax]), SSA, pf, 1947
716	*Sweet was the Song the Virgin Sung (Sweet Christmas Song) (early 17th-century), SATB, pf/org/str, 1948
723	*Luther's Carol for his Son (Luther), TTBB, 1948
727	*Do you Doodle as you Dawdle? (Henry Cowell), chorus, pf, drums ad lib, 1948
728	*Evensong at Brookside: a Father's Lullaby (Harry Cowell), male vv, 1948
731	Do, Do, Do, is C, C, C (Henry Cowell), children's chorus, pf, ?c1948
733	*Ballad of the Two Mothers (Harald), SSATBarB, 1949
750	*To a White Birch (Hagemeyer), chorus, 1950
759	*Song for a Tree (Hagemeyer), SSA, opt. pf, 1950
775	With Choirs Divine (J. T. Shotwell), SSA, 1952
781	Mountain Tree (Hagemeyer), chorus, 1952
782	The Golden Harp, spiritual, 4-pt boys' chorus, 1952
796	Psalm xxxiv, SATB, unacc./org, 1953
801/3	A Thanksgiving for Ruth Strongin (S. R. Cowell), SSATB/S, pf/org/any 5 insts, 1954, no.3 of [6] Memorial Pieces [see also A:801/1]
818	. . .if He please (E. Taylor), chorus, boys' chorus, orch/pf, 1955
819	*The Tree of Life (Taylor), chorus, 1955
829	Lines from the Dead Sea Scrolls, TTTBBB, orch, 1956
873	[untitled, proposed Malayan national anthem], vv, band, 1959
881	Edson Hymns and Fuguing Tunes (L. Edson, Jr.), suite, chorus, orch, 1960; *arr. chorus, org, 881a, ?1960; arr. chorus, band, 881b

121

897a	*Air and Scherzo for Alto Saxophone and Small Orchestra, 1963 [>G:897]
902	*Supplication: Processional (Henry Cowell), org, 2 tpt, 2 trbn, unison vv, timp ad lib, 1962
919	The Creator (G. R. Derzhavin), oratorio, S, A, T, B, chorus, orch, 1963
929	*Ultima actio (J. de Diego, trans. J. Machlis), SSATB, 1964
938	Zapados sonidos, SSAATTBB, tap dancer, 1964

9 other choral works, acc. and unacc., lost

D: SOLO VOCAL
(all for 1v, pf, unless otherwise stated)

92 Jesus was born at Christmas, 1v, unacc., ?c1913; 93 Maternal Love (L. Smith Wood), ?c1913: 100 Follow to the Wild Wood Weeds, 1914; 104/8 That Sir which serves and seeks for gain (Shakespeare), 1914 [see I:104]; 104/9 And will he not come again? (Shakespeare), 1914, [see I:104]; 104/10 If she be made of red and white (Shakespeare), 1914, lost [see I:104]; 104/11 You that choose not by the view (Shakespeare), 1914, lost [see I:104]; 106 Sonnet on the Sea's Voice (G. Sterling), 1914; 123 Among the Rushes (C. Dixon), 1914; 125 The Fish's Toes (Dixon), 1914

129 Bed in Summer (R. L. Stevenson), 1914; 131 Rain (Stevenson), 1914; 134 Time to Rise (Stevenson), 1914; 135 Looking Forward (Stevenson), 1914; 136 At the Seaside (Stevenson), 1914; 145 Where Go the Boats (Stevenson), 1914; 146 A Baby's Smile (Smith Wood), c1914; 151 The Prelude (J. O. Varian), c1914; 152 *St. Agnes Morning (M. Anderson), c1914; 157 My Auntie (Dixon), 1915; 159 A Song of Courage (Dixon), 1915; 161 Jealousy (Dixon), 1915; 164 God of the Future (Varian), 1915; 174 White Death (C. A. Smith), 1915; 175 The Dream Bridge (Smith), 1915

177 I dreamed I lay where flowers were springing (Burns), 1915; 182 Light and Joy (Dixon), 1915; 192 The First Jasmines (R. Tagore), 1v, vn, pf, 1916; 198 The Wisest Wish (Dixon), 1916; 204 Christmas Song (E. R. Veblen), 1916; 207 Invocation (Varian), 1916; 215 March Men of the Earth (Varian), 1v/vv, pf, c1916 [acc. inc.]; 216 Psalm vii [recte Ps. viii], c1916; 222 Oh, could I mount on fairy wings (F. G. Currier), 1917; 226 Look Deep, 1917; 228 Angus Og (Varian), 1917; 230 Consecration (Currier), 1917

238 The Chauldron (Varian), S, A, T, B, pf, ?c1916–17; 244 The Morning Pool (Smith), 1918; 248 Democracy (Varian), 1918–19; 250 April (E. Pound), 1918–19; 251 Mother (T. Helburn), 1918–19; 256 Homing (L. Brower), 1918; 258 System (Stevenson), 1918–19; 261 My Summer (W. Brooks), 1918–19; 268 A Vision (L. Brown), 1918–19; 270 We'll Build our Bungalows

(?Henry Cowell), 1v/vv, pf, ?1918, refrain lost; 274 Prayer for Mary, 1919
276 Psalm cxxi, 1919 [<C:276a]; 278 There is a Light (Varian), 1919; 282 Oh, let me breathe into the happy air (Keats), 1919; 291 The Daga's Song of the Hero Sun (Varian), *c*1919; 296 The Sun's Travels (Stevenson), ?1917–19; 297 To a Skylark (Shelley), 1920; 299 To my Valentine, 1920; 317 Forget me not, *c*1920; 319 Grief Song (Veblen), *c*1920; 322 Before and After (text and tune, T. Glynn), ?1915–20; 329 My Love (Harry Cowell), 1921

331 Auntie's Skirts (Stevenson), 1921; 337 Olivia (Harry Cowell), *c*1921; 344 Allegro and Burden, ?1916–21; 358 Music, when Soft Voices Die (Shelley), 1922; 363 The Song of the Silence (Harry Cowell), 1922; 364 The Dream of My Life, 1v, unacc., ?*c*1922; 365 Sentence (W. Bynner), ?*c*1922; 366 Vox celeste (Harry Cowell), ?*c*1922; 387 *Manaunaun's Birthing (Varian), 1924 [<A:387a]; 400 *Where she Lies (E. St. Vincent Millay), 1924

414 The Fairy Fountain (Harry Cowell), ?*c*1925; 417 Our Sun (Varian), ?*c*1925; 419 Reconciliation (G. W. Russell), T, org, ?*c*1920–25; 420 Shelter my soul, O my love (S. Naidu), ?*c*1920–25; 421 The Willow Waltz, ?*c*1920–25; 425 Carl's Birthday [Ruggles] (?Henry Cowell), ?1926; 436 Dust and Flame (J. Rantz), *c*1927; 455 Renewal, 1929; 474 Milady of Dreams, ?1920–30; 477 *How Old is Song? (Harry Cowell), 1931 [<G:477a]; 492 *Sunset, Rest (C. Riegger), 2 songs, 1933

497 Proletarian Songs and a March, 1v/vv, pf/unacc., ?1930–33: 1 Canned, 2 Free Nations United!, 4 Proletarian Song, 5 We can win together, 6 Working men unite, we must put up a fight! [for no.3 see I:497/3]; 504 Introspection (E. White), 1934; 507 Relativity (S. Giffin), 1934; 509 Plan ahead (C. W. Eliot), ?*c*1934; 538 6 Songs on Mother Goose Rhymes, 1v/vv, pf, 1937: 1 Curly Locks, 2 Polly put the Kettle on, 3 Three Wise Men, 4 Dr. Foster went to Gloucester, 5 Goosey, 6 Tommy Trot

542 3 Anti-modernist Songs, 1938: 1 A sharp where you'd expect a natural, 2 Hark! From the pit a fearsome sound, 3 Who wrote this fiendish "Rite of Spring"?; 575 Up from the Wheelbarrow (O. Nash), 1939; 604 Mice Lament (E. Grainger), 1v, pf-str, 1940; 665 *The Pasture (Frost), 1944 [AP]; 671 *United Nations: Songs of the People (trad.), 1945; 694 *Daybreak (Blake), 1946; 695 *The Donkey (G. K. Chesterton), 1946

698 *March on Three Beats (J. W. Beattie), 1v/vv, pf, 1946; 702 Family Ruellan-Taylor, 3 solo vv, 1946; 760 Signature of Light (Hagemeyer), 1951; 762 Her smile is as sweet as a rose (? Henry Cowell), 1v, ?unacc., 1951; 783 *The Little Black Boy (Blake), 1952, rev. 1954; 803 The Commission (C. McPhee), sym. cantata, 4 solo vv, orch, 1954, not orchd; 808 *Spring Comes Singing (Hagemeyer), 1954; 814 St. Francis' Prayer for Our Day, 4 solo vv, 1955 [AP]

820 Because the Cat (B. A. Davis), ?1951–5; 824 Septet for [5] Madrigal Singers, Cl, and Kbd, 1956; 825 Crane (P. Colum), 1956; 826 I heard in the night (Colum), (1v, pf/cl/va)/(S, fl), 1956; 827 Night Fliers (Colum), 1956: 564 Spring Pools (Frost), ?c1958; 879 High Let the Song Ascend (hymn), 1v, fl, pf, 1960; 891 Music I Heard (C. Aiken), 1961; 910 *Firelight and Lamp (G. Baro), 1962; 935 3 Songs (L. Hughes), 1v, fl/vn, cl, vc, 1964: 1 Demand, 2 Moonlight, 3 Fulfillment; 939 The Eighth-note Jig (R. Brown), ?1960–64; 955 The Word External, ?1917; c80 others, most lost

CHAMBER

E: *5 or more insts*

328a *Exultation, 4 vn, 2 va, 2 vc, db, 1930 [>I:328]; 340 Carl's Birthday [Ruggles], 3 cl, hn, str qt, pf, c1920–21; 380 *Ensemble: Str Qnt with Thunder Sticks, 1924, *rev. 1956, 380b [movts 1 and 2 <movts 1 and 2 of A:443]; 406 A Composition, pf-str, ens, 1925 [movt 1 <movt 1 of A:440; movt 2 <I:406/2a]; 458 *Polyphonica, 12 insts/chamber orch, 1930; 491b *Suite for Ww Qnt, 1934 [>movts 2, 4, 5, 6 of G:491]; 505 *Ostinato pianissimo, 8 perc, 1934; 521 Dance Forms, 3 melody insts, 2 perc, 1936

548 4 Assorted Movts, fl, ob, cl, b cl, bn, hn, pf ad lib, 1938: 1 Hoedown, 2 Taxim, 3 Tala, 4 Chorale; 565 *Pulse, perc, 1939; 639 *Action in Brass, brass qnt, 1943: 1 Dancing Brass, 2 Singing Brass, 3 Fighting Brass; 643 This is America 1943, fanfare, 4 tpt, 3 trbn, tuba, 1943; 684 *Party Pieces (Sonorous and Exquisite Corpses), ?c1945, 20 pieces by Thomson, Cowell, Cage, and Harrison, Cowell contributed to nos.3, 9, 10, 12–20 [arr. fl, cl, bn, hn, pf, by R. Hughes]

705/3b *Ballad, ww qnt, 1956 [>A:705/3a]; 709 *Tall Tale, brass sextet, 1947; 717 Tune Takes a Trip, cl choir/qnt, 1948; 729 Grinnell Fanfare, brass, org, 1948; 772 4 Trumpets for Alan [Hovhaness], 4 tpt, muted pf, 1952; 837 Taxim, Round and F[uguing] T[une], inst ens, 1957, fuguing tune inc.; 851 *Rondo for Brass, 3 tpt, 2 hn, 2 trbn, 1958; 888 Suite, 2 vn, va, vc, db, ?1950–60; 923 *26 Simultaneous Mosaics, cl, vn, vc, pf, perc, 1963

F: *3–4 insts*

24 Pf Quartette, 3 vn, pf, ?1912; 160 Scenario, 2 vn, vc, pf, 1915; 162 Quartett, str qt, 1915; 166 Minuetto, str qt, 1915; 197 *Str Qt [no.1] (Quartett Pedantic), 1916; 223 *Quartet Romantic, 2 fl, vn, va, 1917; 283 *Quartet Euphometric, str qt, 1919; 332 Movt, str qt, 1921; 383 *4 Combinations for 3 Insts, vn, vc, pf, 1924; 408 *7 Paragraphs, vn, va/vn, vc, 1925; 438 4 Little Solos for Str Qt, 1928; 450 *Movt for Str Qt (Str Qt no.2), 1928 [>movt 6 of A:887]

518 *Mosaic Qt (Str Qt no. 3), 1935 [<movts 1–4 of A:887]; 522 *Str Qt no. 4
"United," 1936; 524 *Vocalise, 1v, fl, pf, 1936; 547 *Toccanta, S, fl, vc,
pf, 1940, arr. as Music Lovers' Set of Five, fl, vn, vc, pf, 547b, 1940, lost
[<A:547a]; 556 Return, 3/4 perc, 1939; 595a 58 for Percy, 3 harmonium,
1940 [>A:595]; 628 60 for 3 Sax, 1942; 650 R[uellan]-T[aylor] "Family
Suite," s rec, s/a rec, t rec, 1943; 662 Sonatina, Bar, vn, pf, 1944 [AP]; 664
Hymn and Fuguing Tune no. 4, (s rec, a rec, b rec)/ww/str, 1944 [AP]

668 Sonatina, Bar, vn, pf, 1944; 713 Hymn, Chorale, and Fuguing Tune no. 8,
str qt, 1947 [<movts 5 and 6 of A:788]; 737 *Sailor's Hornpipe: the Sax-
happy Qt, 4 sax, 1949; 741 Christmas for Sidney 1949, s rec, a rec, t rec,
kbd, 1944 [AP]; 779 *Set of Five, vn, pf, perc, 1952; 786 *For 50, s rec, a
rec, t rec, 1953, pubd as no. 2 of 3 Pieces for 3 Rec; 789 Song for Claire, 3
rec, kbd, 1953; 800 Sonata, duet, sopranino/s rec, s rec, a rec, 1954; 802
*Qt for fl, ob, vc, hpd, 1954, arr. fl, ob, vc, harp, 802a, 1962

806 *Pelog, 2 s rec, a rec, 1954 [AP], pubd as no. 1 of 3 Pieces for 3 Rec; 809
*Jig, s rec, s/a rec, a rec, 1955 [AP], pubd as no. 3 of 3 Pieces for 3 Rec;
832 *Str Qt no. 5, 1956; 843 Wedding Anniversary Music, a rec/vn, vn/cl/
hn, vc/bn/hn, 1957 [AP]; 850 *Hymn and Fuguing Tune no. 12, 3 hn,
1958; 890 Sax Qt, 1961; 898 Family Rondo, 3 kotos, 1961; 901 Love on
June 2, 1962, vn, fl, pf, 1962 [AP]; 903 *Trio for fl, vn, harp, 1962; 941
*Trio in 9 Short Movts, vn, vc, pf, 1965; 960 Paragraph, fl, tuba, va, ded.
Ruggles, ?1924/5

G: *2 insts*

71 [A Prince who was Apart]: 1 March, 2 Wedding Music, vn, pf, lost [no. 2
? = no. 12 of J:70]; 74 Rondo, vn, pf, 1913; 104/1 Vn Stucke, vn, pf, 1914
[= no. 1 of I:104]; 150 Minuetto, vn, pf, c1914; 153 Vn Piece no. 1, vn, pf,
?c1914; 158 Vc Sonata, 1915; 180 Vn Piece no. 2: Phantasmagoria, vn, pf,
1915; 199 Air, vn, pf, 1916; 263 Vn Song (Love Song), vn, pf, 1918–19;
264 Va Song, va, pf, 1918–19; 304 Mazurka, e, vn, pf, 1920; 320 Remi-
niscence, vn, pf, c1920; 352 Gavotte, vn, pf, 1922

357 Minuetto, vn, pf, 1922; 368 Chiaroscuro, vn, pf, 1923; 392 Paragraph for
Leo, vn, pf, 1924; 393 Passage, vn, pf, 1924; 397 *Suite, vn, pf, 1924; 398
Trugbild (Phantasmagoria), vn, pf, 1924; 406/2 Duett to St. Cecilia, vn,
pf-str, ?1925/6; 407 Fiddel Piece, vn, pf, 1925; 432 A Remembrance for
Leo Linder, vn, pf, ?1926; 477a How Old is Song?, vn, pf, 1942 [>D:477];
491 *6 Casual Developments, cl, pf, 1933 [<J:491a, movts 2, 4, 5, and 6
<E:491b]; 517 7 Associated Movts, vn, pf, 1935

529 A Bit of a Suite, vn, va, 1937; 532 *3 Ostinati with Chorales, ob, pf, 1937;
552 [4 Pieces for Pereira], vn, pf, 1938, no. 4 inc.; 568 *Triad, tpt, pf, 1939;

597a Ancient Desert Drone, 2 harmonium, 1940 [>A:597]; 611 *Two-Bits, fl, pf, 1941; 649 Carol 1943, 2 rec, 1943; 653 Stonecrop, 2 rec, 1943; 674 Hymn, vn, pf, 1945 [AP; = movt 1 of G:705]; 676 For Sidney, 2 rec, 1945 [AP]

700 *Tom Binkley's Tune, euphonium, pf, 1946; 701 Family Cowell Duet, a rec, b rec, 1946 [AP]; 705 *Vn Sonata, 1946 [movt 1 = G:674, movt 3 <A:705/3a]; 710 *Hymn and Fuguing Tune no.7, va, pf, 1947; 714 122,547th Two Part Invention, s rec, a rec, 1947 [AP]; 730 Set of Two, vn, pf-str, 1948; 736 *4 Declamations with Return, vc, pf, 1949; 756 Duet for Recorders, 1950 [AP]; 758 *Hymn and Fuguing Tune no.9, vc, pf, 1950 [hymn <movt 1 of A:787]

763 Scherzo, s rec, a rec, 1951 [AP]; 766 Duet for Sidney with Love from Henry, vn, vc, 1951 [AP]; 773 Two Part Invention, s rec, a rec, 1952 [AP]; 777 11th Anniversary, s rec, s/a rec, 1952 [AP]; 784 A Set of Four, s rec, a rec, 1952; 791 Duet, s rec, a rec, 1953 [AP]; 793 Merry Christmas to Sidney, 2 rec, 1953 [AP]; 801/6 In Memory of Nehru, (sitar/vīnā/vn/lv), (tambura/ "sanoi"/pipes/harmonium), 1964, no.6 of [6] Memorial Pieces [see also A:801/1]; 804 Invention, a rec, kbd, 1954 [AP]

811 Beethoven Birds, 2 rec/pf, 1955 [AP]; 812 Set of Two, vn, hpd, 1955; 815 Invention, 2 fl/2 rec, 1955 [AP]; 831 Two Part Invention, s rec, a rec, 1956 [AP]; 834 15th Anniversary, 2 tr insts, 1956 [AP]; 835 Sidney Xmas '56, vn, pf, 1956 [AP; = G:862]; 840 Love to Sidney, s rec, a rec, 1957 [AP]; 844 Christmas 1957, s rec, a rec, 1957 [AP]; 845 *Homage to Iran, vn, pf, 1957; 854 Birthday Piece, 2 tr insts, 1958 [AP]

855 [Duet], 2 tr insts, 1958 [AP]; 857 Introduction and Allegro, va, hpd/pf, 1958; 859 Duet, 2 s insts, 1958 [AP]; 862 Love to Sidney, Christmas 1958, s inst, pf, 1958 [AP; = G:835]; 866 Duet, 2 vn, 1959 [AP]; 870 Duet, 2 tr insts, 1959 [AP]; 872 Sidney's Christmas Stretto, 2 tr insts, 1959 [AP]; 875 *Hymn and Fuguing Tune no.13, trbn, pf, 1960; 876 Stretto, 2 tr insts, 1960 [AP]; 880 Love to Sidney, 2 tr insts, 1960 [AP]

883 Love for Sidney, s rec, a rec, 1960 [AP]; 893 Duet: Hymn and Fuguing Tune no.15a, 2 insts, 1961 [AP]; 896 Duet, 2 tr insts, 1961 [AP]; 897 *Air and Scherzo, a sax, pf, 1961 [<B:897a]; 899 Triple Rondo, fl, harp, 1961; 906 Love Christmas 1962, 2 tr insts, 1962 [AP]; 907 Duet, 2 insts, 1962 [AP]; 914 Sixty with Love, vn, vc, 1963 [AP]; 915 Hymn and Fuguing Tune no.15b, vn, vc, 1963; 918 August Duet, 2 vn, 1963 [AP]

921 *Hymn and Fuguing Tune no.16, vn, pf, 1963 [<A:921a]; 924 Christmas 1963, 2 vn, 1963 [AP]; 928 Hymn and Fuguing Tune no.18, s sax, cb sax, 1964; 933 Duet, 2 a rec/2 vn/2 fl/2 ob, 1964 [AP]; 936 For Sidney with Love, s rec, a rec, 1964 [AP]; 937 Stretto for Claflins, 2 insts, 1964; 944

Duet for Sidney, s rec, a rec, 1965 [AP]; 948 Sidney's Tune, s rec, a rec, 1965 [AP]; 950 Duet for Our Anniversary, vn, va/vc, 1965 [AP]; 952 A Melodie for Charlie [Seeger], vn, vc, 1965; 962 For Vn, vn, pf, ?1924–6

H: *solo inst*

280 For Unacc. Vc, 1919; 418 [Presto], vn, *c*1925; 699 *The Universal Fl, shakuhachi, 1946; 798 Hymn and Fuguing Tune no. 10, carillon, ?1952–3, fuguing tune not composed [not = B:813]; 849 Henry's Hornpipe, tr inst, 1958; 852 Andrée's Birthday Song [Andrée Ruellan], tr inst, 1958; 853 Lullaby for Philio, tr inst, 1958; 856 Wedding Rondo [for] Sidney Reisberg, cl, 1958

868 *Iridescent Rondo in Old Modes, accordion, 1959; 877 *Perpetual Rhythm, accordion, 1960, orig. version, 1949, lost; 884 Merry Christmas for Blanche [Walton], tr inst, 1960; 895 Birthday Melody for Blanche [Walton], tr inst, 1960; 913 To my Valentine, 1963 [AP]; 922 *Gravely and Vigorously, in memory of President John F. Kennedy, vc, 1963; 927 Solo for Alto Rec, 1964 [AP]; 931 The Birthday Child, a Day Late, a rec, 1964; 934 Solo for Alto Rec, a rec, t rec ad lib, 1964 [AP]

I: KEYBOARD
(pf solo unless otherwise stated)

5 Waltz, *c*1910; 9 The Wierd Night, *c*1910–11; 10 The Night Sound: a Sonata, 1910–11; 15 Rippling Waters, Waltz, *c*1911; 22 Ghoul's Gallop, ?1912; 27 Op. 1 for Pf, 1912: 1 School March, 2 Tarantelle, 3 Lullaby, 4 Flashes of Hell Fire: a Dance of Devils, 5 The Cloudlet, 6 The Frisk, 7 Imaginings, 8 The Last Match, 9 The Lotus, 10 Scherzo, 11 Etude, 12 Sonatine, all lost except nos. 2 and 4; 29 Nocturne, 1913; 30 Freak de concert, 1913 [= no. 13 of J:70]; 31 Polish Dance, 1913

32 Prelude no. 2, 1913 [= no. 1 of J:70]; 33 Prelude [no. 1] after the Style of Bach, 1913 [= no. 2 of J:70]; 34 Valse lente, 1913 [= no. 3 of J:70]; 35 Bersuse, 1913 [= no. 6 of J:70]; 36 Fairys Dance no. 3 in a Popular Style, 1913 [= no. 7 of J:70]; 37 Invention quasi Bach, a tre voce, 1913 [= no. 8 of J:70]; 38 Brownie's Dance, 1913 [= no. 10 of J:70]; 40 Savage Suite, 1913: 1 Savage Dance, 2 Savage Music, 3 War Dance, 4 Sad Fragment, 5 Melodie, 6 Fire Dance, 7 Funeral March of Natives, 8 Joy Dance, inc., 9 A Savage Rhythm, 10 A War [no. 8 = no. 16 of J:70]

41 A Fragment, 1913; 42 Etude-cadenza, 1913; 43 Lullaby, 1913; 44 Hunting Song, 1913; 45 The Awakening, 1913; 46 Message from Mars, 1913; 47 Quasi Mozart, 1913; 48 Largo, 1913; 51 Etude, d, 1913; 54 Wrinkle Rag,

1913 [= no.4 of J:70]; 55 Love Dance (Valse), 1913 [= no.14 of J:70]; 56 3 Sonatas, 1913: 1 Sonata, A, inc., 2 Sonate, E♭, 3 Sonate, B; 57 Romance, 1913 [= no.11 of J:70]; 58 Dirge, 1913

59 Adventures in Harmony (A Novelette), 1913; 60 Sounds from the Conservatory, 2 pf, 1913; 63 Album Leaflet, 1913; 64 Hash, 1913; 65 Mist Music no.1, 1913 [= no.17 of J:70]; 66 Mist Music no.2, 1913; 73 The Anaemic Rag (A Burlesque), 1913 [= no.9 of J:70]; 75 Etude [no.2], C, 1913; 76 Valse, 1913; 78a The Cauldron, ?1913–18 [arr. from lost pf piece]; 81 Sprites' Dance, 1913 [= Wind Spirits' Dance, no.15 of J:70]

82 [Christmas-thoughts Pieces], 1913: 1 Etude-chimes, 2 Xmas Thoughts for Baby, 3 Reindeer Dance, 4 Xmas Bells, 5 Xmas Stocking Dance, 6 Watching for Santa, 7 The Tin Soldier, 8 The Xmas Tree, 9 Valse, 10 Tarantelle, 11 March, 12 For Phyllis, 1913, nos.9–12 lost; 83 Sonate progressive, 1913: 1 Classic, 2 Romantic, 3 Modern, 4 Humoreske; 84 Orchestra Stucke, 1913 [?>lost orch work]; 86 Descriptive Piece, 1913; 87 The Battle Sonata, 1913; 91 [Andante], A♭, ?c1913

92 Jesus was born at Christmas, ?c1913; 94 Theme, with 3 variations, 1914; 97 In the Tropics, 1914; 98 Sea Picture, 1914 [= no.5 of J:70]; 99 Etude no.3, 1914; 102 Piece, 1914; 104 [Musical Letters to Mrs. Veblen], 1914: 2 Dance, 3 Maid and Hero, 4 Theme, 5 Tango Theme, 6 *Anger Dance "Mad Dance," 7 Modern Stucke, lost, 12 (Etude) Classic, 13 Etude no.4 "The Winds," 14 Themelet, 15 Valse, 16 Snake Piece [for no.1, see G:104/1, for nos.8–11, see D:104/8–11]

105 Vio doloroso, 1914; 108 Imitations in Style of Various Composers: Chopin, Brahms, Schumann, Grieg, 4 pieces, 1914; 109 Popular Melodie, 1914; 114 Sonate Movt, F, 1914; 115 Sonate Movt, f, 1914; 119 Sonate Movt, c♯, 1914; 120 Resumé in 10 Movts, 1914: 1 Savage Music, 2 Choral Music, 3 Contrapuntal Music, 4 Classic Sonate, 5 Folk Music, lost, 6 Romantic, 7 Operatic, 8 Oriental, 9 Modern, 10 Futurist; 139 Skylight, 1914

213 [Dynamic Motion and encores]: 1 *Dynamic Motion, 1916, 2 *What's This?, 1st encore, 1917 [<A:213/2a], 3 *Amiable Conversation, 2nd encore, 1917, 4 *Advertisement, 3rd encore, 1917, 5 *Antinomy, 4th encore, 1917, 6 *Time Table, 5th encore, 1917; 214 The Rogues' Gallery: Portraits, 1916, 8 pieces, all lost except no.6 Mrs. Bartlett; 217 Letter [to J. O. Varian], ?1915–16; 219/1 *The Tides of Manaunaun, ?1917 [= no.1 of J:219, no.1 of I:354; <no.1 of B:605]

224 Sixth Etude (A Tragedy), 1917; 225 Sonate, 1917, movt 4 inc.; 227 Prelude and Canon, 1917; 229 Olive, 1917; 234 Antique Dance, 1917; 239 [untitled], A♭, ?c1916–17; 240 Prelude, ?c1916–17; 243 Telegram, ?1916–17; 262 Child's Song, 1918–19; 269 [Waltz], ?1918–19; 273 Sonate, c, 1919; 279

Prelude interrhythmique, 1919; 281 Sonate Movt, B, 1919; 292 [Expressivo], *c*1919; 294 Mrs. Barrett, ?1917–19; 295 One Moment, Please, ?1917–19; 298 Prelude specifique, 1920; 300 Fugue, A, 1920

302 Fugue, c, 1920; 303 Double Fugue, c, 1920; 305 Vestiges, 1920 [<A:305a]; 307 *Fabric, 1920; 308 The New Born, 1920; 310 Prelude diplomatique, 1920; 312 For Xmas '20: an Idiosyncrasy, 1920; 315 Episode, b♭, 1920; 323 Episode [no.2], d, 1921; 324 *Episode [no.3], g♯, 1921; 326 Singing Waters, 1921; 327 Romance, E♭, 1921; 328 *Exultation, 1921 [<E:328a, <no.2 of B:605]; 335 Xmas 1921, 1921

336 Tom's Waltz, for Tom Moss to Play, 1921; 339 Cantabile, *c*1920–21; 342 March, *c*1920–21; 350 Dance Obsequious, 1922; 353 [Ings]: 1 *Floating, ?1922, 2 *Frisking, ?1922, 3 *Fleeting, 1917, 4 *Scooting, 1917, 5 *Wafting, 1917, 6 *Seething, 1917, 7 *Whisking, 1917, 8 *Sneaking, 1917, 9 *Swaying, 1924, 10 Sifting, 1917, lost, 11 Wafting no.2, 1917, 12 Landscape no.3; Trickling, 1917, 13 Whirling, ?1930, lost, 14 Rocking, 1955 [nos. 1–6 orig. pubd as series, Six Ings, repr. with nos.7–9 as Nine Ings]

354 3 Irish Legends: 1 *The Tides of Manaunaun, ?1917, 2 The Hero Sun, 1922, 3 The Voice of Lir, 1920 [no.1 = I:219/1, <no. 1 of B:605]; 355 *It isn't It, 1922, pubd as Scherzo; 361 Scherzo, 1922; 362 Seven and One Fourth Pounds, 1922; 367 The Sword of Oblivion, pf-str, *c*1920–22; 369 The Vision of Oma, 1923; 370 *The Aeolian Harp, pf-str, *c*1923; 371 Love Song, ?*c*1923; 372 Love Song, ?*c*1923; 377 A Rudhyar, 1924; 378 Xmas Greetings for Olive, 1924

381 Exuberance, 1924; 382 The Fire of the Cauldron, 1924; 384 The Harp of Life, 1924 [<no.3 of B:605]; 388 March of the Feet of the Eldana, 1924; 389 2 Movts for Pf, 1924: 1 *Piece for Pf with Strings, 2 Allegro maestoso–Largo–Con moto, inc.; 390 Paragraph, 1924; 395 *The Snows of Fuji-yama, 1924; 399 The Trumpet of Angus Og (The Spirit of Youth), 1918–24; 401 Chromatic Inst Fugue, ?1924; 403 March of the Fomer, ?*c*1924

405 *The Banshee, pf-str, 1925 [<movt 1 of B:452]; 406/2a Duett to St. Cecilia, pf-str, 1925 [>movt 2 of E:406]; 409 *Prelude for Org, 1925; 412 The Battle of Midyar, ?*c*1925; 415 Irish Jig, ?*c*1925 [<A:415a]; 422 [?F. L.] D. on Birthday, ?*c*1920–25; 426 Domnu, the Mother of Waters, 1926; 429 *Maestoso (Marked Passages), 1926 [<movt 3 of A:443]; 433 The Sleep Music of the Dagna, pf-str, 1926; 435 How Come?, 1927

442 When the Wind Chases You, 1928; 446 [10 children's pieces for piano], 1928: 1 *The Nimble Squirrel, 2 *An Irish Jig, 3 *The Spanish Fiesta, 4 *In Colonial Days, 5 *The Hand Organ Man, titles of nos.6–10 unknown, nos.1–5 pubd as by Henry Dixon; 447 *The Fairy Bells, pf-str, by 1928 [<movt 3 of B:452]; 448 The Leprechaun, pf-str, 1928 [<movt 2 of B:452]; 449 I Wish

I had an Ice Cream Cone, 1928; 451 *2 Woofs, 1928; 453 *The Fairy Answer, pf-str, 1929; 454 Euphoria, 1929; 456 Next to Last, ?pf, ?1919–29

462 *Sinister Resonance, 1930; 463 *Dve piesy [2 pieces]: 1 V ritme "rilya," irlandskiĭ tanets, 1928 [Lilt of the reel], 2 Tigr [Tiger], 1930 [no.1 <A:463/ 1a and b, no.4 of B:605; no.2 >inc. pf piece]; 469 March of Invincibility, 1930; 470 Whirling Dervish, 1930; 473 For a Child, ?1920–30; 479 [Gig], 1931; 484b 2 Appositions, 1932 [>A:484]; 487 Rhythm Study, 1932; 489 Expressivo, ?1928–32; 496 On the 8th Birthday of the Princess (Magic Music): a Measure for Each Year, ?1930–33

497/3 Move Forward!, no.3 of Proletarian Songs and a March, D:497, ?1930– 33, inc.; 514 *The Harper Minstrel Sings, 1935; 515 *The Irishman Dances, 1935; 530 Back Country Set: Reel, Jig, Hornpipe, 1937; 543b *Celtic Set (1941) [>A:543]; 543c *Celtic Set, 2 pf (1941) [>A:543]; 549 Set of 2 Movts, 1938: 1 Deep Color, 2 High Color, 1938; 550 Wedding March, 1938 [<A:550a]; 557 *Rhythmicana, 1938; 560 [Jig], ?pf, ?c1938; 564 *Amerind Suite, 1939: 1 The Power of the Snake, 2 The Lover Plays his Flute, 3 Deer Dance

607 Christmas Duet (Noel), pf 4 hands, 1940; 613 Granny O'Toole's Hornpipe, 1941; 614 *Homesick Lilt, 1941; 631 *Square Dance Tune, 1942; 635 *Processional, org, 1942; 646 2nd Anniversary, 1943 [AP]; 651 Hymn and Fuguing Piece, 1943 [<A:651a]; 654 Fabric Ending (Finale), ?1943; 658 *Mountain Music, 1944; 660a Hymn and Fuguing Tune no.3, c1948 [AP; >A:660]; 667 *Kansas Fiddler, 1944: 1 Fiddle Air, 2 Fiddle Jig, 3 Fiddle Hornpipe, 4 Fiddle Reel; 670 Elegie for Hanya Holm, ?1941–4

678 For Sidney Christmas 1945, 1945 [AP]; 683 Lookit! I'm a Cowboy, ?c1945; 685 Playing Tag is Keen, ?c1945; 696 Hymn and Fuguing Tune no.6, kbd, 1946 [AP; fuguing tune <movt 4 of A:697, part <1:711]; 703 Irish Epic Set, pf-str, kbd, 1946; 711 6th Two Part Invention for Sidney, 1947 [AP; part >1:696]; 718 Invention for Sidney, ?kbd, 1948 [AP]; 720 *All Dressed Up, 1948; 721 Deirdre of the Sorrows, 1948; 724 7th Two-part Invention, 1948 [AP]; 725 *The Good Old Days, 1948

726 Two Part Invention, 1948 [AP]; 734 Madman's Wisp, 1949: 1 Throwing the Curse, 2 Dancing the Spell; 735 Two Part Invention, kbd/2 rec, 1949 [AP]; 738 *Pa Jigs them all Down (Perpetual Jig), 1949; 739 *Pegleg Dance, 1949; 740 Two Part Invention, 1949 [AP]; 749 Two Part Invention, kbd, 1950 [AP]; 751 Two Part Invention, kbd, 1950 [AP]; 752 Two Part Invention with [pedal point on] G, 1950 [AP]; 754 *Two Part Invention in 3 Parts, 1950 [AP]; 755 Improvisation, 1950; 764 10th Anniversary, 1951 [AP]; 780 Invention, 1952 [AP]; 799 *Toccatina, 1954

801/2 Chorale to the Memory of Marie K. Thatcher, org, 1954, no.2 of [6] Memorial Pieces [see also A:801/1]; 801/4 Used in Org Piece for Allen

McHose's Mother-in-law, org, 1961, no.4 of [6] Memorial Pieces [see also A:801/1]; 817 Ground and Fuguing Tune, org, 1955; 822 *Bounce Dance, 1956; 828 *Sway Dance, 1956; 841 Wedding Music, ded. H. and E. Rugg, 1957; 847 Wedding Piece for Krissi and Davy, 1957; 860 Jim's B'day, 1958; 886 *Set of Four, pf/hpd, 1960; 889 Perpetual Motion, 1961 [AP]; 900 *Hymn and Fuguing Tune no.14, org, 1962; 905 September 27, 1962, 1962 [AP]; 920 The Twenty-second, pf/(vn, vc), 1963 [AP]; 949 Tune for Avery [Claflin], pf/(vn, vc), 1965; 953 Polyphonicas nos.1 and 2, ?1916; 956 Clusteriana no.1, ?1916–17

J: MUSIC FOR DANCE AND DRAMA

70   Music for Creation Dawn (incidental music, T. Kanno), 27 pieces, pf, 1913: nos.1–17 composed separately [see I:32, 33, 34, 54, 98, 35, 36, 37, 73, 38, 57, G:71/2, I:30, 55, 81, 40/8, 65], 18 Sunset Music, 19 Fairy's Dance no.2, 20 Thy lily bells, 21 Extacy, 22 Sad Music, 23 Music for Saavashi, 24 Dance Music for Sagano, 25 Sleepy Music, 26 Extra Music: Melodie, 27 Moonlight Music (the finale); Carmel, CA, 16 Aug 1913, Cowell

184   Red Silence (incidental music, Jap. drama, F. L. Giffin), 10 pieces, speaker, fl, vn, vc, pf, 1915, no.7 inc., no.8 lost; San Francisco, 20 Jan 1916

219   The Building of Bamba (Irish mythological opera, 14 scenes, Varian), solo vv, mixed chorus, pf, 1917, inc., Halcyon, CA, 18 Aug 1917; rev. 1930, 219a, Halcyon, 7 Aug 1930, cond. Cowell [scene 1 = I:219/1, no.1 of I:354 <no.1 of B:605]

423   Atlantis (ballet, 9 movts), S, A, Bar, pf, orch, 1926

457   Men and Machines (dance music, E. Findlay), pf, 1930; Brooklyn, NY, 27 Feb 1930

476   Steel and Stone (dance music, C. Weidman), ?pf, 1931, lost, New York, 4 Feb 1931; arr. as Dance of Work, 10 insts, 476a, New York, 5 Jan 1932, cond. A. Weiss

482   Dance of Sport (dance music, Weidman), orig. entitled Competitive Sport, pf, also arr. fl, ob, cl, bn, str, 482a, 1931; New York, 5 Jan 1932

483   Heroic Dance (dance music, ded. M. Graham), 10 insts, ?1931; *arr. pf, 483a, ?1931

491a   Six Casual Developments (dance music, Graham), chamber orch, 1934, lost; New York, 25 Feb 1934, cond. L. Horst [>G:491]

495   Three Dances of Activity (dance music, S. Delza), fl, pf, perc, 1933, lost: 1 Labor, 2 Play, 3 Organization; New York, 10 Dec 1933

500   Trojan Women (dance music, R. Radir), chamber orch, 1934

513   Fanati (incidental music, prol., 5 scenes, R. E. Welles), vv, pf, perc, 1935, lost; Palo Alto, CA, 7 June 1935

516   Salutation (dance music, H. Holm), fl, pf, perc, 1935, lost; Millbrook, NY, 28 Feb 1936

534   Sarabande (dance music, Graham), ob, cl, perc, 1937, lost; Bennington, VT, 30 July 1937, cond. Horst

537   Deep Song (dance music, Graham), ww, perc, 1937, lost; New York, 19 Dec 1937, cond. Horst

539   Ritual of Wonder (dance music, M. Van Tuyl), pf, perc, ?c1937

563   Les mariés de la Tour Eiffel (incidental music, J. Cocteau), pf, perc, 1939: 1 *Hilarious Curtain-opener, 2 *Ritournelle, 3 Two Ritournelles, 4 The Train Finale; Seattle, 24 March 1939, pf, dir. J. Cage

596   Fanfare: Variations (dance music, Van Tuyl), chaconne with 7 variations, 1940; Oakland, CA, 27 July 1940

606   King Lear (incidental music, Shakespeare), male chorus, pf, orch, 1940; New York, 14 Dec 1940, dir. E. Piscator

609   *Trickster (Coyote) (dance music, E. Hawkins), ww, perc, 1941; New York, 20 April 1941

622   Hanya Holm Music (dance music, Holm), pf, 1941, inc.: 1 Dance of Introduction, 2 Evocation, 3 For a Dancer; no.1, New York, 17 March 1941

624   Woman in War (dance music, S. Chen), pf, 1942, lost; New York, 23 April 1942

627   Mr. Flagmaker (film music, M. E. Bute), SAATB, wind, ?pf, str, 1942

630   Banners: a Choreographic Chorale (dance music, 2 scenes, Whitman), S, chorus, chamber ens, 1942

637   Killer of Enemies (dance music, Hawkins), 1942, lost

644   Chinese Partisan Fighter (dance music, Chen), pf, 1943, lost; Redlands, CA, 27 Aug 1943

666   Derwent and the Shining Sword (incidental music, radio play, Bute), 1944

680   Hamlet (incidental music, Shakespeare), male vv, inst ens, 1945

743   O'Higgins of Chile (opera, 3, Harald), 1949, not orchd

753   A Full Moon in March (dance music, G. Lippincott, W. B. Yeats), male v/hn/vc/trbn, pf, 1950; Fargo, ND, 1 Dec 1950

761   Clown (dance music, Hawkins), pf, 1951

768   The Morning of the Feast (incidental music, M. Connelly), solo vv, inst ens, 1952

805   Changing Woman (dance music, J. Erdman), pf, drums, harmonium, 1954; San Francisco, 18 Dec 1954
836   Music for Ploesti (film music), ?1955–6, inc.
885   Here by the Water's Edge (film music, C. Pratt, L. Hurwitz), cl, bn, tuba, str, 1960, inc.

K: ARRANGEMENTS
525   C. Ives: Calcium Light Night, 6 wind, 2 drums, 2 pf, arr. and ed., 1936
572   J. S. Bach: Christ lag in Todesbanden BWV278, arr. band, 1939
588   F. Chopin: Polonaise, arr. band, 1936–40, lost
589   C. W. von Gluck: Andante, arr. orch ens, 1936–40, lost

folksong arrangements
612   *The Lost Jimmie Whalen (American trad.), 4vv, 1941
623   La Valenciana (Iberian trad.), S, A, mixed chorus, fl, bn, 2 gui, castanets, tap dancer, 1942
633   Ballynure Ballad (Irish trad.), chorus, bagpipe, 1942
672   *The Irish Girl (Irish trad.), SATB, pf, 1945
742   *Lilting Fancy (Nickelty, Nockelty) (Irish trad.), SATB, 1949
794   *Garden Hymn for Easter, SATB, 1953
795   *Granny does your dog bite?, SATB, 1953

Principal publishers: Associated, Boosey & Hawkes, C. Fischer, Peer-Southern, Peters, Presser, G. Schirmer

BIBLIOGRAPHY

M. Bauer: "New Musical Resources," *MM*, vii/3 (1929–30), 43
N. Slonimsky: "Henry Cowell," *American Composers on American Music*, ed. H. Cowell (Stanford, CA, 1933/*R*1962)
A. Farwell: "Pioneering for American Music," *MM*, xii (1934–5), 116
C. Seeger: "Henry Cowell," *Magazine of Art*, xxxiii (1940), 288
E. Gerschefski: "Henry Cowell," *ACAB*, iii/4 (1953–4), 3, 18
J. S. Harrison: "Cowell: Peck's Bad Boy of Music," *ACAB*, iii/4 (1953–4), 5
H. Brant: "Henry Cowell – Musician and Citizen," *The Etude*, lxxv (1957), no.2, p.15; no.3, p.20; no.4, p.22
J. Edmunds and G. Boelzner: *Some Twentieth-century American Composers*, i (New York, 1959), 37ff [incl. further bibliography]
H. Weisgall: "The Music of Henry Cowell," *MQ*, xlv (1959), 484
J. Cage: "The History of Experimental Music in the United States," *Silence* (Middletown, CT, 1961/*R*1973), 67
E. Helm: "Henry Cowell – American Pioneer," *MusAm*, lxxxii/4 (1962), 32

O. E. Albrecht: "Henry Cowell (1897–1965)," *JAMS*, xix (1966), 432

G. Chase: "Henry Cowell," *Inter-American Institute for Musical Research Yearbook*, ii (1966), 98

R. F. Goldman: "Henry Cowell (1897–1965): a Memoir and an Appreciation," *PNM*, iv/2 (1966), 23

various authors: "Henry Cowell: a Dancer's Musician," *Dance Scope* (1966), spr., 6

H. Oesch: "Henry Cowell, Pionier und Aussenseiter der Neuen Musik," *Melos*, xl (1973), 287

S. E. Gilbert: " 'The Ultramodern Idiom': a Survey of New Music," *PNM*, xii/1–2 (1973–4), 282

O. Daniel: "American Composer Henry Cowell," *Stereo Review*, xxxiii/6 (1974), 72

B. Saylor: *The Writings of Henry Cowell*, ISAMm, vii (Brooklyn, NY, 1977)

"Three Libraries to House Cowell Music and Recordings," *Clavier*, xvii/5 (1978), 56

B. Silver: "Henry Cowell and Alan Hovhaness: Responses to the Music of India," *Contributions to Asian Studies*, xii (1978), 54

D. S. Augustine: *Four Theories of Music in the United States, 1900–1950: Cowell, Yasser, Partch, Schillinger* (diss., U. of Texas, 1979)

R. H. Mead: "Cowell, Ives and *New Music*," *MQ*, lxvi (1980), 538

——: *Henry Cowell's New Music, 1925–1936: the Society, the Music Editions, and the Recordings* (Ann Arbor, 1981)

H. Gleason and W. Becker: "Henry Cowell," *20th-century American Composers*, Music Literature Outlines, ser. iv (Bloomington, IN, rev. 2/1981), 58 [incl. further bibliography]

M. L. Manion: *Writings about Henry Cowell: an Annotated Bibliography*, ISAMm, xvi (Brooklyn, NY, 1982)

F. Koch: *Reflections on Composing: Four American Composers: Elwell, Shepherd, Rogers, Cowell* (Pittsburgh, 1983)

R. H. Mead: "The Amazing Mr. Cowell," *American Music*, i/4 (1983), 63

H. W. Hitchcock: "Henry Cowell's *Ostinato Pianissimo*," *MQ*, lxx (1984), 23

D. Hall: "New Music Quarterly Recordings – a Discography," *Journal* [Association of Recorded Sound Collections], xvi/1–2 (1984), 10

R. O. Devore: *Stylistic Diversity within the Music of Five Avant-garde American Composers, 1929–1945* (diss., U. of Iowa, 1985) [also incl. Becker, Crawford, Riegger, and Ruggles]

B. Saylor: "The Tempering of Henry Cowell's 'Dissonant Counterpoint'," *Essays on Modern Music*, ed. M. Brody, ii (Boston, 1985), 3

W. Lichtenwanger: *The Music of Henry Cowell: a Descriptive Catalog*, ISAMm (Brooklyn, NY, 1986)

134

GEORGE GERSHWIN

Richard Crawford
Wayne Schneider

CHAPTER FIVE

George Gershwin

1. BOYHOOD. Gershwin's parents, Moshe Gershovitz and Rose Bruskin, immigrated to the USA in the 1890s from Russia and settled in New York, where they met and married in 1895. George Gershwin [Jacob Gershvin] was born in Brooklyn on 26 September 1898. He shared the heritage of Irving Berlin, Jerome Kern, Richard Rodgers, and many other songwriters who dominated American popular music between the two world wars: all were New Yorkers of European-Jewish background.

Neither of Gershwin's parents was musical. His father drifted from job to job, and between 1895 and 1917 the Gershwins occupied at least 22 different residences in Brooklyn and Manhattan. But while their financial situation was often precarious, they avoided poverty. The family lived under one roof until long after the four children were grown, and although his parents did not provide George with an environment in which learning and the arts were cultivated, their legacy to him included an artistic collaborator in the person of his older brother Ira, who wrote the lyrics for most of his songs.

Gershwin's boyhood was marked by an interest in athletics and an indifference to school. Prompted later in life by interviewers to recall his early musical experiences, he remembered having stood rapt on a sidewalk on 125th Street in Harlem, perhaps as early as 1904, listening to a player piano grind out Anton Rubinstein's Melody in F. But music was seldom heard at home until 1910, when the Gershwins bought their first piano.

Though it had been intended for Ira, George quickly took it over; he progressed rapidly in lessons with neighborhood teachers and about 1912 was accepted as a pupil of Charles Hambitzer, a musician of talent and taste. Hambitzer recognized "genius" in Gershwin and sought to open up the world of classical music to his pupil, taking him to concerts and assigning him pieces by composers such as Chopin, Liszt, and Debussy. In 1914, however, Gershwin turned to a musical world closer to home when he dropped out of New York's High School for Commerce and went to work for Jerome H. Remick & Co., a music publishing firm on Tin Pan Alley, for $15 per week.

Remick hired the 15-year-old Gershwin as a song plugger – a salesman who promoted the firm's songs chiefly by playing and singing them for performers. Endless hours at the keyboard improved his playing: he cut his first piano rolls in 1915 (by 1926 he had made more than 100), and he became a skilled vocal accompanist. He also began to compose songs and piano pieces of his own, though with no encouragement from his employers. Finally, he aspired to move from Tin Pan Alley, with its emphasis on single songs written to commercial formulas, to the Broadway musical stage, where men like Jerome Kern, whom he had come to admire especially, were applying a more highly developed musical artistry to writing scores for entire shows.

2. FROM BROADWAY TO "RHAPSODY IN BLUE." Gershwin left Remick & Co. in March 1917 and by July was working as the rehearsal pianist for *Miss 1917*, a show by Kern and Victor Herbert. After the show opened in November at the Century Theater, he stayed on as the organizer of and accompanist for popular concerts held there on Sunday evenings. His talent as a composer was also noticed. Although he had previously published only two songs and a raglike piano piece, in February 1918 Max Dreyfus, the head of Harms publishing company, offered him

$35 per week for the right to publish any songs he might compose in the future. Before the year was out, three Broadway shows carried songs by Gershwin, and he had served for a time as the accompanist to the Broadway star Nora Bayes in the review *Ladies First*. Soon thereafter he composed his first full Broadway score, for *La La Lucille* (produced by Alex A. Aarons), which opened on 26 May 1919 and received 104 performances. Several months before his 21st birthday, Gershwin had a reputation as a good pianist, as well as a Broadway show on the boards, several independent songs in print, and a publisher awaiting more.

The beginning of the 1920s saw Gershwin realize much of the promise of his earlier years. *Swanee*, recorded in 1920 by the popular singer Al Jolson, was his first hit song, yielding some $10,000 in composer's royalties in that year alone. For Broadway, under contract to the producer George White, he composed the music for five annual reviews, called *George White's Scandals*, in 1920–24. Working for other producers he supplied the scores for such shows as *A Dangerous Maid* (1921), *Our Nell* (1922), and *Sweet Little Devil* (1924), and he contributed songs to many more. He composed for the London musical stage as well: *The Rainbow* (1923) and *Primrose* (1924). The latter was a success, and he followed it in the same year with *Lady, be Good!*, the first of his shows for which Ira wrote all the lyrics; it included the songs *Fascinating rhythm* and *Oh, lady, be good!*, both of which became standards of the American song repertory.

In 1924 Gershwin became famous. He did so not by writing more successful musicals or hit songs but by composing and then performing, in a highly publicized concert organized by the dance band leader Paul Whiteman, a work that gained immediate recognition: the *Rhapsody in Blue* for piano and orchestra. First performed in New York's Aeolian Hall on 12 February, the *Rhapsody* owed much of its impact to the circumstances of its first appearance and to Whiteman's promotional skill. The concert was billed as "An Experiment in Modern Music," and it purported to show that a new, rhythmically vivacious kind of dance music called jazz – a music that most concert musicians and critics of the time thought slapdash in execution and conducive to poor musicianship – was improved when performed in the "symphonic" arrangements that were the specialty of Whiteman's band. Identified in preconcert publicity as a "jazz concerto," the *Rhapsody* was written to demonstrate that jazz-based materials need not be confined to short pieces. The Aeolian Hall concert achieved a sense of occasion: Whiteman had invited many prominent classical musicians and New York's leading critics. Questions about the destiny of American music were very much in the air, and critics such as Carl Van Vechten and Gilbert Seldes were arguing that vernacular idioms should vitalize American fine arts of the future. Gershwin's *Rhapsody* won the audience's approval and the critics' attention. It also won renown for its composer. No longer simply another talented American songwriter, he was thereafter recognized as a historical figure – the man who had brought "jazz" into the concert hall.

Although many listeners found *Rhapsody in Blue* a dramatic departure from Gershwin's previous compositions, it can be perceived as a reaffirmation of his boyhood interest in classical music. During his early years on Tin Pan Alley, Gershwin seems to have set classical-music studies aside. As he turned his attention more towards composing than playing, however, he recognized a need to improve his craft. By 1917 he had begun to study harmony, counterpoint, orchestration, and musical form with Edward Kilenyi, continuing at least to 1921. His first classical piece, the *Lullaby* for string quartet, was apparently composed as a harmony exercise for Kilenyi. His second, a brief opera called *Blue Monday*, was written to open the second act of *George White's Scandals of 1922* but was withdrawn after the first performance. On 1 November 1923 Gershwin accompanied the Canadian soprano

Eva Gauthier in a recital at Aeolian Hall that helped to set the stage for Whiteman's concert less than three months later; in a program that ranged from songs by Purcell and Bellini to works by Schoenberg, Hindemith, and Bartók, Gauthier included compositions by Gershwin, Kern, Berlin, and Walter Donaldson. In the context of both Gershwin's career and New York's concert life, the startling musical juxtapositions of *Rhapsody in Blue* were not entirely without precedent.

3. YEARS OF CELEBRITY AND EXPANSION. Growing fame and affluence (between 1924 and 1934 he received more than a quarter of a million dollars from performances, recordings, and rental fees of the *Rhapsody in Blue* alone) brought about changes in Gershwin's life. In 1925 he moved his family from an apartment to a five-story town house in a fashionable neighborhood on New York's upper west side. About the same time he began to develop his interest in the visual arts by collecting paintings, sculptures, prints, and drawings, and by becoming a painter himself. (His collection included works by Picasso, Modigliani, Utrillo, Pascin, Thomas Hart Benton, and many other modern artists; in December 1937, several months after his death, 39 of his own paintings were exhibited in New York.) He also became known as a figure in New York theatrical and literary society, enlivening and often dominating parties with his piano playing. ("I'd bet on George any time," the playwright George S. Kaufman once remarked, "in a 100-yard dash to the piano.")

After the success of the *Rhapsody*, new patterns emerged in Gershwin's activity as a composer. He continued to write scores for the musical theater, though at a slower rate (ten full scores and one collaboration in the ten years 1926–35, compared with 16 full scores and several more collaborations in the previous seven years, 1919–25). But he gave more and more of his time and energy to concert music, continuing to study with a succes-

11. *George Gershwin (center) with his brother Ira (right) and Fred Astaire during rehearsals for the film "Shall we Dance," 1937*

sion of teachers among whom were Rubin Goldmark (three lessons in 1923), Wallingford Riegger (for several months in the late 1920s), and Henry Cowell (intermittently between 1927 and 1929). He devoted much of the summer of 1925 to composing the Concerto in F for piano and orchestra, commissioned by Walter Damrosch and the New York SO. The Preludes for Piano were introduced the next December as part of a recital in which he accompanied the contralto Marguerite d'Alvarez. During much of 1928 Gershwin was occupied with the composition of the tone poem *An American in Paris*, written in part during a trip to Europe from mid-March to June. Traveling with Ira, Ira's wife, and his sister Frances (who later married Leopold Godowsky, Jr.), Gershwin was welcomed as a musical celebrity; he met many composers, including Prokofiev, Milhaud, Poulenc, Ravel, Walton, and Berg, and heard both *Rhapsody in Blue* and the Concerto in F played in his honor by French musicians. In the summer of 1929 he made his début as a conductor in an open-air concert at Lewisohn Stadium in New York where before an audience of more than 15,000 he conducted the New York PO in *An American in Paris* and *Rhapsody in Blue*, playing the piano part of the latter himself. A few months later, in October 1929, he signed a contract to compose a "Jewish opera," to be called *The Dybbuk*, for the Metropolitan Opera, but he never fulfilled that commission. Even during his first stay in Hollywood (from November 1930 to February 1931), however, Gershwin maintained his commitment to concert music; while he and Ira wrote the score for the film *Delicious* (for which they were paid $100,000) and began the Broadway operetta *Of Thee I Sing*, he also composed most of his Second Rhapsody for Piano and Orchestra.

One of Gershwin's most remarkable accomplishments was that he managed this broadening of his musical activities and interests without sacrificing his popularity. Rather than being intimidated by success, he reveled in it, accepting adulation calmly as no

143

more than his due. By the early 1930s his fame, his earning power, and the range of his works made Gershwin unique among American musicians.

Having established himself as a composer of ambition and talent, Gershwin turned his attention more to the music that had first won him wide audience approval and composed some of his most successful musicals and operettas: *Strike up the Band* (1927; revised 1930), *Girl Crazy* (1930), and *Of Thee I Sing* (1931), which won a Pulitzer Prize. (*Let 'em Eat Cake* and *Pardon my English*, both from 1933, were less successful.) He was apparently never happier than when performing his own music; he accepted a two-week engagement at New York's Roxy Theater in 1930 playing *Rhapsody in Blue* with the Whiteman band during showings of *The King of Jazz*, a film about Whiteman; he continued his concerts (16 August 1932 and 9–10 July 1936 at Lewisohn Stadium; 1 November 1932 at the Metropolitan Opera) and tours (14 January–11 February 1934, with Leo Reisman's orchestra; 15 December 1936–11 February 1937, last tour); and he talked and played on a radio program, "Music by Gershwin," broadcast by CBS in 1934–5. Nor did he lose his touch as a composer of popular songs. In June 1936 he and Ira signed a contract with RKO film studios, and by August they had moved to Hollywood. The songs they supplied for *Shall we Dance* (1937), *A Damsel in Distress* (1937), and *The Goldwyn Follies* (1938) were among their best. In addition, Gershwin never stopped his study and composition of concert music. While taking lessons with Joseph Schillinger (1932–6) he wrote the *Cuban Overture* (1932), a set of variations on the song *I got rhythm* (1934), and his magnum opus, *Porgy and Bess* (1935; see fig. 12).

The idea of composing a full-length opera based on Dubose Heyward's novel *Porgy* about life among the black inhabitants of "Catfish Row" in Charleston, South Carolina, first occurred to Gershwin when he read the book in 1926. Subsequently it had been the basis of a successful play, and Heyward had been approached by Al Jolson, who hoped to use the story for a musical show in which he would play the lead in blackface. This plan was rejected, however, and in October 1933 Heyward and the Gershwin brothers signed a contract with the Theatre Guild in New York, the same organization that had produced *Porgy* as a play. Gershwin began the score in February 1934; during most of the next summer he stayed in South Carolina, composing and absorbing local color. A news release from Charleston reported his promise that, if the opera turned out as he hoped, it would "resemble a combination of the drama and romance of *Carmen* and the beauty of *Meistersinger*." By early 1935 the composition was finished, and Gershwin spent the next several months orchestrating the work. Billed as "an American folk opera," *Porgy and Bess* opened in New York in October 1935 – in a Broadway theater and not an opera house. It ran for only 124 performances, however, and even a subsequent tour failed to earn enough to recoup the original investment; in spite of Gershwin's vaunted record of success, his last and most ambitious work for the stage was at first a financial failure.

Few events in the history of American music were more shocking than Gershwin's death, when he was at the height of his success and seemingly on the threshold of new musical achievements. Through the first half of 1937, although he had experienced flashes of discomfort, dizziness, and emotional despondency, he continued to work; he planned to compose a ballet, to be called *Swing Symphony*, for the *Goldwyn Follies*. On 9 July he fell into a coma. A brain tumor was diagnosed and emergency surgery was performed, but on the morning of 11 July 1937 George Gershwin died in Hollywood at the age of 38. Four days later, after memorial services in New York and Hollywood, he was buried in Mount Hope Cemetery, Hastings-on-Hudson, New York.

4. GERSHWIN AS A SONGWRITER. Throughout his professional life Gershwin was first and foremost a songwriter, composing songs for Tin Pan Alley, the Broadway stage, and Hollywood films; and it was within the framework of the American popular song that he learned and polished his craft. The songwriter's ultimate goal was to reach a mass audience, to please not just himself, or fellow musicians, critics, or posterity, but a large, anonymous group of people whose acceptance was expressed in a willingness to buy his work. The challenge of songwriting was stiff: to create, using a conventional verse-refrain form and a restricted musical idiom, songs that would catch public fancy more effectively than those of dozens of other songwriters.

Gershwin as a songwriter is best understood as one of a group of American composers who dominated the field between World War I and 1950: Berlin, Kern, Rodgers, Porter, Arlen, and others. The achievements of these men were remarkable by any measure. They set a high standard of professional craftsmanship in a genre traditionally open to amateurs and dilettantes. Although they worked in a commercialized medium that restricted the range of innovation, they altered and expanded the musical idiom of the popular song, making it into a characteristic form of American expression. Within that expanded idiom, each found a distinctive personal style and each composed songs that remained in fashion even as fashion changed. One might, in fact, be excused for questioning precisely what, apart from the acceptance of a certain set of textual and musical conventions, separates these composers' "popular songs" from pieces usually classified as "art songs."

When Gershwin reached maturity at about the end of World War I, the style of the American popular song was characterized by major–minor diatonicism and the beginnings of a rhythm that was at once relaxed, flexible, and driving, showing the influence of Afro-American dance. Gershwin and his contem-

146

12. Sheet-music cover of the first edition of the song "Bess you is my woman" from Gershwin's "Porgy and Bess" (1935)

poraries enriched the melodic and harmonic vocabulary with modulations, melodic chromaticism, and unexpected plunges into remote harmonic territory, plunges rationalized by prompt returns to the main key, for phrases seldom exceed eight bars in length. At the same time they learned from jazz musicians a more aggressive, swinging beat, which by the mid-1930s had pervaded popular song. The swing beat opened up weak and strong beats alike to the possibility of accent, and by repeating patterns of accents it retained continuity; from the swing beat popular song gained both variety of rhythmic detail and coherence.

While scholarly research on Gershwin has not yet progressed enough to allow a proper evaluation of his role in the evolution of the American popular song style, a brief survey of traits in a few of his best-known songs will suggest something of his artistry and stylistic development. Two favorites from Gershwin's early years show his mastery of song types introduced by others: *Swanee* is in the square-cut, striding, declamatory style of George M. Cohan; and *The man I love*, in which the pervasiveness of one melodic motif is offset by shifting harmonies, employs a tonal idiom and a flexible beat similar to Jerome Kern's earlier songs and to operetta. *The man I love*, a slow, romantic song of a type often called a ballad, was followed by others whose choruses, dominated by melodic figures beginning on an offbeat, invite rubato: *Someone to watch over me* (1926), *But not for me* (1930), and *Embraceable you* (1930). In each of these songs the title phrase or a variant of it appears as both a verbal refrain and as the chorus's last words. All three, and all of the songs mentioned below, carry deft lyrics by Ira Gershwin, who once wrote wryly of his craft: "Since most of [my] lyrics . . . were arrived at by fitting words mosaically to music already composed, any resemblance to actual poetry, living or dead, is highly improbable."

Although in songs like *Strike up the band* (1927), *Of thee I sing*

(1931), and *Love is sweeping the country* (1931) Gershwin continued to write in the slightly old fashioned, eupeptic style of *Swanee*, he is remembered more for songs like *Fascinating rhythm* (1924) and *I got rhythm* (1930), both dominated by rhythmic innovations, and especially syncopation. *I got rhythm* was introduced by Ethel Merman in the musical *Girl Crazy*. Its circulation in different versions and contexts reflects a fact about many popular songs: once introduced in public, their interpretive fate depends upon as broad a range of performers as choose to sing or play them. In *George Gershwin's Song-book* (1931) the composer published his own elaborate solo piano arrangement, and two years later he composed a set of variations on it for piano and orchestra. Between the mid-1930s and the early 1950s the song was recorded by popular singers (Jane Froman) and pianists (Victor Arden), by swing bands (Glenn Miller) and "pops" orchestra leaders (Andre Kostelanetz), and by jazz performers (Benny Goodman, Red Norvo, Chick Webb). Moreover, the harmonic progressions of *I got rhythm*, disengaged from the original melody, set to new ones, and retitled *Cotton Tail* or *Little Benny* or *Crazeology*, or any one of a number of other names, served as the most common 32-bar structure in the jazz tradition. Composed in *AABA* form, with four eight-bar phrases (Gershwin's two-bar extension of the last phrase is usually omitted by jazz performers), *I got rhythm* embodies a harmonic scheme of utmost simplicity. The *A* section is built on the most basic chords in the key of B♭ (I, II, and V); the *B* section (the "bridge" or "release") provides some variety by jumping briefly into the relative minor, then moving back to the tonic through the circle of 5ths. It is easy to understand the tune's appeal to jazz musicians of the middle of the century, whose art was dominated by improvisations on simple borrowed harmonic patterns.

In addition to rhythm songs and ballads, the Gershwins also mastered a medium-tempo song style with a relaxed, swinging

Ex. 1 from *Nice work if you can get it* (1937)

(a)

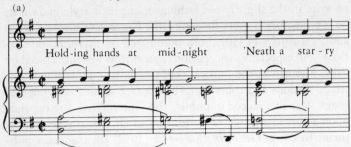

Hold-ing hands at mid-night 'Neath a star-ry sky, Nice work if you can get it, and you can get it if you try.

(b)

Nice work if you can get it, And if you get it ___ Won't you tell me how?

beat – a style created by their own generation of songwriters. Such songs as *'S wonderful* (1927), *They can't take that away from me* (1937), and *Nice work if you can get it* (1937) show them at home in a sophisticated, jazz-tinged idiom. *Nice work* neatly exemplifies this kind of song. There is a strong contrast within the *A* section of the chorus, where the smooth, stepwise descent of the first four bars is followed by a sharp, syncopated upturn (ex. 1*a*). After a bridge in the relative minor, which reaches a climax on "Who could ask for anything more?" (a quotation from *I got rhythm*), the last phrase of the *AABA* form brings an added twist: the singer, until now posing as an authority on the joys of successful romance, reveals in a two-bar extension of the phrase

151

that he has been speaking more from imagination than experience. Here the music, after preparing for a cadence identical to those of the first and second phrases, delivers one that is different, yet so offhandedly satisfying that it seems inevitable (ex. 1*b*). The words keep emotion at an arm's length, treating love as a rational game, and the song wears its craftsmanship as lightly as its narrator does his solitude. Its general tone of civility and its adroitly inventive details of musical construction, absorbed by the relaxed insistence of its rhythm, combine to create a sensibility that is typical of Gershwin's songs.

5. CONCERT WORKS AND "PORGY AND BESS." Already well known before his public career as a "classical" composer began, Gershwin was surely one of the most conspicuous musical apprentices in history. Rather than inflating his classical credentials, he was candid about them and even risked public displays of naiveté. Isaac Goldberg, his first biographer, reported that after accepting the commission for the Concerto in F, Gershwin "went out to buy a book on musical form to find out how . . . a concerto was constructed." Whatever the state of his theoretical knowledge, Gershwin entered the concert world with assets that no other American composer of his generation enjoyed. A proven master of melody, he was also accustomed to having his works judged by audiences. And because his music consistently gained approval, he wrote with the confidence that his talents outweighed his deficiencies. That confidence was borne out by his composing – in less than 12 years, while maintaining separate careers as a songwriter, pianist, and conductor – four large-scale works of enduring appeal: the *Rhapsody in Blue*, the Concerto in F, *An American in Paris*, and *Porgy and Bess*.

The melodies of Gershwin's concert works are surely the chief reason the works hold their place in the repertory. They share with many of his popular songs a trait that helps to imprint them firmly on the listener's memory: the opening material is consistently restated before moving on to a contrast. This is most conspicuous in the soaring, lyric, if somewhat square themes of *Rhapsody in Blue*, in the first movement of the Concerto, and in *An American in Paris*, but it can also be found in more fragmentary material. The *Rhapsody*, for example, begins with two highly distinctive phrases, each of which first stands on its own, yet within a short time each becomes the first phrase of a larger melody with an *AABA* design.

Some thematic phrases that Gershwin restates are themselves built from repetitions of smaller motifs. The Rachmaninoff-like opening of the Concerto's third movement, which is repeated four times in the first 38 bars, begins with a statement and restatement of a two-bar figure. The first 20 bars of *An American in Paris* contain a full statement and restatement of an eight-bar theme that presents the same one-bar motif six times. This technique is found not only in Gershwin's themes but in introductory, transition, and development sections as well. The Concerto opens with an introduction of 50 bars, of which all but about six are devoted to statements and restatements of three different figures; the transition out of the first thematic section of *An American in Paris* (rehearsal nos. 20–23) is similarly structured. Although in these and other such passages phrase units may occasionally be three or five bars long, four-bar units are by far the most common, and their absence, as at the start of the Concerto's third movement, creates a sense of disruption. Tending towards symmetry both in the pairing of opening phrases and in the reliance on parallel units of two, four, and eight bars, Gershwin's melodic materials seem designed to impose regularity and coherence even in the ear of an inattentive listener.

If Gershwin's melodic structures are somewhat old-fashioned for a composer writing concert music in the 1920s and 1930s, the tonal vocabulary on which they are based is more modern.

Perhaps the most striking characteristic of Gershwin's melodies is their reliance on blue notes. Sometimes they function as blatant dissonances, as in one theme of the *Rhapsody*, where on strong beats they clash with the bass (ex.2). At other times they soften the melodic contour with sinuous grace. In the *Rhapsody*'s opening theme, the presence of both major and minor 7ths in the second chord, and of both major and minor 3rds in the melody (bars 2–3) proves the aptness of the work's title before even four bars have passed (ex.3, p.155). In the Concerto, blues-tinged tonality appears more subtly in the opening theme, which avoids

Ex.2 *Rhapsody in Blue* (fig.12)

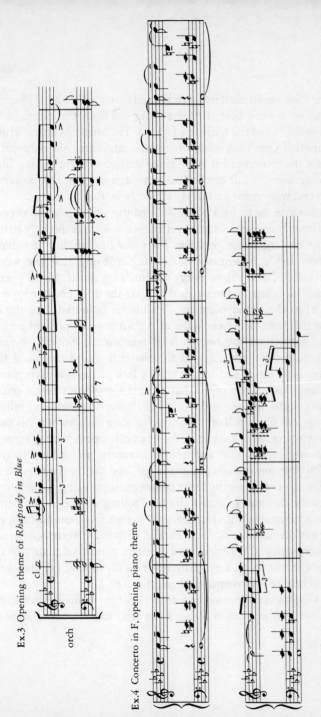

Ex.3 Opening theme of *Rhapsody in Blue*

orch

Ex.4 Concerto in F, opening piano theme

155

the tonic chord until its tenth bar and then touches it only briefly, and on a weak beat, before moving on from the raised to the lowered 3rd of the tonic triad (ex.4). The blues idiom sometimes supplied Gershwin with a harmonic structure: not only did he base the second of his three piano preludes on the 12-bar blues progression, but it can be heard through much of the Concerto's second movement and in *An American in Paris*.

Because the melodic idiom of Gershwin's concert works depends so heavily on Afro-American elements, it seems especially fitting that his largest composition, *Porgy and Bess*, should be a drama about black Americans. Nor is it surprising that the work's melodic idiom – from Porgy's identifying motif, to the opera's main love duet, to the satirical songs of the drug peddler Sportin' Life, to the choral numbers – should be saturated with the inflected 3rds, 5ths, and 7ths of Afro-American popular music, and sometimes touched with its syncopated, driving rhythm. Opera critics have objected to arias that sound too much like Broadway songs and to the score's lack of organic, symphonic integration. Black critics have found Gershwin's evocations of their music inauthentic. For all of these criticisms, and others, *Porgy and Bess* is full of moments that show Gershwin at his most convincing. Act 1 scene ii, for example, opens with a scene of mourning. A soloist and chorus alternate, the soloist singing with abandon at the top of her range, and the chorus responding with an ever darkening series of chords, supporting a whole-tone descent through an octave, like the tolling of a bell. The chords are generated by the voice-leading: against five descending upper voices the bass line ascends. Parallel octaves between soprano and tenor, alto and baritone, lend a certain primitive quality to the passage; yet only a keenly inventive ear could have calculated the freshness of the harmonic progression (ex.5).

Gershwin's approach to formal structure in his concert works shows him as a practical composer who took care that growing

Ex.5 *Porgy and Bess*, opening of Act 1 scene ii

technique did not overshadow expression. *Rhapsody in Blue*, reportedly composed in three weeks, draws much of its vitality from its juxtapositions of piano and orchestra, and of jazz-like and classical materials. Its essence lies more in these juxtapositions, and in the strength of its melodies, than in its overall shape. As Leonard Bernstein wrote: "It can be a five-minute piece or a six-minute piece or a twelve-minute piece. And in fact all these things are being done to it every day. It's still the *Rhapsody in Blue*." A more ambitious undertaking than the *Rhapsody*, the Concerto filled several months of Gershwin's time and even received a trial performance before its delivery to Damrosch and the New York SO. Like the *Rhapsody*, it also uses sharp juxtapositions, but its integration through cyclic form and thematic transformation, both standard 19th-century techniques for unifying large instrumental works, reflects Gershwin's study. While the Concerto's third movement introduces new themes, it also recalls the main lyric theme of the first movement (speeded up and punctuated by rests), a lyric theme from the last part of the

157

second movement, a jauntier, blues-based theme from earlier in the second movement, and finally a climactic, "grandioso" return of the main theme of the first movement. More than the earlier *Rhapsody*, the Concerto forms a convincing organic whole whose impact derives as much from its entire structure as from its separate parts.

In that way the Concerto also outdoes the tone poem *An American in Paris*, whose structure was apparently inspired by an elaborate program. For all of its élan, *An American in Paris* is more or less a medley of excellent tunes, varied and extended, and clad in attractive orchestral garb. Gershwin's treatment of the main lyric theme recalls his own piano playing and the arrangements he published in his *Song-book*. In each restatement of the melody, he varies the orchestration and the harmony, or the "responses" to the theme's opening "call," but the melody itself remains intact. While Gershwin borrowed from jazz his blues tonality and rhythmic syncopation, his fondness for reiterating the same melodies, with only cosmetic variations, distinguishes him sharply from such jazz musicians as Armstrong, Ellington, and Henderson, for whom melody, however important, was always subject to decoration, embellishment, and playful alteration.

Few today would deny Gershwin's place in the history of American music, though perhaps it is not quite the one claimed for him by some of his contemporaries. For them he was an important historical figure because he brought together separate musical worlds: jazz and classical traditions in his concert pieces, black-American folk music and opera in *Porgy and Bess*. Such matters of musical taxonomy no longer seem as significant today; rather it is the eagerness of audiences, nearly half a century after Gershwin's death, to hear many of his songs and concert works, and the willingness of musicians to perform them with skill and commitment, that is remarkable.

WORKS

Only published songs listed for stage works and film scores; for fuller details see Jablonski and Stewart (2/1973) and Schwartz (1973). Songs marked with an asterisk were completed by Kay Swift from Gershwin's tune notebooks with lyrics provided by Ira Gershwin. Unless otherwise stated lyrics for all songs are by Ira Gershwin. Most of Gershwin's music for the theater was not orchestrated by the composer although he may have scored some works from the mid-1920s on. Most extant MSS are in DLC.

STAGE WORKS
(all first performed in New York unless otherwise stated)

Title, genre; song title (lyricist)	Book author	First performance	Remarks
Half Past Eight, revue		Empire Theatre, Syracuse, NY, 9 Dec 1918	
La La Lucille, musical comedy	F. Jackson	Henry Miller Theatre, 26 May 1919	
The best of everything (B. G. DeSylva, A. J. Jackson)			
From now on (DeSylva, Jackson)			
Nobody but you (DeSylva, Jackson)			
Somehow it seldom comes true (DeSylva, Jackson)			
Tee-oodle-um-bum-bo (DeSylva, Jackson)			
There's more to the kiss than the x-x-x (I. Caesar)			
George White's Scandals of 1920, revue	A. Rice, G. White	Globe Theatre, 7 June 1920	
Idle dreams (Jackson)			
My lady (Jackson)			
On my mind the whole night long (Jackson)			
Scandal Walk (Jackson)			
The songs of long ago (Jackson)			
Tum on and tiss me (Jackson)			

159

Title, genre; song title (lyricist)	Book author	First performance	Remarks
A Dangerous Maid, musical comedy	C. W. Bell	Atlantic City, NJ, 21 March 1921	
Boy wanted (Arthur Francis [pseud. I. Gershwin])			
Dancing shoes (Francis)			
Just to know you are mine (Francis)			
The simple life (Francis)			
Some rain must fall (Francis)			
George White's Scandals of 1921, revue	A. Baer, White	Liberty Theatre, 11 July 1921	
Drifing along with the tide (Jackson)			
I love you (Jackson)			
She's just a baby (Jackson)			
South sea isles (Jackson)			
Where East meets West (Jackson)			
Blue Monday (opera "Ala Afro-American," DeSylva, 1)		Globe Theatre, 28 Aug 1922	unpubd; orchd W. H. Vodery; orig. part of George White's Scandals of 1922, withdrawn after 1st perf.
		concert perf., Carnegie Hall, 29 Dec 1925	reorchd F. Grofé
retitled 135th Street			
George White's Scandals of 1922, revue	W. C. Fields, Rice, White	Globe Theatre, 28 Aug 1922	orig. incl. Blue Monday, see above
Across the sea (DeSylva, E. R. Goetz)			
Argentina (DeSylva)			
Cinderelatives (DeSylva)			
I found a four leaf clover (DeSylva)			
I'll build a stairway to paradise (DeSylva, Francis [pseud. I. Gershwin])			

Oh, what she hangs out (DeSylva)			
Where is the man of my dreams (DeSylva, Goetz)			
Our Nell, ? musical comedy	B. Hooker, A. E. Thomas	Nora Bayes Theatre, 4 Dec 1922	incl. other songs by W. Daly
By and by (Hooker)			
Innocent ingenue baby (Hooker)			collab. Daly
My old New England home (Hooker)			
Walking home with Angeline (Hooker)			
The Rainbow, revue	A. de Courville, N. Scott, E. Wallace	Empire Theatre, London, 3 April 1923	
Beneath the eastern moon (C. Grey)			
Good-night, my dear (Grey)			
In the rain (Grey)			
Innocent lonesome blue baby (Grey, Hooker)			tune same as that of Innocent ingenue, 1922
Moonlight in Versailles (Grey)			
Oh! Nina (Grey)			
Strut lady with me (Grey)			
Sweetheart (I'm so glad that I met you) (Grey)			
Sunday in London town (Grey)			
George White's Scandals of 1923, revue	W. K. Wells, White	Globe Theatre, 18 June 1923	
Let's be lonesome together (DeSylva, Goetz)			
The life of a rose (DeSylva)			
Lo-la-lo (DeSylva)			
(On the beach at) How've-you-been (DeSylva)			
There is nothing too good for you (DeSylva, Goetz)			
Throw her in high! (DeSylva, Goetz)			
Where is she? (DeSylva)			
You and I (DeSylva, Goetz, B. MacDonald)			

Title, genre; song title (lyricist)	Book author	First performance	Remarks
Sweet Little Devil, musical comedy	F. Mandel, L. Schwab	Astor Theatre, 21 Jan 1924	
Hey! Hey! Let 'er go! (DeSylva)			
The Jijibo (DeSylva)			
Mah-jongg (DeSylva)			
Pepita (DeSylva)			
Someone believes in you (DeSylva)			
Under a one-man top (DeSylva)			
Virginia (DeSylva)			
George White's Scandals of 1924, revue	Wells, White	Apollo Theatre, 30 June 1924	
I need a garden (DeSylva)			
Kongo Kate (DeSylva)			
Mah-jongg (DeSylva)			
Night time in Araby (DeSylva)			
Rose of Madrid (DeSylva)			
Somebody loves me (DeSylva, MacDonald)			
Tune in (to station J. O. Y.) (DeSylva)			
Year after year (DeSylva)			
Primrose, musical comedy	G. Bolton, G. Grossmith	Winter Garden Theatre, London, 11 Sept 1924	vs (1924)
Boy wanted (D. Carter, I. Gershwin)			
Isn't it wonderful? (Carter, I. Gershwin)			
Naughty baby (Carter, I. Gershwin)			
Some far-away someone (Carter, I. Gershwin)			
That new-fangled mother of mine (Carter)			tune same as that of At half past seven, 1923
This is the life for a man (Carter)			
Wait a bit, Susie (Carter, I. Gershwin)			

Lady, be Good!, musical comedy	Bolton, F. Thompson	Liberty Theatre, 1 Dec 1924	
Fascinating rhythm			
The half of it, dearie, blues			
Hang on to me			
Little jazz bird			
Oh, lady, be good!			
So am I			
Tell me More, musical comedy	Thompson, Wells	Gaiety Theatre, 13 April 1925	
Baby! (DeSylva, I. Gershwin)			
Kickin' the clouds away (DeSylva, I. Gershwin)			
My fair lady (DeSylva, I. Gershwin)			
Tell me more! (DeSylva, I. Gershwin)			
Three times a day (DeSylva, I. Gershwin)			
Why do I love you? (DeSylva, I. Gershwin)			
Tip-toes, musical comedy	Bolton, Thompson	Liberty Theatre, 28 Dec 1925	
Looking for a boy			
Nice baby! (Come to Papa!)			
Nightie-night			
Sweet and low-down			
That certain feeling			
These charming people			
When do we dance?			
Song of the Flame, operetta	O. Hammerstein II, O. Harbach	44th Street Theatre, 30 Dec 1925	incl. other songs by H. Stothart
Cossack Love Song (Don't forget me) (Hammerstein, Harbach)			collab. Stothart
Midnight bells (Hammerstein, Harbach)			
The signal (Hammerstein, Harbach)			
Song of the flame (Hammerstein, Harbach)			collab. Stothart
Vodka (Hammerstein, Harbach)			collab. Stothart

Title, genre; song title (lyricist)	Book author	First performance	Remarks
You are you (Hammerstein, Harbach)			collab. Stothart
Oh, Kay!, musical comedy	Bolton, P. G. Wodehouse	Imperial Theatre, 8 Nov 1926	
Clap yo' hands			
Dear little girl (I hope you've missed me)			
Do, do, do			
Fidgety Feet			
Heaven on earth (H. Dietz, I. Gershwin)			
Maybe			
Oh, Kay! (Dietz, I. Gershwin)			
Someone to watch over me			
Strike up the Band, operetta [1st version]	G. S. Kaufman	Shubert Theatre, Philadelphia, 5 Sept 1927	
Military dancing drill			
The man I love			
Seventeen and twenty-one			
Strike up the band			
Yankee doodle rhythm			
Funny Face, musical comedy	P. G. Smith, Thompson	Alvin Theatre, 22 Nov 1927	
The babbit and the bromide			
Dance along with you			
Funny face			
He loves and she loves			
High hat			
Let's kiss and make up			
My one and only			
'S wonderful			
The world is mine			
Rosalie, musical comedy	Bolton, W. A. McGuire	New Amsterdam Theatre, 10 Jan	incl. other songs by Romberg

Ev'ry body knows I love somebody   tune same as that of Dance along with you, 1927

How long has this been going on?
Oh gee! Oh joy! (I. Gershwin, Wodehouse)
Say so! (I. Gershwin, Wodehouse)   1928

Treasure Girl, musical comedy — V. Lawrence, Thompson — Alvin Theatre, 8 Nov 1928
Feeling I'm falling
Got a rainbow
I don't think I'll fall in love today
I've got a crush on you
K-ra-zy for you
Oh, so nice
What are we here for?
Where's the boy? Here's the girl!

Show Girl, musical comedy — McGuire, J. P. McEvoy — Ziegfeld Theatre, 2 July 1929
Do what you do! (I. Gershwin, G. Kahn)
Harlem Serenade (I. Gershwin, Kahn)
I must be home by twelve o'clock (I. Gershwin, Kahn)
Liza (All the clouds'll roll away) (I. Gershwin, Kahn)
So are you! (I. Gershwin, Kahn)

Strike up the Band, operetta [2nd version] — M. Ryskind, after Kaufman — Times Square Theatre, 14 Jan 1930 — vs (1930)
Hangin' around with you
I mean to say
I want to be a war bride
I've got a crush on you
Mademoiselle in New Rochelle
Soon

165

Title, genre; song title (lyricist)	Book author	First performance	Remarks
Strike up the band			
Girl Crazy, musical comedy	Bolton, J. McGowan	Alvin Theatre, 14 Oct 1930	vs (1954)
Bidin' my time			
Boy! What love has done to me!			
But not for me			
Could you use me?			
Embraceable you			
I got rhythm			
Sam and Delilah			
Treat me rough			
Of Thee I Sing, operetta	Kaufman, Ryskind	Music Box Theatre, 26 Dec 1931	vs (1932)
Because, because			
The illegitimate daughter			
Love is sweeping the country			
Of thee I sing			
Who cares?			
Wintergreen for President			
Pardon my English, musical comedy	H. Fields	Majestic Theatre, 20 Jan 1933	
Isn't it a pity?			
I've got to be there			
Lorelei			
Luckiest man in the world			
My cousin in Milwaukee			
So what?			
Where you go I go			

Let 'em Eat Cake, operetta Blue, blue, blue Let 'em eat cake Mine On and on and on Union square	Kaufman, Ryskind	Imperial Theatre, 21 Oct 1933	sequel to Of Thee I Sing, 1931
Porgy and Bess (American folk opera, I. Gershwin, DuBose Heyward, after play by DuBose and Dorothy Heyward: Porgy)	DuBose Heyward	Alvin Theatre, 10 Oct 1935	vs (1935)

Act 1: Jasbo Brown Blues; Summertime; A woman is a sometime thing; Here come de honey man; They pass by singin'; Oh little stars; Gone, gone, gone; Overflow; My man's gone now; Leavin' for the promise' lan'

Act 2: It take a long pull to get there; I got plenty o' nuttin'; Buzzard Song; Bess you is my woman; Oh, I can't sit down; I ain' got no shame; It ain't necessarily so; What you want wid Bess?; Oh, doctor Jesus; Strawberry Woman; Crab Man; I loves you, Porgy; Oh, hev'nly father; Oh, de Lawd shake de heavens; Oh, dere's somebody knockin' at de do'; A red headed woman

Act 3: Clara, Clara; There's a boat dat's leavin' soon for New York; Good mornin', sistuh!; Oh, Bess, oh where's my Bess; Oh Lawd, I'm on my way

SONGS FOR SHOWS BY OTHER COMPOSERS
(all first performed in New York unless otherwise stated)

Song title (lyricist)	Show title (genre, book author)	First performance	Remarks
Making of a girl (H. Atteridge)	The Passing Show of 1916 (revue, H. Atteridge)	Winter Garden Theatre, 22 June 1916	music mainly by O. Motzan and S. Romberg; Making of a girl, collab. Romberg
You-oo just you (Caesar)	Hitchy-koo of 1918 (revue, G. MacDonough)	Globe Theatre, 6 June 1918	music mainly by R. Hubbell
The Real American Folk Song (Francis [pseud. I. Gershwin])	Ladies First (musical comedy, H. B. Smith)	Broadhurst Theatre, 24 Oct 1918	music mainly by A. B. Sloane
Some wonderful sort of someone (S. Greene)	ibid.		
I was so young (you were so beautiful) (A. Bryan, Caesar)	Good Morning, Judge (musical comedy, F. Thompson)	Shubert Theatre, 6 Feb 1919	music mainly by L. Monckton and H. Talbot
There's more to the kiss than the x-x-x (Caesar)	ibid.		
Some wonderful sort of someone (Greene)	The Lady in Red (? musical comedy, A. Caldwell)	Lyric Theatre, 12 May 1919	music mainly by R. Winterberg; Some wonderful sort of someone, rev. for this show
Something about love (L. Paley)	ibid.		
Come to the moon (Paley, N. Wayburn)	Capitol Revue (revue)	Capitol Theatre, 24 Oct 1919	music by many composers
Swanee (Caesar)	ibid.		
Limehouse nights (DeSylva, J. H. Mears)	Morris Gest Midnight Whirl (revue, DeSylva, J. H. Mears)	Century Grove, Century Theatre, 27 Dec 1919	music by many composers
Poppyland (DeSylva, Mears)	ibid.		
We're pals (Caesar)	Dere Mabel (? musical comedy)	Academy of Music, Baltimore, 2 Feb 1920	music by many composers
Oo, how I love to be loved by you (Paley)	Ed Wynn's Carnival (revue, E. Wynn)	New Amsterdam Theatre, 5 April 1920	music mainly by E. Wynn
Waiting for the sun to come out (Francis [pseud. I. Gershwin])	The Sweetheart Shop (?revue, Caldwell)	Knickerbocker Theatre, 31 Aug 1920	music mainly by H. Felix

Song title (lyricist)	Show title (genre, book author)	First performance	Remarks
Lu Lu (A. Jackson)	Broadway Brevities of 1920 (revue, B. Traynor, A. Gortlier)	Winter Garden Theatre, 29 Sept 1920	music by many composers
Snowflakes (Jackson)	ibid.		
Spanish love (Caesar)	ibid.		
My log-cabin home (Caesar, DeSylva)	The Perfect Fool (revue, Wynn)	George M. Cohan Theatre, 7 Nov 1921	music mainly by Wynn
No one else but that girl of mine (Caesar)	ibid.		
Someone (Francis [pseud. I. Gershwin])	For Goodness Sake (? musical comedy, F. Jackson)	Lyric Theatre, 20 Feb 1922	music mainly by W. Daly and P. Lannin
Tra-la-la (Francis)	ibid.		
Do it again (DeSylva)	The French Doll (? musical comedy, A. E. Thomas)	Lyceum Theatre, 20 Feb 1922	music by many composers
The Yankee Doodle Blues (Caesar, DeSylva)	Spice of 1922 (revue, J. Lait)	Winter Garden Theatre, 6 July 1922	music by many composers
That American boy of mine (Caesar)	The Dancing Girl (? musical comedy, Atteridge, Caesar)	Winter Garden Theatre, 24 Jan 1923	music mainly by A. Goodman and Romberg
I won't say I will but I won't say I won't (DeSylva, Francis [pseud. I. Gershwin])	Little Miss Bluebeard (? musical comedy, A. Hopwood)	Lyceum Theatre, 28 Aug 1923	music by many composers
At half past seven (DeSylva)	Nifties of 1923 (revue, S. Bernard, W. Collier)	Fulton Theatre, 25 Sept 1923	music by many composers
Nashville nightingale (Caesar)	ibid.		
That lost barber shop chord	Americana (revue, McEvoy)	Belmont Theatre, 26 July 1926	music by many composers
By Strauss	The Show is On (revue, D. Freedman, M. Hart)	Winter Garden Theatre, 25 Dec 1936	music by many composers

Gershwin also contributed songs to the revues Piccadilly to Broadway (1920), Blue Eyes (1921), and Selwyn's Snapshots (1921), although none of these was published.

SONGS FOR FILMS
(*musicals unless otherwise stated*)

Film title, song title (lyricist)	Date, production company	Remarks
The Sunshine Trail, silent film	1923, Thomas H. Ince	music as acc. for film, perf. by pf/ens
The sunshine trail (Francis [pseud. I. Gershwin])		
Delicious	3 Dec 1931, Fox	screenplay by Bolton and S. Levien
Blah, blah, blah		
Delishious		
Katinkitschka		
Somebody from somewhere		
Shall we Dance?	7 May 1937, RKO Radio	screenplay by A. Scott and E. Pagano
(I've got) Beginner's luck		
Let's call the whole thing off		
Shall we dance		
Slap that bass		
They all laughed		
They can't take that away from me		
A Damsel in Distress	19 Nov 1937, RKO Radio	screenplay by S. K. Lauren, E. Pagano, and Wodehouse
A foggy day		
I can't be bothered now		
The jolly tar and the milk maid		
Nice work if you can get it		
Stiff upper lip		
Things are looking up		
The Goldwyn Follies, revue	23 Feb 1938, Goldwyn-United Artists	screenplay by B. Hecht; Gershwin died during filming, Vernon Duke completed Gershwin's songs and supplied others
I love to rhyme		
I was doing all right		
Love is here to stay		
Love walked in		

The Shocking Miss Pilgrim   1946, 20th Century-Fox   screenplay by G. Seaton
*Aren't you kind of glad we did?
*The Back Bay Polka
*Changing my tune
*For you, for me, for evermore
*One, two, three

Kiss me, Stupid   1964, United Artists   screenplay by B. Wilder and I. A. L. Diamond
*All the livelong day (and the long, long night)
*I'm a poached egg
*Sophia

MISCELLANEOUS PUBLISHED SONGS
(listed by year of first performance)

1916: When you want 'em, you can't get 'em, when you've got 'em, you don't want 'em (M. Roth)

1919: O land of mine, America (M. E. O'Rourke)

1920: Yan-kee (Caesar)

1921: Dixie Rose (Caesar, DeSylva); In the heart of a geisha (F. Fisher); Swanee Rose (Caesar, DeSylva) [tune same as that of Dixie Rose]; Tomale (I'm hot for you) (DeSylva)

1925: Harlem River Chanty [orig. composed for Tip-toes, but not used]; It's a great little world! [orig. composed for Tip-toes, but not used]; Murderous Monty (and light-fingered Jane) (D. Carter) [composed for London production of Tell Me More, 1925]

1926: I'd rather charleston (Carter) [composed for London production of Lady, be Good!, 1926]; Show me the town [orig. composed for Oh, Kay!, but not used]; Something about love (L. Paley) [composed for London production of Lady, be Good!, 1926]

1928: Beautiful gypsy [orig. composed for Rosalie, but not used; tune same as that of Wait a bit, Susie, 1924]; Rosalie [orig. composed for Rosalie, but not used]

1929: Feeling sentimental [orig. composed for Show Girl, but not used]; In the mandarin's orchid garden

1931: Mischa, Yascha, Toscha, Sascha [orig. composed for Delicious, but not used]

1932: You've got what gets me [composed for film version of Girl Crazy, RKO 1932]

1933: Till then

1936: King of swing; Strike up the band for U.C.L.A. [tune same as Strike up the band, 1927, 1930]

1937: Hi-ho! [orig. composed for Shall we Dance, but not used]

1938: Just another rhumba [orig. composed for The Goldwyn Follies, but not used]; *Dawn of a new day

ORCHESTRAL

Rhapsody in Blue, pf, jazz band, orchd Grofé, 1924, rev. orchestration for full orch by Grofé, 1926; New York, 12 Feb 1924, Gershwin, cond. Whiteman [Gershwin's orig. 2-pf score unpubd; solo pf and 2-pf pubd versions not Gershwin's arrs.]

Concerto in F, pf, orch, 1925; New York, 3 Dec 1925, Gershwin, cond. Damrosch [orig. pubd as 2-pf score; pubd orch version rev. F. Campbell-Watson]

An American in Paris, tone poem, 1928; New York, 13 Dec 1928, cond.

Damrosch [Gershwin's orig. 2-pf score unpubd; pubd orch version arr. F. Campbell-Watson, pubd 2-pf version rev. G. Stone]

Second Rhapsody for Piano and Orchestra, 1931; Boston, 29 Jan 1932, Gershwin, cond. Koussevitzky [orig. MS unpubd, pubd rev. version by R. McBride]

Cuban Overture, orig. entitled Rumba, 1932; New York, 16 Aug 1932, cond. A. Coates

"I got Rhythm" Variations, pf, orch, 1934; Boston, 14 Jan 1934, Gershwin, cond. C. Previn [orig. MS unpubd, pubd rev. version by W. C. Schoenfeld]

Catfish Row: Suite from Porgy and Bess, 1935–6, unpubd; Philadelphia, 21 Jan 1936, cond. A. Smallens

OTHER WORKS

Chamber: Lullaby, str qt, *c*1919–20; Short Story, orig. Novelette for pf, arr. S. Dushkin for vn, pf, *c*1923–5, New York, 8 Feb 1925, Dushkin, Gershwin

Pf: Rialto Ripples, collab. W. Donaldson, *c*1916; Three-quarter Blues (Irish Waltz), early 1920s; [3] Preludes for Piano, orig. entitled Novelettes, *c*1923–6; Impromptu in 2 Keys, *c*1924 [?for a show]; Merry Andrew, by 1928 [orig. dance piece in Rosalie, 1928]; George Gershwin's Song-book, 18 arrs. of refrains from Gershwin's songs, ded. K. Swift, 1931; 2 Waltzes, C, by 1933 [orig. as 2-pf piece in Pardon my English, 1933, arr. pf solo by I. Gershwin, S. Chaplin]; Promenade, by 1937 [orig. as inst interlude, Walking the Dog, in Shall we Dance, 1937, transcr. pf solo by H. Borne]

INDEX TO PUBLISHED SONGS
(dates refer to year of first performance)

Across the sea, 1922; A foggy day, 1937; All the livelong day (and the long, long night), 1964; A red headed woman, 1935; Aren't you kind of glad we did?, 1946; Argentina, 1922; At half past seven, 1923; A woman is a sometime thing, 1935; The babbitt and the bromide, 1927; Baby!, 1925; The Back Bay Polka, 1946; Beautiful gypsy, 1928; Because, because, 1931; Beneath the eastern moon, 1923; Bess you is my woman, 1935; The best of everything, 1919; Bidin' my time, 1930; Blah, blah, blah, 1931

Blue, blue, blue, 1933; Boy wanted, 1921, 1924; Boy! What love has done to me!, 1930; But not for me, 1930; Buzzard Song, 1935; By and by, 1922; By Strauss, 1936; Changing my tune, 1946; Cinderelatives, 1922; Clap yo' hands, 1926; Clara, Clara, 1935; Come to the moon, 1919; Cossack Love Song (Don't forget me), 1925; Could you use me?, 1930; Crab Man, 1935; Dance along with you, 1927; Dancing shoes, 1921; Dawn of a new day, 1938; Dear little girl (I hope you've missed me), 1926; Delishious, 1931

Dixie Rose, 1921; Do, do, do, 1926; Do it again, 1922; Do what you do!,

1929; Drifting along with the tide, 1921; Embraceable you, 1930; Ev'ry body knows I love somebody, 1928; Fascinating rhythm, 1924; Feeling I'm falling, 1928; Feeling sentimental, 1929; Fidgety feet, 1926; For you, for me, for evermore, 1946; From now on, 1919; Funny face, 1927; Gone, gone, gone, 1935; Good mornin', sistuh!, 1935; Good-night, my dear, 1923; Got a rainbow, 1928; The half of it, dearie, blues, 1924; Hangin' around with you, 1930

Hang on to me, 1924; Harlem River Chanty, 1925; Harlem Serenade, 1929; Heaven on earth, 1926; He loves and she loves, 1927; Here come de honey man, 1935; Hey! Hey! Let 'er go!, 1924; High hat, 1927; Hi-ho!, 1937; How long has this been going on?, 1927, 1928; I ain' got no shame, 1935; I can't be bothered now, 1937; Idle dreams, 1920; I don't think I'll fall in love today, 1928; I'd rather charleston, 1926; I found a four leaf clover, 1922; I got plenty o' nuttin', 1935; I got rhythm, 1930

I'll build a stairway to paradise, 1922; The illegitimate daughter, 1931; I loves you, Porgy, 1935; I love to rhyme, 1938; I love you, 1921; I'm a poached egg, 1964; I mean to say, 1930; I must be home by twelve o'clock, 1929; I need a garden, 1924; Innocent ingenue baby, 1922; Innocent lonesome blue baby, 1923; In the heart of a geisha, 1921; In the mandarin's orchid garden, 1929; In the rain, 1923; Isn't it a pity?, 1933; Isn't it wonderful?, 1924; It ain't necessarily so, 1935; It's a great little world!, 1925

It take a long pull to get there, 1935; I've got a crush on you, 1928, 1930; I've got beginner's luck, 1937; I've got to be there, 1933; I want to be a war bride, 1930; I was doing all right, 1938; I was so young (you were so beautiful), 1919; I won't say I will but I won't say I won't, 1923; Jasbo Brown Blues, 1935; The Jijibo, 1924; The jolly tar and the milk maid, 1937; Just another rhumba, 1938; Just to know you are mine, 1921; Katinkitschka, 1931; Kickin' the clouds away, 1925

King of swing, 1936; Kongo Kate, 1924; K-ra-zy for you, 1928; Leavin' for the promise' lan', 1935; Let 'em eat cake, 1933; Let's be lonesome together, 1923; Let's call the whole thing off, 1937; Let's kiss and make up, 1927; The life of a rose, 1923; Limehouse nights, 1919; Little jazz bird, 1924; Liza (All the clouds'll roll away), 1929; Lo-la-lo, 1923; Looking for a boy, 1925; Lorelei, 1933; Love is here to stay, 1938; Love is sweeping the country, 1931; Love walked in, 1938

Luckiest man in the world, 1933; Lu Lu, 1920; Mademoiselle in New Rochelle, 1930; Mah-jongg, 1924; Making of a girl, 1916; The man I love, 1924, 1927; Maybe, 1926; Midnight bells, 1925; Military dancing drill, 1927; Mine, 1933; Mischa, Yascha, Toscha, Sascha, 1931; Moonlight in Versailles, 1923; Murderous Monty (and light-fingered Jane), 1925; My cousin in Milwaukee, 1933; My fair lady, 1925; My lady, 1920; My log-cabin home, 1921; My man's gone now, 1935; My old New England home, 1922

My one and only, 1927; Nashville nightingale, 1923; Naughty baby, 1924; Nice baby! (Come to papa!), 1925; Nice work if you can get it, 1937; Nightie-night, 1925; Night time in Araby, 1924; Nobody but you, 1919; No one else but that girl of mine, 1921; Of thee I sing, 1931; Oh, Bess, oh where's my Bess, 1935; Oh, de Lawd shake de heavens, 1935; Oh, dere's somebody knockin' at de do', 1935; Oh, Doctor Jesus, 1935; Oh gee! Oh joy!, 1928; Oh, hev'nly Father, 1935; Oh, I can't sit down, 1935

Oh, Kay!, 1926; Oh, lady, be good!, 1924; Oh Lawd, I'm on my way, 1935; Oh little stars, 1935; Oh! Nina, 1923; Oh, so nice, 1928; Oh, what she hangs out, 1922; O land of mine, America, 1919; On and on and on, 1933; One, two, three, 1946; On my mind the whole night long, 1920; On the beach at how've-you-been, 1923; Oo, how I love to be loved by you, 1920; Overflow, 1935; Pepita, 1924; Poppyland, 1919; The Real American Folk Song, 1918; Rosalie, 1928; Rose of Madrid, 1924

Sam and Delilah, 1930; Say so!, 1928; Scandal Walk, 1920; Seventeen and twenty-one, 1927; Shall we dance, 1937; She's just a baby, 1921; Show me the town, 1926; The signal, 1925; The simple life, 1921; Slap that bass, 1937; Snowflakes, 1920; So am I, 1924; So are you!, 1929; Somebody from somewhere, 1931; Somebody loves me, 1924; Some far-away someone, 1924; Somehow it seldom comes true, 1919; Someone, 1922; Someone believes in you, 1924; Someone to watch over me, 1926

Some rain must fall, 1921; Something about love, 1919, 1926; Some wonderful sort of someone, 1918, rev. 1919; Song of the flame, 1925; The songs of long ago, 1920; Soon, 1930; Sophia, 1964; South sea isles, 1921; So what?, 1933; Spanish love, 1920; Stiff upper lip, 1937; Strawberry woman, 1935; Strike up the band, 1927, 1930; Strike up the band for U.C.L.A., 1936; Strut lady with me, 1923; Summertime, 1935; Sunday in London town, 1923; The sunshine trail, 1923; Swanee, 1919

Swanee Rose, 1921; Sweet and low-down, 1925; Sweetheart (I'm so glad that I met you), 1923; 'S wonderful, 1927; Tee-oodle-um-bum-bo, 1919; Tell me more!, 1925; That American boy of mine, 1923; That certain feeling, 1925; That lost barber shop chord, 1926; That new-fangled mother of mine, 1924; There is nothing too good for you, 1923; There's a boat dat's leavin' soon for New York, 1935; There's more to the kiss than the x-x-x, 1919; These charming people, 1925; They all laughed, 1937

They can't take that away from me, 1937; They pass by singin', 1935; Things are looking up, 1937; This is the life for a man, 1924; Three times a day, 1925; Throw her in high!, 1923; Till then, 1933; Tomale (I'm hot for you),

1921; Tra-la-la, 1922; Treat me rough, 1930; Tum on and tiss me, 1920; Tune in (to Station J. O. Y.), 1924; Under a one-man top, 1924; Union Square, 1933; Virginia, 1924; Vodka, 1925; Wait a bit, Susie, 1924; Waiting for the sun to come out, 1920

Walking home with Angeline, 1922; We're pals, 1920; What are we here for?, 1928; What you want wid Bess?, 1935; When do we dance?, 1925; When you want 'em, you can't get 'em, when you've got 'em, you don't want 'em, 1916; Where East meets West, 1921; Where is she?, 1923; Where is the man of my dreams, 1922; Where's the boy? Here's the girl!, 1928; Where you go I go, 1933; Who cares?, 1931; Why do I love you?, 1925; Wintergreen for President, 1931; The world is mine, 1927

Yan-kee, 1920; The Yankee Doodle Blues, 1922; Yankee doodle rhythm, 1927, 1928; Year after year, 1924; You and I, 1923; You are you, 1925; You-oo just you, 1918; You've got what gets me, 1932

Principal publishers: Chappell, New World

BIBLIOGRAPHY

CATALOGUES AND BIBLIOGRAPHIES

A Catalogue of the Exhibition Gershwin: George the Music, Ira the Words (New York, 1968)

C. M. Schwartz: *George Gershwin: a Selective Bibliography and Discography*, Bibliographies in American Music, no. 1 (Detroit, 1974)

LIFE AND WORKS

P. Whiteman and M. M. McBride: *Jazz* (New York, 1926)

I. Goldberg: *Tin Pan Alley: a Chronicle of the American Popular Music Racket* (New York, 1930, rev. and enlarged 2/1961 as *Tin Pan Alley: a Chronicle of American Popular Music*)

——: *George Gershwin: a Study in American Music* (New York, 1931, rev. and enlarged 2/1958)

F. Jacobi: "The Future of Gershwin," *MM*, xv (1937–8), 3

M. Armitage, ed.: *George Gershwin* (New York, 1938)

O. Levant: "My Life, or The Story of George Gershwin," *A Smattering of Ignorance* (New York, 1940), 147–210

D. Ewen: *The Story of George Gershwin* (New York, 1943)

Rhapsody in Blue: the Jubilant Story of George Gershwin and his Music (Hollywood, CA, 1945)

V. Duke: "Gershwin, Schillinger, and Dukelsky," *MQ*, xxxiii (1947), 102

V. Arvey: "George Gershwin through the Eyes of a Friend," *Opera and Concert*, xiii/4 (1948), 10, 27

Bibliography

E. Kilenyi, Sr.: "George Gershwin as I Knew Him," *The Etude*, lxviii (1950), 11

W. Mellers: "Gershwin's Achievements," *MMR*, lxxxiii (1953), 13

V. Duke: *Passport to Paris* (Boston, 1955)

D. Ewen: *A Journey to Greatness* (New York, 1956; rev. and enlarged 2/1970 as *George Gershwin: his Journey to Greatness*)

E. Jablonski: "Gershwin after 20 Years," *Hi-Fi Music at Home*, iii/3 (1956), 22 [incl. discography]

M. Armitage: *George Gershwin: Man and Legend* (New York, 1958)

E. Jablonski and L. D. Stewart: *The Gershwin Years* (Garden City, NY, 1958, rev. 2/1973)

I. Gershwin: *Lyrics on Several Occasions* (New York, 1959)

R. Payne: *Gershwin* (New York, 1960)

E. Jablonski: "Gershwin on Music," *MusAm*, lxxxii/7 (1962), 32

——: "George Gershwin," *Hi Fi/Stereo Review*, xii/5 (1967), 49

C. M. Schwartz: *The Life and Orchestral Works of George Gershwin* (diss., New York U., 1969)

R. Kimball and A. Simon: *The Gershwins* (New York, 1973)

C. M. Schwartz: *Gershwin: his Life and Music* (Indianapolis, 1973) [incl. catalogue of works and full bibliography]

E. Jablonski: "Gershwin at 80: Observations, Discographical and Otherwise, on the 80th Anniversary of the Birth of George Gershwin, American Composer," *American Record Guide*, xli (1977–8), no.11, pp.6, 58; no.12, pp.8, 57

D. Jeambar: *George Gershwin* (Paris, 1982)

E. Knight: "Charles Martin Loeffler and George Gershwin: a Forgotten Friendship," *American Music*, iii (1985), 452

N. Rorem: "Living with Gershwin," *Opera News*, xlix/13 (16 March 1985), 10

E. Jablonski: "George Gershwin: the Education of a Natural," *Ovation*, vii/1 (1986), 9

K. LaFave: "Gershwin, Hollywood, and the Unanswered Question," *Keynote*, x/6 (1986), 8

W. Youngren: "How Gershwin Played It," *The Atlantic*, cclvii/5 (1986), 81

D. Ewen: *American Songwriters* (New York, 1987)

J. Rockwell: "The Genius of Gershwin still Inspires Composers," *New York Times* (8 March 1987), §II, 23

A. M. Schlesinger, Jr.: "How History Upstaged the Gershwins," *New York Times* (5 April 1987), §II, 6

MUSICAL STUDIES

C. E[ngel]: "Views and Reviews," *MQ*, xii (1926), 299 [on Conc. in F]

H. O. Osgood: *So this is Jazz* (Boston, 1926)

G. Gershwin: "The Relation of Jazz to American Music," *American Composers on American Music*, ed. H. Cowell (Palo Alto, CA, 1933/*R*1962)

B. Atkinson and O. Downes: " 'Porgy and Bess,' Native Opera, Opens at the Alvin," *New York Times* (11 Oct 1935), 30

I. Kolodin: "Porgy and Bess: American Opera in the Theatre," *Theatre Arts Monthly*, xix (1935), 853

P. Rosenfeld: "Gershwin," *Discoveries of a Music Critic* (New York, 1936), 264, 384

V. Thomson: "George Gershwin," *MM*, xiii (1935–6), 13 [on *Porgy and Bess*]

Library of Congress Quarterly Journal, iv (1946–7), 65; xii (1954–5), 127; xvii (1959–60), 19–50; xviii (1960–61), 13; xxiv (1967), 47–82; xxv (1968), 50–91; xxvi (1969), 21; xxvii (1970), 51–83; xxviii (1971), 45; xxix (1972), 48 [reports on acquisitions by E. N. Waters and others]

F. C. Campbell: "Some Manuscripts of George Gershwin," *Manuscripts*, vi (1953–4), 66

L. Bernstein: "A Nice Gershwin Tune," *Atlantic Monthly*, cxcv/4 (1955), 39; repr. in *The Joy of Music* (New York, 1959)

R. Ellsworth: "Americans on Microgroove: Part II," *HiFi*, vi (1956), 60

H. Keller: "Rhythm: Gershwin and Stravinsky," *Score and I.M.A. Magazine*, no.20 (1957), 19

D. Baskerville: *Jazz Influence on Art Music to Mid-century* (diss., UCLA, 1965) [incl. chap. on *Porgy and Bess*]

W. Mellers: *Music in a New Found Land* (New York, 1965)

C. M. Schwartz: *Elements of Jewish Music in Gershwin's Melody* (thesis, New York U., 1965)

H. Levine: "Gershwin, Handy and the Blues," *Clavier*, ix/7 (1970), 10

R. Crawford: "It ain't necessarily Soul: Gershwin's *Porgy and Bess* as Symbol," *Yearbook for Inter-American Musical Research*, viii (1972), 17

A. Wilder: "George Gershwin (1898–1937)," *American Popular Song* (New York, 1972), 121–62

W. D. Shirley: "Porgy and Bess," *Library of Congress Quarterly Journal*, xxxi (1974), 97

R. Crawford: "Gershwin's Reputation: a Note on Porgy and Bess," *MQ*, lxv (1979), 257

W. D. Shirley: "Reconciliation on Catfish Row: Bess, Serena, and the Short Score of Porgy and Bess," *Library of Congress Quarterly Journal*, xxxviii (1981)

178

Bibliography

W. D. Shirley: "Notes on Gershwin's First Opera," *ISAM Newsletter*, xi/2 (1982), 8 [on *Blue Monday*]

——: "The 'Trial Orchestration' of Gershwin's Concerto in F," *Notes*, xxxix (1982–3), 570

L. Starr: "Toward a Reevaluation of Gershwin's Porgy and Bess," *American Music*, ii/2 (1984), 25

S. E. Gilbert: "Gershwin's Art of Counterpoint," *MQ*, lxx (1984), 423

J. A. Conrad: *Style and Structure in Songs by George Gershwin, Published 1924–1938* (diss., Indiana U., 1985)

W. J. Schneider: *George Gershwin's Political Operettas "Of Thee I Sing" (1931) and "Let 'Em Eat Cake" (1933), and their Role in Gershwin's Musical and Emotional Maturing* (diss., Cornell U., 1985)

W. D. Shirley: "Scoring the Concerto in F: George Gershwin's First Orchestration," *American Music*, iii (1985), 277

AARON COPLAND

William W. Austin

CHAPTER SIX

Aaron Copland

1. LIFE. Copland's parents immigrated, at different times and by different routes, from villages in the Polish and Lithuanian parts of Russia. His father came to New York as an adolescent, late in the 1870s, after some time in England, where the spelling of his name was established: Harris Morris Copland. His mother, Sarah Mittenthal, had grown up and attended school in a series of Midwestern and Texan cities before arriving in New York in 1881. In the 1890s the family store prospered; Harris Copland became president of the oldest synagogue in Brooklyn. Aaron was born in Brooklyn on 14 November 1900; he was the fifth child, seven years younger than his nearest sister. He learned what she could teach him at the piano and then, on his own initiative, went to Leopold Wolfsohn. After about three years with him, Copland advanced to study piano with Victor Wittgenstein and Clarence Adler. He had already begun to attend New York SO concerts under Damrosch at the Brooklyn Academy of Music. He was stirred by performances by Paderewski, Cyril Scott, Isadora Duncan, and the Diaghilev ballet, particularly in *Scheherazade* and *L'après-midi d'un faune*.

Beginning in 1917, and then more intensively after his graduation from the Boys' High School (1918), Copland studied harmony, counterpoint, and sonata form under Goldmark, whose fidelity to Beethoven, Wagner, and Fuchs increased his pupil's independent enthusiasm for Mussorgsky, Debussy, Ravel, Scriabin, and Scott. Ives's "Concord" Sonata, glimpsed on the piano

183

in Goldmark's studio, attracted Copland, but his teacher prevented him from becoming "contaminated" with it. Copland forgot Ives for a decade. A literary friend, Aaron Schaffer, encouraged his idealism, guided his reading of *Jean-Christophe* and *The Dial*, and urged him to go to Paris. When he was 20, having saved just enough from his allowance and earnings in summer jobs, he set off to attend the new American Conservatory at Fontainebleau near Paris.

There Copland found a "powerful," "exhilarating" teacher in Boulanger; he stayed with her until 1924 and recruited other Americans to join and follow him. Something of the attitude he learned was promptly expressed in his essay on Fauré, whom he called "the French Brahms." His growing skills he employed in the Stravinsky-like rhythms and transparent instrumental sounds of his first big work, music for an unperformed ballet *Grohg* (1922–4), parts of which became the prize-winning *Dance Symphony* (1930). Copland's years in Paris brought fruitful contacts with Roussel, Prokofiev, Milhaud, and Koussevitzky. He attended the Diaghilev ballets, heard Koussevitzky conduct the première of Ravel's orchestration of Mussorgsky's *Pictures*, and studied French piano music under Viñes. Copland was less impressed by Satie than was Thomson, and less impressed by Honegger and Dukas than was Piston. He visited England, Belgium, and Italy; the summers were spent, on Boulanger's advice, in Berlin, Vienna, and Salzburg, where he responded to what he heard of Webern, Bartók, Hába, Hindemith, Weill, and many others. Mahler he took as a useful model of counterpoint as well as orchestration. He began to cultivate an interest in jazz. Wishing to be as recognizably American as Mussorgsky and Stravinsky were Russian, Copland applied some syncopated and polymetric rhythms and some "blue" intervals in his next works, most memorably in the suite *Music for the Theatre* (1925). At the same time he cultivated his own "idea of the grandiose, of the dramatic

13. *Aaron Copland*

and the tragic, which was expressed to a certain extent in the Organ Symphony [1924, proposed by Boulanger for her first American tour] and very much in the *Symphonic Ode* [1927–9, for the 50th anniversary of the Boston SO]." The deliberate Americanism and the grandiosity were characteristics that recurred in various guises and various combinations throughout his later works. He continued to cherish the ideals of economy and refinement represented by Fauré, and to be fascinated by Stravinsky in all his phases. But amid all these diverse lures and standards, Copland developed his own musical personality, growing from his earlier spontaneous affinities with Mussorgsky and Scriabin.

He shared an apartment in Paris with Harold Clurman, then studying dramatic literature at the Sorbonne; Clurman provided the scenario for *Grohg*. Back in New York the two young men responded to the same currents of thought and fashion; their careers ran parallel through the optimistic 1920s, through what Clurman later called "the fervent years" of the 1930s, and thereafter. Clurman's ideas on art and society helped Copland to form his own without the influence of systematic reading or argument. Both were determined to "make clear to our countrymen the value attached in all lands to the idea of the creative personality" and to assert the "possibility of the coexistence of industrialism and creative activity." Their determination, like their friendship, was immune to all successes and failures. Clurman's article (1946) on the critic Paul Rosenfeld gives a valuable account of the young men's early admiration and gratitude, their slightly diverging responses to changing times, and their renewed appreciation of Rosenfeld's individualism.

Copland tried at first in 1924 to establish himself as a private teacher. Soon his compositions won the support of Rosenfeld (though Varèse still claimed Rosenfeld's most rapturous approval), then of the patron Alma Morgenthau Wertheim, of the Boston SO's new conductor Koussevitzky, of the MacDowell Colony, and of the Guggenheim Foundation – he had returned at a lucky moment when advanced New Yorkers were hoping to outdo Diaghilev's Paris. He later joined the League of Composers and, with his reporting, enriched its journal *Modern Music*; he paid due respect to Varèse, Bloch, Cowell, and Carpenter. In the summers of 1926, 1927, and 1929 he was able to go back to Europe to learn more of the latest musical news, to report, and to organize American collaborations. He enlisted Sessions, who continued to live in Europe, to join him in sponsoring an important series of concerts of new music in New York (the Copland–Sessions Concerts, 1928–31). In the next years Copland was among the founders of the Yaddo Festivals, the Arrow Music Press, and the ACA (president, 1937–45). At the New School for Social Research he succeeded Rosenfeld as lecturer to laymen (1927–37). His lectures and articles took enduring shape in the books *What to Listen for in Music* and *Our New Music*, both of which were widely read and admired, and translated into many languages. On the invitation of Chávez, whose music he had extolled with rare enthusiasm, he visited Mexico (1932); he toured Latin America on behalf of the Coordinator of Inter-American Affairs (1941) and the State Department (1947), and in many ways he exemplified the "good neighbor policy" of Franklin Roosevelt – Copland's Americanism was always more neighborliness than chauvinism.

During the terms when Piston took leave (1935, 1944) Copland taught at Harvard. In 1951 he revisited Europe for six months, went to Israel for the first time, and then returned to Harvard for a year as Norton Professor of Poetics – the first American composer in this chair. His lectures, published as *Music and Imagination*, were worthy successors to Stravinsky's *Poetics* and Hindemith's *Composer's World*, without the dogmatism of the former or the bitterness of the latter. In 1940, when Koussevitzky established a summer school at the Berkshire Music

Center to supplement the festivals of the Boston SO there, he turned to Copland as teacher and adviser. Soon Copland became chairman of the faculty, a position he held each summer until he retired in 1965. As a teacher or colleague he generously helped composers from Chávez and Citkowitz to Takemitsu and Del Tredici. His help was always more encouragement than guidance in a particular direction, even though he shyly hoped that younger composers would surpass him and his contemporaries in progressing towards a "solid American tradition." He shared this concern with Piston, Sessions, Thomson, Harris, and Blitzstein, who constituted what he called in 1941 "a nascent American school." Their differences increased with time. Copland's valuing solidarity did not interfere with his support for such composers as Ives, Cowell, and Cage, whose successes he warmly welcomed although their styles did not conform to any tradition he envisioned.

Copland has received many honors: the Pulitzer Prize (1945), the New York Music Critics' Circle award (1945), the Academy of Motion Picture Arts and Sciences "Oscar" (1950), the Gold Medal of the National Institute of Arts and Letters (1956), the Presidential Medal of Freedom (1964), the Commander's Cross of the Order of Merit of the Federal Republic of Germany (1970), the Howland Prize of Yale University (1970), honorary degrees from Princeton (1956), Oberlin, Harvard, Brandeis, and a number of other universities, memberships or fellowships in the American Academy of Arts and Letters (of which Copland was eventually president), the American Academy of Arts and Sciences (Boston), the Accademia di S. Cecilia (Rome), the Royal Academy of Music and the Royal Society of Arts (London), the Academia Nacional de Belles Artes (Buenos Aires), and the University of Chile. He served as director or board member of the American Music Center, the American branch of the ISCM, the Koussevitzky Foundation, the Edward MacDowell Association,

14. Scene from the première of Copland's ballet "Appalachian Spring," performed by the Martha Graham Dance Company at the Coolidge Auditorium, Library of Congress, 30 October 1944

189

the Charles Ives Society, and the Naumburg Foundation, and as advisory editor of *Perspectives of New Music*. The Aaron Copland School of Music was founded in 1982 at Queens College, CUNY.

Between 1959 and 1972 Copland appeared as speaker, pianist, or conductor on 59 television programs, including a series of 12 for the National Educational Television network, several valuable interviews for the BBC, and programs with complete performances of the First Symphony, the Violin Sonata, the *Tender Land* suite, and the 12 Poems of Emily Dickinson. He continued touring as conductor and speaker through another decade before ending his conducting career in 1983 with a performance of *Appalachian Spring* in New York. Copland's recording of a rehearsal of that work is among his most vivid legacies.

2. WORKS. Copland's first considerable piece of chamber music was the trio *Vitebsk* (1929) and his first big piano work the Variations (1930). For orchestra, the early *Grohg* and *Music for the Theatre* were soon followed by a piano concerto, the Short Symphony, a hasty compilation for ballet, *Hear ye! Hear ye!* (1934, for Ruth Page), and a more distinctive major work, *Statements* (1932–5). As the world economic and political crisis deepened and war approached, Copland intensified his concerns for explicit social significance, for the theater (including dance and cinema), and for school music. His short opera for children, with a chorus of parents, *The Second Hurricane* (1936), is the clearest expression of these concerns. A more relaxed, and better-known, expression of related concerns is *El salón México* (1933–6), which led to Copland's permanent contract with Boosey & Hawkes as his publisher.

Beginning in 1938 he produced a series of ballets that reached wide audiences and for a decade exerted wide influence: *Billy the Kid* (1938, commissioned by Lincoln Kirstein for Eugene Loring), *Rodeo* (1942, for Agnes de Mille), and *Appalachian Spring*

(1943–4, for Graham, who chose the title from a poem (*The Dance*) by Hart Crane; see fig. 14). Then the Clarinet Concerto that he wrote for Benny Goodman (1947–8) was used by Robbins for the ballet *Pied Piper*, and the series was continued with *Dance Panels* (1959, revised 1962, for Heinz Rosen, Munich).

Copland's eight scores for films – documentaries and versions of plays by Wilder, Steinbeck, and others – set new standards for Hollywood. The previously established style, which Copland described as "Dvořák-Tchaikovsky generalized music" was replaced by a freedom to choose among all kinds of styles whatever could best "evoke a specific landscape." Copland's own range of rhythms and instrumental effects, as Hamilton has observed, "soon became the common coin of Hollywood hacks," and the freedom for greater variety came into force only over the next decades.

A still different kind of success was the result of a commission from Kostelanetz for one of a series of musical portraits of American heroes by various composers. At first Copland proposed to portray Whitman, but Kern had already started to work on Twain and Kostelanetz wished to avoid another literary figure. Copland next considered Jefferson and finally Lincoln; his friend Thomson, long practiced at musical portraiture, tried to dissuade him from anything so exalted. (Thomson's choice was Fiorello LaGuardia.) But Copland was well enough aware of the dangers, remembering Goldmark's orchestral threnody of 1919, *Requiem suggested by Lincoln's Gettysburg Address*, in which trumpets try to proclaim the American creed. Copland proceeded to make a new kind of portrait; his music, borrowing some American tunes of Lincoln's time and earlier, became the humble prelude and accompaniment for spoken excerpts from Lincoln's addresses and letters. Though he never convinced Thomson that his choice or his procedure was right, and though friends like Berger felt obliged to defend him long afterwards from "the belittling effect the Copland of *Lincoln Portrait* has, for some listeners, on the

15. *Opening of the autograph short score of Copland's "Inscape," 1967*

Copland of the Sextet," still the *Portrait* found many uses, and more performances even than *Appalachian Spring*. Among all the celebrated readers of the Lincoln text, the best was the Lincolnian Illinois statesman and Copland's exact contemporary, Adlai Stevenson. Copland's own reading of the text was more moving; a performance broadcast on television in 1980, with some moments from the rehearsal shown beforehand, demonstrated how he worked with the conductor Bernstein to preserve true meaning through his own nuances in timing.

Berger and Mellers have found worthier successors to the Piano Variations in the Piano Sonata (1939–41), the Violin Sonata (1942–3), the Third Symphony (1944–6), and the Piano Quartet (1950), in which Copland for the first time made extensive use of 12-tone techniques within his free and distinctive harmonic style. The cycle of 12 Poems of Emily Dickinson (1944–50) was singled out by Stravinsky with songs by Ruggles and Babbitt. On the other hand, Copland's full-length opera, *The Tender Land* (1952–4), satisfied neither his large public nor his élite critics, although the orchestral suite became a favorite of some listeners. The orchestration of the Variations (1957) was a further disappointment. Then came the Piano Fantasy (1952–7), a long and complex work. The Nonet for Strings (1960) was regarded by admirers like Salzman as a temporary retreat from dodecaphony; it pleased such older friends as Kirkpatrick.

For the opening of Philharmonic Hall at Lincoln Center, New York, Copland composed *Connotations* (1962) and for the New York PO's 125th anniversary *Inscape* (1967; see fig. 15). To listeners and critics at their first performances these pieces seemed to reveal Copland as a follower of new trends. Looking back in 1970, Bernstein, who had regarded him in the 1930s and 1940s as "a substitute father," recalled how in the 1950s young composers "gradually stopped flocking to Aaron; the effect on him – and therefore on American music – was heartbreaking." Perhaps just because Bernstein could not make *Connotations* compelling in performance, as he had so many of the earlier works, it seemed to him that Copland "tried to catch up – with twelve-tone music, just as it too was becoming old-fashioned to the young." But Copland himself never expressed "heartbreak." He was as little dismayed by misunderstanding and neglect as he was spoiled by official honors. As always, Copland's main concern continued to be the mysterious process of "exteriorising inner feelings." Always he was exploring his own "inscape" and finding the sounds with the right "connotations" to let any imaginative listener "relive in his own mind the completed revelation of the composer's thought."

Moreover, in the *Dance Panels* (1959), the *Music for a Great City* (1964), and the Duo for Flute and Piano (1971) he continued his explorations by means of triads and major scales, as he had done since *Music for the Theatre*. He found fresh ideas in these, in new relations between them and in the chromatic and dissonant materials that were also long familiar to him. *Night Thoughts* (1972) continued a progression from the Variations through the Sonata and the Fantasy, while the two *Threnodies* (1971, 1973) added weight to the list of chamber music; all three of these later works cast new light and shadow on all that had come before them, and they suggest a closer relationship to Ives and Stravinsky. His work as a whole has escaped chronological pigeonholes, and critics have recognized the integrity of Copland's style and the range of his concerns at every stage of his development.

3. STYLE. Copland's orchestration is well described by Thomson: "plain, clean-colored, deeply imaginative . . . theatrically functional . . . it has style." *Appalachian Spring* offers particularly interesting examples of Copland's orchestration, because the well-known suite for full orchestra may be compared with the original scoring for 13 instruments (flute, clarinet, bassoon, piano, and

strings). Both confirm all of Thomson's points.

In the first climax (ex.1, fig.9) the discreet and ingenious doublings of the fuller version make a continually changing blend: the trumpets lead the slow lyric melody while the strings, piano, and xylophone pursue the leaping counterpoint; the tutti lasts for only two chords before the oboes and clarinets drop out; then the flutes rest for a deep chord with divided trumpets in unison with the horns; then the xylophone falls silent; then, after an extension of the phrase, the oboes and clarinets replace the piano. The same passage in the original version keeps the lyrical melody in the strings, the leaping counterpoint in the flute, clarinet, and piano; the bassoon is important just before and after the passage, linking larger continuities with a subordinate motif. In Copland's words as reported by Cole (*Tempo*, no.76, 1966), "orchestral know-how consists in keeping instruments out of each other's way" and, as Cole pointed out, in both early and late works this "know-how" serves for extreme clarity in counterpoint. The sound is never quite conventional, nor complacent in its novelty. Moreover, the sounds are always at the service of what Copland has called "the expressive idea," recognizing in each timbre and combination of timbres a specific "emotional connotation." Above all, the ever-changing details of sound are planned to express the emotional development of the whole work. The beginning and end of *Appalachian Spring*, with the "white tone" of the clarinet set off against hushed strings, makes the perfect frame for the clarinet's one long solo – its statement of the Shaker dance-prayer *The Gift to be Simple*, which is the theme for a set of variations. Often Copland's orchestration seems magically simple. When he added brass, drums, cymbals, glockenspiel, and xylophone to the originally very limited range of colors, he risked losing the simplicity. But his way of using the new timbres saved it.

With respect to rhythm, Copland's orchestral music is different from his piano and chamber music. The difference in notation is greater than that in sound, because Copland's experience in rehearsing convinced him of the lasting advantages of a traditional placement of bar-lines. But the orchestral music relies more often and for longer stretches on traditional patterns of dance and march, with steady tempos enlivened by odd accents and phrasings. (The complex rhythms of the Second Symphony are unmatched by anything in the later orchestral music.) The lively theme in ex. 1 (fig. 9) establishes a four-bar norm as well as the emphatic four-beat norm; the lyrical theme has four phrases in asymmetrical balance – 16 beats, 13, 12, and 15 – so that there are occasional bars that take three or five beats instead of four. Regularity is reinforced by the transitional fugato; then the overlapping entry of the theme makes a surprise; the fading-out of the passage, after the example, permits the *marcato* motif to break up into fragments and when, after a silent bar, motion resumes, there is even a bar of 7/8 before regularity returns. (In most of his music there are effective passages in 5/8 and 7/8, but no whole movement maintains such a meter.) In slower passages Copland calls for fluctuations of tempo as well as changes of meter and accent. Such fluctuations are used with particular virtuosity in the *Dance Panels*, where a waltz is more a lingering memory or shy hope than a whirling dance. His rhythms in solo instrumental music are often so subtle that the most elaborate notation cannot specify them precisely, but a performer who is at home with the style and who studies each piece thoroughly can make them convincing.

The combination of nervously animated and trance-like swaying rhythms is present in most of Copland's works, each time with a different relation between the contrasting types. In *Appalachian Spring* Carter has noted the procedures by which the animation is restrained and subdued. (Carter's Piano Sonata, written just after *Appalachian Spring*, may owe more to Copland in this respect than in harmony or timbre.) In Copland's Piano Sonata the slow finale, with bell effects, goes to an extreme of the trance type. In the Piano Fantasy, *Connotations*, and *Inscape*, there are marvelous transitions that bind the fast central movements into the slow beginnings and endings.

Copland's way of using familiar intervals is no more conventional than his orchestration, and no more indebted to Stravinsky or any other model. He finds new contexts for conventional intervals, without relying on them to shape his phrases, much less his long forms. When his contexts are very dissonant and chromatic, he still returns occasionally to triads, or to bare 5ths, 6ths, and particularly 10ths, for the sake of their sound and for the emotional connotations that he values so much. The critic Theodore Chanler remarked on Copland's characteristic 10ths in the works of the 1920s; they are still prominent in *Appalachian Spring* and *Inscape*. Very often he prefers a wide-spaced texture of few notes, alternating dissonance with pure consonance and playing with enharmonic ambiguities – for instance, the germinal diminished 4th or major 3rd of the Piano Variations. When he makes a major scale dominate, as in the phrases of *Appalachian Spring* shown in ex. 1, Copland provides pungent clashes between melody and accompaniment, and he makes his abrupt cadences on a tonic with only its major 3rd. He leads up to this passage through a modulating fugato (ex. 1, fig. 8) with free collisions of the parts.

In many characteristic passages there are few clear harmonic progressions; even if a clear tonic and dominant are implied, the voice-leading may prolong indefinitely a single chord of approximately subdominant character. Forte has analyzed the third Piano Blues to show this procedure convincingly. In *Appalachian Spring*, however, perfect cadences are frequent; what keeps the music moving is melodic expectation.

A melody like that of the trumpet in ex. 1 (fig. 9) is rare, yet

198

Ex.1 *Appalachian Spring*, 1943-4

199

it could be recognized as Copland's even without its instrumentation and counterpoint. It avoids the leading tone of the scale; it emphasizes the tonic as a high note, but otherwise touches the tonic only lightly; and it conforms to no accompanying triad, but rather suggests a broken 4th chord, with the repeated rising 4ths and the falling 7th.

This melody returns at three important points in the ballet, transformed each time. At the end of the Allegro, soft strings play the melody while a solo flute gasps the last fragments of the dance; here the melody's phrases are regularized to 14 beats each. Then at the end of the central Presto, before the variations on the Shaker tune (rehearsal number 51), a solo violin and oboe in octaves play a variant of the melody, with the concluding downward leap expanded to a 10th, but with the rhythm compressed to phrases of only eight and six beats. Finally, at the end of the work, flute and strings play the melody stretched out to phrases of 20 beats or more, and with its final leap quieted, first to a 5th and at last to a step onto the tonic. These variants of the melody, together with some motivic connections with other melodies, give coherence and a satisfying shape to the whole ballet; they make it a more symphonic composition than the suites derived from *Billy*, *Rodeo*, and *Our Town*. The final form of Copland's melody is like the gift of simplicity referred to in the Shaker text; it is no mere coda after the glorified variations but a fulfillment to which all the variations and the intervening hesitant prayer had led.

The Shaker tune in *Appalachian Spring* is an exception among all Copland's borrowed melodies: it is the only one that he does not modify with syncopation or changing meter, the only one that he dwells on through a set of variations. His earliest ventures in borrowing were travesties of *The Star-Spangled Banner* and Mendelssohn's Wedding March in *Hear ye! Hear ye!* In *El salón México*, *Billy the Kid*, *Rodeo*, and the *Lincoln Portrait*, the tunes may be presented straight once or twice, but generally durations are stretched unexpectedly or notes omitted, motifs are detached, new phrases are formed, so that the flow of the music is by no means determined by the tunes; and the forms never resemble Thomson's rondos. In the *Lincoln Portrait* there is something like an Ivesian blending of tunes: a hint of *Yankee Doodle* links the lyric *Springfield Mountain* and the boisterous *Camptown Races*. Even in the simplest arrangements of *Old American Songs*, Copland tampers with rhythms, at least between phrases, and in the accompaniments. *Simple Gifts* is one of the songs in his first set, and here its accompaniment is altogether different from that in any of the ballet's variations – most of the chords are syncopated. In *Appalachian Spring* the exceptional procedure may be essential to make clear the communal expression, for the sober tune and the Shaker community in which it was used are not so familiar as *So long, old Paint*, nor so colorful as *El mosco* and its Mexican dance hall atmosphere. (*Simple Gifts*, after Copland made it famous, was adopted into the repertories of schools, churches, and the popular "folksingers" of the 1960s.) If all these borrowings are simpler than the melodies of the Piano Variations, the simplicity of *Simple Gifts* is extraordinary, and Copland's use of the tune is in fine accord with its simplicity. Moreover, *Appalachian Spring* is a marvelous movement towards *Simple Gifts*; the music acknowledges the claims of solitariness and the possibilities of violence, but always turns toward true simplicity.

After *Appalachian Spring* and *The Tender Land*, Copland's interest in borrowed melodies was apparently exhausted; even the influence of such melodies on his own melodic invention declined. He never depended on them to the extent that Vaughan Williams, Janáček, and Bartók depended on what they had absorbed from folk music. Yet in all the works that led up to *Appalachian Spring*, as Carter observed, "there is a keen awareness in the choice of folk-material and in their handling that transforms everything

201

into the Coplandesque." After that work Copland proceeded to develop his own kinds of declamatory and lyrical melody. Listeners all over the world continued to respond to the individual quality he had given so many borrowed melodies, and to recognize that quality in more and more of his music.

WORKS

(all published unless otherwise stated)

OPERAS

The Second Hurricane (school play-opera, E. Denby), 1936, New York, 21 April 1937, Henry Street Settlement Music School, cond. L. Engel

The Tender Land (opera, 2, H. Everett, after E. Johns), 1952–4, New York, 1 April 1954, New York City Opera, cond. Schippers; rev. 3 acts, 1955, Oberlin, OH, 20 May 1955; orch suite, 1956, Chicago, 10 April 1958, Chicago SO, cond. Reiner

BALLETS

Grohg, 1922–5, unpubd; excerpt Cortège macabre, orch, 1922–3, Rochester, 1 May 1925, cond. Hanson, unpubd; excerpts arr. as Dance Symphony, 1930, Philadelphia, 15 April 1931, cond. Stokowski; excerpt Dance of the Adolescent, arr. 2 pf, before 1932

Hear ye! Hear ye!, 1934, Chicago, 30 Nov 1934, cond. Ganz, unpubd

Billy the Kid, 1938, Chicago, 6 Oct 1938; orch suite, 1939, New York, 9 Nov 1940, NBC SO, cond. W. Steinberg; excerpts Prairie Night, Celebration, Waltz, n.d.; excerpts arr. 2 pf, n.d., New York, 17 Oct 1946, U. Appleton, M. Field

Rodeo, 1942, New York, 16 Oct 1942, cond. F. Allers; arr. pf, 1962; Rodeo: 4 dance episodes, orch, 1942, Boston, 28 May 1943, Boston Pops Orch, cond. Fiedler; excerpt Hoedown, str (1945)

Appalachian Spring, fl, cl, bn, pf, 4 vn, 2 va, 2 vc, db, 1943–4, Washington, DC, 30 Oct 1944, cond. Horst; suite, full orch, 1945, New York, 4 Oct 1945, New York PO, cond. Rodzinski; suite, orch, 1970, Los Angeles, 14 Aug 1970, Los Angeles PO, cond. Copland; complete ballet, orch, 1954, Philadelphia, Philadelphia SO, 1954; excerpt Variations on a Shaker Song, school orch (1967)

Dance Panels, 1959, rev. 1962, Munich, 3 Dec 1963, cond. Copland; arr. 2 pf, 1965; suite, orch, 1966, Ojai, CA, 1966, cond. I. Dahl

The City, dir. O. Serlin, 1939, unpubd; excerpt Sunday Traffic incl. in Music for Movies, see ORCHESTRAL

Of Mice and Men (after Steinbeck), dir. L. Milestone, 1939, unpubd; excerpts incl. in Music for Movies

Our Town (after Wilder), dir. S. Wood, 1940; orch suite, 1940, Boston, 7 May 1944, Boston Pops Orch, cond. Bernstein; 3 excerpts arr. pf, 1944; excerpts incl. in Music for Movies

North Star (after L. Hellman), dir. Milestone, 1943, unpubd; excerpts Song of the Guerrillas and The Younger Generation pubd separately, see CHORAL

The Cummington Story, 1945, unpubd; excerpt In Evening Air, arr. pf, 1966

The Red Pony (after Steinbeck), dir. Milestone, 1948; orch suite, 6 scenes, 1948, Houston, 30 Oct 1948, Houston SO, cond. Kurtz; band suite, 4 scenes, 1966

The Heiress (after James: Washington Square), dir. W. Wyler, 1948, unpubd

Something Wild (after A. Karmel, J. Garfein), dir. Garfein, 1961, unpubd ·

ORCHESTRAL

Symphony, org, orch, 1924, New York, 11 Jan 1925, Boulanger, New York SO, cond. W. Damrosch; arr. without org as Symphony no. 1, 1928, Berlin, 9 Dec 1931, Berlin SO, cond. Ansermet; Prelude, chamber orch, 1934

Music for the Theatre, suite, 1925, Boston, 20 Nov 1925, Boston SO players, cond. Koussevitzky

Piano Concerto, 1926, Boston, 28 Jan 1927, Copland, Boston SO, cond. Koussevitzky

Symphonic Ode, 1927–9, Boston, 19 Feb 1932, Boston SO, cond. Koussevitzky; rev. 1955

Short Symphony (Symphony no. 2) [arr. chamber sextet], 1932–3, Mexico City, 23 Nov 1934, Orquesta Sinfónica de México, cond. Chávez

Statements: Militant, Cryptic, Dogmatic, Subjective, Jingo, Prophetic, 1932–5, New York, 7 Jan 1942, New York PO, cond. Mitropoulos

El salón México, 1933–6, Mexico City, 27 Aug 1937, Orquesta Sinfónica de México, cond. Chávez

Music for Radio (Prairie Journal), 1937, New York, 25 July 1937, CBS RO, cond. H. Barlow

An Outdoor Overture, 1938, New York, 16 Dec 1938, High School of Music and Art Orch, cond. A. Richter; arr. band, 1941, New York, June 1942, Goldman Band, cond. Copland

Quiet City [arr. chamber piece], eng hn, tpt, str, 1939, New York, 28 Jan 1941, Saidenberg Little SO, cond. D. Saidenberg

From Sorcery to Science, puppet show score, 1939, New York World's Fair, 12 May 1939, unpubd

John Henry, chamber orch, 1940, New York, 5 March 1940, CBS SO, cond. Barlow; rev. 1952

Fanfare for the Common Man, brass, perc, 1942, Cincinnati, 12 March 1943, Cincinnati SO, cond. Goossens

Lincoln Portrait, speaker, orch, 1942, Cincinnati, 14 May 1942, W. Adams, Cincinnati SO, cond. Kostelanetz

Music for Movies [from film scores The City, Of Mice and Men, Our Town], small orch, 1942, New York, 17 Feb 1943, Saidenberg Little SO, cond. Saidenberg

Letter from Home, 1944, New York, 17 Oct 1944, cond. P. Whiteman; rev. 1962

Jubilee Variation on theme of Goossens, 1944, Cincinnati, 23 March 1945, Cincinnati SO, cond. Goossens.

Danzón cubano [arr. 2 pf piece], 1944, Baltimore, 17 Feb 1946, Baltimore SO, cond. R. Stewart

Symphony no.3, 1944–6, Boston, 18 Oct 1946, Boston SO, cond. Koussevitzky

Clarinet Concerto, cl, str, harp, pf, 1947–8, New York, 6 Nov 1950, Goodman, NBC SO, cond. Reiner

Preamble for a Solemn Occasion, speaker, orch, 1949, New York, 10 Dec 1949, Olivier, Boston SO, cond. Bernstein; arr. org, C. Weinrich, 1953; arr. band, 1973

Orchestral Variations [arr. pf piece], 1957, Louisville, 5 March 1958, Louisville Orch, cond. Whitney

The World of Nick Adams (television score), 1957, Columbia Television Network, 10 Nov 1957, cond. A. Antonini, unpubd

Connotations, 1962, New York, 23 Sept 1962, New York PO, cond. Bernstein

Music for a Great City [based on film score Something Wild], 1964, London, 26 May 1964, London SO, cond. Copland

Down a Country Lane [arr. pf piece], school orch, 1964, London, 20 Nov 1964, London Junior Orch, cond. E. Read

Emblems, band, 1964, Tempe, AZ, 18 Dec 1964, Trojan Band of the U. of Southern California, cond. W. Schaefer

CBS (Signature), 1967, CBS television, 29 Jan 1967

Inscape, 1967, Ann Arbor, 13 Oct 1967, New York PO, cond. Bernstein

Inaugural Fanfare (Ceremonial Fanfare), wind, 1969, Grand Rapids, MI, June 1969, Grand Rapids SO, cond. G. Millar; rev. 1975

3 Latin American Sketches: Estribillo, Paisaje mexicana, Danza de Jalisco, 1972, New York, 7 June 1972, New York PO, cond. Kostelanetz

CHAMBER

Capriccio, vn, pf; Poème, vc, pf; Lament, vc, pf; 2 Preludes, vn, pf; Piano Trio, inc.; all *c*1916–21, unpubd

2 Pieces, str qt: Rondino, 1923, Fontainebleau, France, 1924; Lento molto, 1928, New York, 6 May 1928; arr. str orch, 1928

Lento espressivo, str qt, *c*1923, New York, 18 Oct 1984, Alexander Qt

2 Pieces, vn, pf: Nocturne, Ukelele Serenade, 1926, Paris, 1926, Dushkin, Copland

Movement for String Quartet (Lento espressivo), str qt, *c*1923, New York, 18 Oct 1984, Alexander Qt

2 Pieces, vn, pf: Nocturne, Ukelele Serenade, 1926, Paris, 1926, Dushkin, Copland

Vitebsk, Study on a Jewish Theme, pf trio, 1929, New York, 16 Feb 1929, W. Gieseking, A. Omnou, R. Maas

Miracle at Verdun (incidental music, H. Chlumberg), 1931, 16 March 1931, unpubd

Elegies, vn, va, 1932, New York, 2 April 1933, C. Karman, I. Karman.

Sextet [arr. Short Symphony], cl, pf, str qt, 1937, New York, 26 Feb 1939

The Five Kings (incidental music, Shakespeare scenes), 5 insts, 1939, unpubd

Quiet City (incidental music, I. Shaw), cl, sax, tpt, pf, 1939, unpubd

Violin Sonata, 1942–3, New York, 17 Jan 1944, Posselt, Copland; arr. cl, pf, 1983, Rochester, 1983, M. Webster, B. Lister-Sink

Piano Quartet, 1950, Washington, DC, 29 Oct 1950, A. Schneider, Katims, F. Miller, Horszowski

Nonet, 3 vn, 3 va, 3 vc, 1960, Washington, DC, 2 March 1961, cond. Copland

Duo, fl, pf, 1971, Philadelphia, 3 Oct 1971, E. Shaffer, H. Menuhin

Threnody I: Igor Stravinsky, in memoriam, fl, str trio, 1971, London, ?April 1972, London Sinfonietta

Vocalise [arr. vocal piece], fl, pf, 1972, D. Dwyer

Threnody 11 [based on Night Thoughts, pf]: Beatrice Cunningham, in memoriam, G-fl, str trio, 1973, Ojai, CA, 1 June 1973

KEYBOARD

Moment musical, pf, 1917; Danse caractéristique, pf duet/orch, 1918; Waltz Caprice, pf, 1918; Sonnets I, III, 1918–20; Piano Sonata, G, 1920–21; all unpubd

Sonnet II, pf, *c*1919, New York, 26 Oct 1985, B. Lerner

Scherzo humoristique: Le chat et la souris, pf, 1920, Fontainebleau, 21 Sept 1921, Copland

205

Three Moods: Embittered, Wistful, Jazzy, pf, 1920–21, 1981, L. Smit

Petit Portrait, pf, 1921

Passacaglia, pf, 1921–2, Paris, Jan 1923, D. Ericourt

Sentimental Melody, pf, 1926, 1927, Copland

Piano Variations, 1930, New York, 4 Jan 1931, Copland; orchd 1957

Dance of the Adolescent [arr. excerpt from ballet Grohg], 2 pf, before 1932

Sunday Afternoon Music, pf, The Young Pioneers, pf, 1935, New York, 24 Feb 1936, Copland

Piano Sonata, 1939–41, Buenos Aires, 21 Oct 1941, Copland

Episode, org, 1940, March 1940, W. Strickland

Danzón cubano, 2 pf, 1942, New York, 9 Dec 1942, Copland, Bernstein; orchd 1944

Our Town [arr. film score], 3 excerpts, pf, 1944

2 Piano Pieces: Midday Thoughts, Proclamation for Piano, 1944–82, New York, 28 Feb 1983, B. Lerner

4 Piano Blues, 1947, 1934, 1948, 1926, no.4, Montevideo, 1942, H. Balzo

Piano Fantasy, 1952–7, New York, 25 Oct 1957, Masselos

Preamble for a Solemn Occasion [arr. orch piece], org, 1953

Down a Country Lane, pf, 1962

Rodeo [arr. ballet], 1962

Danza de Jalisco, 2 pf, 1963; orchd 1972

Dance Panels [arr. ballet], 2 pf, 1965

In Evening Air [arr. excerpt from film score The Cummington Story], pf, 1966

Night Thoughts (Homage to Ives), pf, 1972, Fort Worth, 30 Sept 1973, V. Viardo

Midsummer Nocturne, pf, 1977

CHORAL

4 Motets, 1921, Fontainebleau, 1924, Paris-American-Gargenville Chorus, cond. M. Smith

The House on the Hill (E. A. Robinson), SSAA, 1925, New York, spr. 1925, Women's U. Glee Club, cond. G. Reynolds

An Immorality (Pound), S, SSA, pf, 1925, New York, spr. 1925, Women's U. Glee Club, cond. G. Reynolds

Into the Streets May First (A. Hayes), unison vv, pf, 1934, New York, 29 April 1934, Workers Music League

What do we plant? (H. Abbey), SSA, pf, 1935, New York, Henry Street Settlement Girls Glee Club

Lark (G. Taggard), B, SATB, 1938, New York, 13 April 1943, Collegiate Chorale, cond. R. Shaw

Las agachadas (Sp. trad.), SSAATTBB, 1942, New York, 25 May 1942, Schola
Cantorum, cond. H. Ross

Song of the Guerrillas (I. Gershwin), Bar, TTBB, pf, 1943 [from film score
North Star]

The Younger Generation (I. Gershwin), SATB, pf, 1943 [from film score North
Star]

In the Beginning (Genesis), Mez, SATB, 1947, Cambridge, MA, 2 May 1947,
N. Tangeman, Robert Shaw Chorale, cond. Shaw

Stomp your Foot, The Promise of Living [from opera The Tender Land], SATB,
pf, *c*1954, arr. orch, Tanglewood Festival Orch and Chorus, 8 Aug 1957

Canticle of Freedom (J. Barbour), 1955, Cambridge, MA, 8 May 1955, Chorus
and Orch of the Massachusetts Institute of Technology, cond. K. Liepmann;
rev. 1965, Atlanta, 19 Oct 1967, Atlanta SO, cond. Shaw

SONGS

(for 1v. pf, unless otherwise stated)

Melancholy (J. Farnol), 1917; Spurned Love (T. B. Aldrich), 1917; After Ant-
werp (E. Cammaerts), 1917; Night (A. Schaffer), 1918; A Summer Vacation,
1918; My heart is in the east, 1918; Simone (R. de Gourment), 1919; Music
I heard (C. Aiken), 1920; all unpubd

Old Poem (Waley), 1920, Paris, 10 Jan 1922, C. Hubbard and Copland

Pastorale (E. P. Mathers), 1921, Paris, 10 Jan 1922, Hubbard and Copland

Alone (Mathers) [arr. va, pf], 1922, New York, 4 Dec 1985, J. DeGaetani,
unpubd

As it fell upon a day (R. Barnefield), S, fl, cl, 1923, Paris, 6 Feb 1924, A.
MacLeish

Poet's Song (Cummings), 1927, New York, 11 Oct 1935, E. Luening

Vocalise, S/T, pf, 1928, New York, 11 Oct 1935, Luening

12 Poems of Emily Dickinson, 1944–50, New York, 18 May 1950, A. Howland,
Copland; 8 Poems orchd, 1958–70, New York, 14 Nov 1970, G. Killebrew

Old American Songs [arrs.]: The Boatmen's Dance [D. Emmett, 1843], The
Dodger [collected Lomax], Long Time Ago [1830s], Simple Gifts [Shaker,
1840s, ed. E. D. Andrews, 1940], I bought me a cat, 1950, Aldeburgh, 17
July 1950, P. Pears, Britten; arr. medium v, orch, Los Angeles, 7 Jan 1955,
W. Warfield, Los Angeles PO, cond. A. Wallenstein

Old American Songs, set 2 [arrs.]: The Little Horses [collected Lomax], Zion's
Walls [attrib. J. G. McCarry, ed. G. P. Jackson, 1942], The Golden Willow
Tree [version of The Golden Vanity], At the River [R. Lowry, 1865], Ching-
a-ring Chaw [1830s], 1952, Ipswich, MA, 1953, W. Warfield, Copland;
arr. medium v, orch, Ojai, CA, 25 May 1958, G. Bumbry, Ojai Festival
Orch, cond. Copland

Dirge in Woods (Meredith), 1954, Fontainebleau, 1954
Laurie's Song [from opera The Tender Land], S, pf, *c*1954

MSS in *DLC*

Principal publisher: Boosey & Hawkes

WRITINGS

What to Listen for in Music (New York, 1939, 2/1957)
Our New Music (New York, 1941, rev. and enlarged 2/1968 as *The New Music 1900–1960*)
Music and Imagination (Cambridge, MA, 1952, repr. 1959)
Copland on Music (New York, 1960) [selected essays]

For a list of articles see Smith, 1955, and Gleason and Becker, 1981

BIBLIOGRAPHY

BIBLIOGRAPHIES, DISCOGRAPHIES

D. Hamilton: "Aaron Copland: a Discography of the Composer's Performances," *PNM*, ix/1 (1970), 149

——: "The Recordings of Copland's Music," *HiFi*, xx/11 (1970), 52

H. Gleason and W. Becker: "Aaron Copland," *20th-century American Composers*, Music Literature Outlines, ser. iv (Bloomington, IN, rev. 2/1981), 33

C. Oja: "Aaron Copland," *American Music Recordings* (New York, 1982), 62

J. Skowronski: *Aaron Copland: a Bio-bibliography* (Westport, CT, 1985)

LIFE AND WORKS

V. Thomson: "Aaron Copland," *MM*, ix (1932), 67

A. Berger: *Aaron Copland* (New York, 1953) [review by H. Clurman, *Saturday Review*, xxxvi (28 Nov 1953), 36]

J. F. Smith: *Aaron Copland: his Work and Contribution to American Music* (New York, 1955) [incl. letters and summaries of writings]

R. F. Goldman: "Aaron Copland," *MQ*, xlvii (1961), 1

W. H. Mellers: *Music in a New Found Land* (London, 1964), 81

H. Cole: "Aaron Copland," *Tempo*, no.76 (1966), 2; no.77 (1966), 9

B. Northcott: "Copland in England," *Music and Musicians*, xviii/3 (1969), 34

L. Bernstein: "Aaron Copland: an Intimate Sketch," *HiFi*, xx/11 (1970), 53

E. Valencia: "Aaron Copland, el hombre, el músico, la leyenda," *Heterofonia*, iv/24 (1972), 9, 47

P. Dickinson: "Copland at 75," *MT*, cxvi (1975), 967

D. Rosenberg and B. Rosenberg: "Aaron Copland," *The Music Makers* (New York, 1979), 31

L. Kerner: "Aaron Copland's Time and Place," *Village Voice* (10 Dec 1980), 95

Bibliography

J. Rockwell: "Copland Conducts Copland at Tanglewood," *New York Times* (7 July 1980)

E. Rothstein: "Fanfares for Aaron Copland at 80," *New York Times* (9 Nov 1980), §D, p.21

W. Schuman: Tribute to Aaron Copland, Kennedy Center Honoree, 1979, *American Record Guide*, xliv/1 (1980), 6

R. Silverman: "Aaron Copland: Happy Birthday," *Piano Quarterly*, xxvii (1980), 5 [with articles also by L. Smit and D. Newlin]

H. W. Hitchcock: "Aaron Copland and American Music," *PNM*, xix (1980–81), 31 [with musical tributes by many composers, incl. Berger, Del Tredici, Diamond, Kirchner, Orrego-Salas, Persichetti, Ramey, Rorem, Shapero, Talma, and Thomson]

V. Perlis: "Copland and the BSO: a Lasting Friendship," [The Boston SO:] *The First Hundred Years*, ed. C. E. Hessberg and S. Ledbetter (Boston, 1981), 28

E. Salzman: "Aaron Copland: *the* American Composer is Eighty," *Stereo Review*, xlvi/2 (1981), 66

A. Copland and V. Perlis: *Copland 1900 through 1942* (New York, 1984–) [autobiography] [review of vol.1 by A. Berger, *New York Review of Books*, xxxii/3 (1985), 21]

E. B. Fein: "Copland at 85: Fanfare for an Uncommon Man," *New York Times* (15 Nov 1985)

P. Ramey: "Aaron Copland, Genial Patriarch of American Music," *Ovation*, vi/10 (1985), 11

N. Rorem: "Aaron Copland: 'He is like a song-filled Rock of Gibraltar'," *New York Times* (10 Nov 1985), §II, 1

J. Hiemenz: "Aaron Copland at 85: the Birthday Tributes," *MusAm*, xxxvi/4 (1986), 2

V. Perlis: "A New Chance for 'Tender Land'," *New York Times* (26 April 1987), §II, 21

INTERVIEWS

E. T. Cone: "Conversations with Aaron Copland," *PNM*, vi/2 (1968), 57

"Interview with Aaron Copland," *1st American Music Conference: Keele 1975*, 4

N. Kenyon: "The Scene Surveyed: Nicholas Kenyon Talks to Aaron Copland," *Music and Musicians*, xxiv/3 (1975), 22

P. Rosenwald: "Aaron Copland Talks about a Life in Music," *Wall Street Journal* (14 Nov 1980), 31

L. Smit: "A Conversation with Aaron Copland," *Keyboard*, vi/11 (1980), 6 [with musical tributes by 12 composers, incl. K. Emerson's *Variations on Simple Gifts*]

C. Gagne and T. Caras: "Aaron Copland," *Soundpieces: Interviews with American Composers* (Metuchen, NJ, 1982), 101

WORKS, GENERAL STUDIES

P. Rosenfeld: "Copland without the Jazz," *By Way of Art* (New York, 1928) 266

——: "Aaron Copland's Growth," *New Republic*, lxvii (27 May 1931), 46

F. Sternfeld: "Copland as Film Composer," *MQ*, xxxvii (1951), 161

H. Overton: "Copland's Jazz Roots," *Jazz Today*, i (1956), 40

R. Evett: "The Brooklyn Eagle," *Atlantic Monthly*, ccxxxiv (1969), 135

H. Cole: "Popular Elements in Copland's Music," *Tempo*, no.95 (1971), 4

N. Kay: "Aspects of Copland's Development," *Tempo*, no.95 (1971), 23

D. Matthews: "Copland and Stravinsky," *Tempo*, no.95 (1971), 10

D. Young: "The Piano Music," *Tempo*, no.95 (1971), 15

S. Lipman: "Copland as American Composer," *Commentary*, lxi (1976), 70

C. Palmer: "Aaron Copland as Film Composer," *Crescendo International* (1976), May

T. Magrini: "Per una critica del 'populare' in Aaron Copland," *Ricerchi musicali*, ii/2 (1978), 5

B. Northcott: "Notes on Copland," *MT*, cxxii (1980), 686

P. Ramey: "Copland and the Dance," *Ballet News*, ii/5 (1980), 8

L. Starr: "Copland's Style," *PNM*, xix (1980–81), 68

N. M. Case: *Stylistic Coherency in the Piano Works of Aaron Copland* (diss., Boston U., 1984)

N. Butterworth: *The Music of Aaron Copland* (New York, 1986)

STUDIES OF PARTICULAR WORKS

P. Rosenfeld: "Musical Chronicle," *The Dial*, lxxviii (1925), 258 [Symphony]

A. Berger: "The Piano Variations of Aaron Copland," *Musical Mercury*, i (1934), 85

A. Goldberg: "Salome and New Ballets Occupy Chicago Stage," *MusAm*, liv/19 (1934), 11 [*Hear ye! Hear ye!*]

C. Sand [pseud. of C. Seeger]: "Copeland's [sic] Recital at Pierre Degeyter Club," *Daily Worker* (22 March 1934), 5 [several pieces]

C. M. Smith: "Copland's Hear ye! Hear ye!," *MM*, xii (1935), 86

P. Rosenfeld: "Current Chronicle," *MQ*, xxv (1939), 372 [*An Outdoor Ov.*, *The City*, *Billy the Kid*, and others]

J. Kirkpatrick: "Aaron Copland's Piano Sonata," *MM*, xix (1942), 246

A. Berger: "Copland's Piano Sonata," *Partisan Review*, x (1943), 187

E. Carter: "Theatre and Films," *MM*, xxi (1943), 50 [*North Star*]

——: "What's New in Music," *Saturday Review*, xxviii (20 Jan 1945), 13 [Vn Sonata, pf arrs. of *Our Town* and *Billy the Kid*]

——: "New Publications," *Saturday Review*, xxix (26 Jan 1946), 34 [*Appalachian Spring*]

Bibliography

A. Forte: *Contemporary Tone Structures* (New York, 1955), 63 [Piano Blues no.3]

A. Berger: "Aaron Copland's Piano Fantasy," *Juilliard Review*, v/1 (1957), 13

W. H. Mellers: "The Tender Land," *MT*, ciii (1962), 245

A. Salzman and P. Des Marais: "Aaron Copland's Nonet: Two Views," *PNM*, i/1 (1962), 172

P. Evans: "Copland on the Serial Road: an Analysis of Connotations," *PNM*, ii/2 (1964), 141

W. H. Mellers: "The Teenager's World," *MT*, cv (1964), 500 [on *Second Hurricane*]

R. P. Locke: *Aaron Copland's Twelve Poems of Emily Dickinson* (diss., Harvard U., 1970)

D. Whitwell: "The Enigma of Copland's Emblems," *Journal of Band Research*, vii/2 (1972), 5

D. Young: "Copland's Dickinson Songs," *Tempo*, no.103 (1972), 33

E. Salzman: "Copland's Appalachian Spring," *Stereo Review*, xxxix/4 (1974), 108

R. Swift: "Aaron Copland: Night Thoughts," *Notes*, xxxi (1974–5), 158

R. M. Daugherty: *An Analysis of Aaron Copland's "Twelve Poems of Emily Dickinson"* (diss., Ohio State U., 1980)

J. Anderson: "Dance: Copland Conducts for Graham," *New York Times* (18 June 1982), §C, p.8 [*Appalachian Spring*]

P. Fuller: *Copland and Stravinsky* (diss., UCLA, 1982) [*Appalachian Spring*]

D. Conte: *A Study of Aaron Copland's Sketches for Inscape* (diss., Cornell U., 1983)

OTHER LITERATURE

V. Thomson: "The Cult of Jazz," *Vanity Fair*, xxiv/4 (1925), 54

M. Graham: "The Dance in America," *Trend*, i/1 (1932), 5

A. Mendel: "What is American Music?"; "The American Composer," *Nation*, cxxxiv (1932), 524, 578

P. Rosenfeld: "A Musical Tournament," *New Republic*, lxxi (15 June 1932), 119

V. Thomson: *The Musical Scene* (New York, 1945), 125

H. Clurman: "Paul Rosenfeld," *MM*, xxiii (1946), 184

V. Thomson: *The Art of Judging Music* (New York, 1948), 51, 74, 161, 201

——: *Music Right and Left* (New York, 1951), 120

R. Sessions: *Reflections on the Music Life in the United States* (New York, 1956), 156

I. Stravinsky and R. Craft: *Dialogues and a Diary* (New York, 1963), 47

V. Thomson: *Virgil Thomson* (New York, 1966), 71, 138, 146, 243, 277, 411

H. Clurman: *All People are Famous (Instead of an Autobiography)* (New York, 1974)

A. Croce: "The Blue Glass Goblet," *New Yorker*, l (6 May 1974), 130

211

W. Schuman: "Americanism in Music: a Composer's View," *Music in American Society 1776–1976*, ed. G. McCue (New Brunswick, NJ, 1977), 15

M. Siegel: "The Cake with the Stripper Inside," *Hudson Review*, xxxi (1978), 137

C. J. Oja: "The Copland-Sessions Concerts and their Reception in the Contemporary Press," *MQ*, lxv (1979), 212

C. Alexander: *Here the Country Lies: Nationalism and the Arts in 20th-century America* (Bloomington, IN, 1980)

B. Zuck: *A History of Musical Americanism* (Ann Arbor, MI, 1980)

R. Friedberg: *American Art Song and American Poetry* (Metuchen, NJ, 1981), 117

L. Bernstein: *Findings* (New York, 1982), 57, 284, 314, 336

M. Lederman: *The Life and Death of a Small Magazine (Modern Music, 1924–1946)*, ISAMm, xviii (Brooklyn, NY, 1983)

A. H. Levy: *Musical Nationalism: American Composers' Search for Identity* (Westport, CT, 1983)

A. Porter: "American Symphonists," *New Yorker*, lviii (31 Jan 1983), 94

R. M. Meckna: *The Rise of the American Composer-critic: Aaron Copland, Roger Sessions, Virgil Thomson, and Elliott Carter in the Periodical "Modern Music"* (diss., U. of California, Santa Barbara, 1984)

M. Meckna: "Copland, Sessions, and *Modern Music*: the Rise of the Composer-critic in America," *American Music*, iii/2 (1985), 198

ELLIOTT CARTER

Bayan Northcott

CHAPTER SEVEN

Elliott Carter

1. LIFE. Elliott Cook Carter, Jr., was born in New York on 11 December 1908 and educated at the Horace Mann School and at Harvard (1926–32, BA in English, MA in music). From 1932 to 1935 he studied at the Ecole Normale de Musique in Paris and privately with Boulanger. After returning to the USA he became music director of Ballet Caravan until 1940 and a regular contributor to *Modern Music* until 1946. In 1939 he married the sculptor Helen Frost-Jones, by whom he had one son. The suite from his ballet *Pocahontas* won the Juilliard Publication Award in 1940. From 1940 to 1942 he was on the faculty of St. John's College, Annapolis, teaching music and related subjects, and from 1943 to 1944 he worked as a consultant in the Office of War Information. In 1945 his *Canonic Suite* for four alto saxophones was awarded a BMI Publication Prize and his *Holiday Overture* won first prize in the Independent Music Publishers Contest; he also received a Guggenheim Fellowship. He was professor of composition at the Peabody Conservatory from 1946 to 1948, and at Columbia University from 1948 to 1950.

In 1950 a second Guggenheim Fellowship and a grant from the National Institute of Arts and Letters enabled him to work in seclusion in Arizona on his String Quartet no.1. This won first prize in the International Quartet Competition at Liège, Belgium, in 1953, and in the same year Carter received a fellowship to the American Academy in Rome, where he worked on his Variations for Orchestra, commissioned by the Ford Foun-

215

dation for the Louisville Orchestra. In 1955–6 he was professor of composition at Queens College, New York; in 1956 he was elected a member of the National Institute of Arts and Letters, and his Sonata for flute, oboe, cello, and harpsichord received the Naumburg Prize. In 1958 he taught at the Salzburg Seminars. In 1960 his String Quartet no.2 won the Pulitzer Prize and the Critics' Circle Award, and in 1961 the same work gained the UNESCO Prize, also being nominated "best received contemporary classical composition" by the National Academy of Recording Arts and Sciences. Also in 1961 Carter received the Sibelius Medal and the Critics' Circle Award for his Double Concerto.

From 1960 to 1962 Carter was professor of composition at Yale. In 1963 he was elected a member of the American Academy of Arts and Sciences (Boston) and was appointed composer-in-residence at the American Academy in Rome. The following year he held a similar appointment in Berlin, where he worked on his Piano Concerto. In 1965 he received the Brandeis University Creative Arts Award, and in 1967 the Harvard Glee Club Medal. That year he returned for another year as composer-in-residence at the American Academy in Rome, also spending some of 1968 at the Villa Serbelloni at Bellagio, Italy, where he worked on his Concerto for Orchestra, commissioned by the New York PO for its 125th anniversary year. In 1969 he was elected a member of the American Academy of Arts and Letters.

In 1971 Carter was awarded the Gold Medal of the National Institute of Arts and Letters and he spent more time at the Villa Serbelloni, working on his String Quartet no.3. In 1967 he was appointed to teach composition at the Juilliard School and was also named Andrew D. White Professor-at-Large of Cornell University. He has also taught at the Dartington and Tanglewood summer schools and served in the League of Composers, the ISCM, and the ACA. He has received honorary doctorates from the New England Conservatory of Music (1961), Swarthmore

College (1965), Princeton University (1967), Ripon College (1968), Oberlin College, and Boston, Yale, and Harvard universities (1970), as well as the Peabody Conservatory (1974) and the University of Cambridge (1983). He received the Handel Medallion in 1978, the Ernst von Siemens Prize in 1981, the Edward MacDowell Medal in 1983, the George Peabody Medal in 1984, and the National Medal of Arts in 1985.

Carter's reputation, which grew steadily from the 1950s, rests squarely on a cumulative sequence of large-scale works; at its best his music sustains an energy of invention that is unrivalled in contemporary composition. He has avoided conducting or playing in public on the grounds of "poor performing nerves," but his writings on music cover an impressive range: he has published articles on many aspects of 20th-century music including the works of Ives, Piston, Riegger, Stravinsky, and Wolpe. A collection of these, *The Writings of Elliott Carter: an American Composer looks at Modern Music,* edited by E. Stone and K. Stone, was published in 1977.

2. EARLY WORKS. Carter had the good fortune to grow up during a progressive period of New York's cultural life. At the age of 16 he met Ives, who encouraged him to compose and took him to concerts. During his schooldays he heard not only *The Rite of Spring* and *Pierrot lunaire*, but also many first performances of Varèse, Ruggles, Ives himself, and later the young Sessions and Copland. Scriabin was another early enthusiasm. Scholar friends introduced him to Indian and Balinese music, and he took the opportunity of a visit to Vienna with his businessman father in 1925 to purchase all the available scores of the Second Viennese School, including Schoenberg's newly published Piano Suite op. 25. Meanwhile his interest in the modern movement also extended to Proust, Joyce, Eisenstein, the German expressionist painters, and the visiting Moscow Arts Theater.

217

Wide reading in modern literature, together with subsidiary courses in mathematics, German, and Greek, also occupied much of his time at Harvard, which he chose largely in order to attend Koussevitzky's adventurous concerts with the Boston SO. But singing Bach in the Glee Club and sharing a room with the Elizabethan specialist Stephen Tuttle aroused his interest in the music of earlier centuries and he profited from the technical advice of Holst, who appeared as visiting professor for 1931–2. Vacations were spent exploring the German classics at the Salzburg and Munich festivals. Nonetheless, it was studying a range of material from Machaut to Stravinsky and furthering his command of strict counterpoint in up to 12 parts under Boulanger that proved crucial in focusing his musical understanding and technique. Contact with Stravinsky and the conducting of a French madrigal group were other musical gains of his years in Paris, during which observation of the events surrounding the Stavisky affair also matured his political outlook.

The darkening situation in Europe and the Depression to which he returned in 1935 were to affect his compositional direction. His first major orchestral score, the ballet suite *Pocahontas* (1938–9), displays variously the influence of Stravinsky and Hindemith, the English virginalists, and that mild vein of indigenous lyricism exemplified by Piston, but not a trace of German expressionism. Carter has explained that although the modern movement has remained for him a permanent core of ideas, the expressionist aesthetic had at that point come to seem like part of the madness that led to Hitler. His reaction was towards moderation and the practical. This took the form, on the one hand, of participation in a liberal arts college scheme to deploy music as a link study between mathematics, the sciences, and the ancient and modern languages and literature, and, on the other, of a deliberate simplification of compositional style towards a hoped-for accessibility.

218

16. Elliott Carter

This aim was undoubtedly achieved in the fresh, unpretentious diatonicism of such works as the *Three Poems of Robert Frost* (1943) and *The Harmony of Morning* (1944). Other works of this period nevertheless presage aspects of his mature style. Continual variation of material and its extension into sustained melodic paragraphs are already features respectively of the pellucidly bitonal *Pastoral* (1940) and the warmly intimate *Elegy* (1943) for cello and piano. The first movement of the Symphony no. 1 (1942) belies the New England calm of its Coplandesque opening in subsequent flights of contrapuntal dialectic, while the ostensibly "popular" *Holiday Overture* (1944) not only employs a "Jacobean" technique of cross-rhythms in ways comparable with the quite independent usages of Michael Tippett but also superimposes slabs of contrasting texture and tempos for the first time in Carter's work.

3. TRANSITION. These developments, together with a rereading of Freud towards the end of World War II, led Carter increasingly to feel that the neoclassical aesthetic represented an evasion of vital areas of feeling and expression. In the fine Piano Sonata (1945–6) he accordingly attempted to free himself from traditional schemata by deriving his compositional substance from the interrelations of the tone-color and playing technique of the instrument itself. The hierarchical superimpositions of octaves, 5ths, 4ths, and 3rds that comprise the work's harmony embody the characteristic overtone resonances of the piano. Carter exploited his fundamental chord of 5ths, B–F♯–C♯–G♯–D♯–A♯, right from the beginning, setting up a tension between chordal paragraphs founded on B and A♯ that soon issues in arpeggios and then tirades of toccata-like figuration, constant in pulse but continually varied in rhythmic grouping. Only later, and in passing, do such textures separate out into something resembling theme and accompaniment. The magnificent second-movement

fugue is similarly evolved out of, and dissolved back into, the fundamental chords.

Carter's next three works have a somewhat retrospective quality, as though he now felt the need to tidy away the loose ends of a "first period" before going on. Neoclassical gestures from then recent Stravinsky, notably the Symphony in Three Movements, are to be heard again in *The Minotaur* (1947), if for the last time in Carter's output. The declamatory male-voice choruses, *Emblems* (1947), have similarly remained the last of his choral works, and the Woodwind Quintet (1948), a kind of Les Six-type divertimento, is the last of his genre pieces, though the frenetic energy of its part-writing also looks forward to the next phase.

4. WORKS OF 1948–59. In the Sonata for cello and piano (1948) Carter resumed his exploitation of instrumental character itself by emphasizing the differences between his two protagonists. Although this contrast is still subsidiary to the character forms of the two inner movements – an "out-of-doors" scherzo and an impassioned elegy – the opposition of melodic content, tone, articulation, and pace between the two instruments during large stretches of the outer movements is so great as almost to create the impression that the players are simultaneously improvising independently. The "almost" is crucial, as the work adumbrated Carter's abiding aesthetic quest for a "focused freedom" and several of his most far-reaching coordinating techniques for the first time. Instead of relying on a received harmonic vocabulary, he permeated and "framed" his progressions by a recurrent chromatic aggregate of interlocking 3rds (the second movement is his last piece to bear a key signature), while by superimposing opposing rhythms – for instance, triplets on quintuplets – and shifting the basic pulse from one to another, he hit on the device later known as "metric modulation," a means of gearing contin-

221

ually fluctuating speeds in precise notation.

The drive and eloquence such techniques had helped to release in what is one of the finest 20th-century cello sonatas now encouraged Carter in a wider rethinking of the elements of musical discourse. He turned once more to the music of Ives, to the rhythmic formulations of Cowell's *New Musical Resources* and Nancarrow's earliest studies for player piano, and to medieval, oriental, and African music for devices to create modern equivalents of the dynamic continuities in the classics that interested him, notably the elliptical coherences of middle-period Haydn and the techniques of superimposition in the operatic ensembles of Mozart, Verdi, and Mussorgsky. Meanwhile he practiced elaborating structures from deliberately restricted materials in the Eight Etudes and a Fantasy for woodwind quartet (1949–50) and the Eight Pieces for four timpani (1950–66).

Scruples about outstripping the stamina of players and audiences notwithstanding, Carter at last felt compelled to allow the urgencies of his new explorations free play in a large-scale work. The monumental String Quartet no.1 (1950–51) superimposes independent melodies in polymetric relationships as complex as 3 against 7 against 15 against 21; and the pitch materials of its entire 40 minutes relate not to tonality but to a tetrachord, E–F–G♯–A♯, from which every interval may be obtained by permutation. Even more impressive, however, is the work's grandly unified sweep through four movements. These comprise a tumultuous opening stretch of seething four-part counterpoint opening out into a more aerated scherzo, not without resemblances to that of Berg's *Lyric Suite*, which in turn gives way to an Adagio where the contrast of tranced upper strings against passionate recitatives from viola and cello represents the widest point of textural definition before the volatile concluding variations work back again towards heterophony. Yet the whole vast sequence is also conceived as a kind of parenthesis in the opening cello cadenza, which the first violin resumes at the end.

Far from languishing in obscurity as Carter had feared, the String Quartet no. 1 rapidly established his international reputation, encouraging him to rethink the possibilities of two further traditional ensembles with comparable boldness. Having worked hitherto with equal voices, he took Sylvia Marlowe's commission for the Sonata for flute, oboe, cello, and harpsichord (1952) as an opportunity to develop the structural possibilities of a group dominated by one. Here the somewhat acid timbre of the harpsichord is amplified by the other instruments, and its typical gestures are anticipated, echoed, and modified in terms of their individual characters. The long diminuendo that comprises the first movement, for instance, reflects the gradual subsidence of the fuzz of upper partials which the other instruments catch and reverberate from the harpsichord's percussive opening attack, while the capacity of the latter for precise, rapid figuration touches off some of Carter's most spontaneous flights of metrical modulation in the delectable finale.

With the Variations for Orchestra of 1954–5 (see fig. 17) Carter faced the problem of deploying his greatly expanded sense of textural functions in an ensemble that retains the 19th-century concept of monolithic chordal tuttis in its very balance of forces. His solution was to build the work around not one but three elements, the theme itself and two ritornellos, the one a descending line that gets faster in its reappearances, the other a fast rising gesture transformed in reverse. As the three are frequently superimposed, Carter was able to create not only layered tuttis of considerable richness and power (ninth variation), but also a scherzando music by rapid switches of spotlight (first variation). Implicit here is yet another textural dimension to be developed in later pieces: the sense of perspective in bringing one idea into foreground definition while another simultaneously sinks back into an indistinct accompanying role. The overall trajectory is a

223

reversal of the First Quartet's: starting from textural multiplicity, Carter worked inwards to a static neutrality in the fifth variation, which isolates the characteristic harmonies of the whole, and then out again towards variety. Whether or not the resemblance of the climax of the finale to Debussy's *Jeux* (a work with a comparable "time sweep") is deliberate, it remains the last moment in Carter's music to sound at all derivative.

With the String Quartet no.2 (1959) Carter achieved at last an "auditory scenario for the players to act out with their instruments" that is virtually independent of received formal procedures. Each instrument is assigned a different "vocabulary" of characteristic intervals, rhythms, and expressive gestures, the parts evolving not in terms of constant themes against varied backgrounds, but rather in terms of constant fields of possibilities realized in continually varied foreground shapes – as it were, the same tones of voice uttering ever new sentences. The conversational metaphor, which Carter doubtless derived from the precedent of Ives's Second Quartet, also accounts for the continuous nine-section form which is the direct result of the various controversies, dominations, and agreements among the four players. As these interactions proceed more or less at the speed of human speech, projecting the work presents difficulties that can be mitigated to some extent by spacing the players wider apart than usual, but that largely disappear in the fullness of quadraphonic recording.

5. THE CONCERTOS. If the Second Quartet attempts to communicate meaning largely in terms of its own devising, the Double Concerto (1961) dramatizes the process of becoming meaningful. Its quasi-palindromic shape, a process of integration going backwards after the midpoint, arose from Carter's decisions first to assign contrasting intervallic and rhythmic sets to the solo piano and harpsichord and to back each with a differently

17. *Opening of the autograph MS of Variation 6 from Carter's Variations for Orchestra, 1954–5*

constituted ensemble, and second to deploy the keyboards as intermediaries between the percussion and pitch-sustaining instruments in the groups. At the start antiphonal percussion establishes the basic rhythmic oscillations, suggesting the "giant polyrhythms" that underlie the whole structure – a procedure reversed at the end to produce a memorable image of dissolution. Moving inwards, these are gradually associated with the intervallic sets and the combined figures then developed in characteristic gestures by the keyboards in long concertante dialogues that lead towards and away from the work's center. This comprises the most sustained and expressive treatment of the pitch materials in a glowing chorale-like passage for wind and strings during which the soloists and percussion are reduced to simple retarding and accelerating patterns. Despite the innumerable local incidents, parentheses, and contradictions with which this scheme is animated and the almost bewildering ductility and friskiness of the keyboard writing, the Double Concerto probably remains Carter's most convincing cyclic structure.

The Piano Concerto (1964–5), by contrast, is sequential in form and develops the Beethovenian kind of confrontation between disparate forces to be sensed behind a number of earlier Carter passages. In the first half the piano presents a mosaic of contrasting, mostly lyrical character-paragraphs, often supported only by a "companionate" concertino of seven solo wind instruments and strings. The few orchestral irruptions, however, prove ominous precursors to the second half. In this the ripieno strings gradually pile up into densely inert chords while brass and woodwind tick monotonously away in polyrhythms that slowly approach synchronization, the combined effect of which is progressively to subdue the piano despite repeated attempts to break out and a series of long concertino solos offering "irrelevant suggestions." At breaking-point, the piano is assailed by the orchestra at its most brutal and insensitive, but survives as its quiet self. Unlike

226

the previous works, the Piano Concerto has a somewhat heavy *espressivo* quality that doubtless befits its pessimistic scenario but may also reflect its innovative pitch system, in which varying superimpositions of three-note chords are extracted from a background formulation of two 12-note chords, one for the piano and concertino, and one for the orchestra.

Yet the flexibility with which Carter could handle an even more elaborate version of the same technique (with chords of five and seven notes) is just one of the ways in which the Concerto for Orchestra (1968–9) comprises both his most synoptic and his most exhilarating achievement. An evocation of the "poetry of change" inspired by verses of St. John Perse's *Vents*, it combines both cyclic and sequential procedures. There are four "close-up" movements, each dominated by a different concertino pack, in the background of which, however, sounds of the other three are continually to be heard. Another continuity, developed from the Variations, is the progressive slowing of the second-movement music against the quickening of the fourth, while the whole structure is "framed" in an awesome impressionist approach and retreat of the entire material at the beginning and end. After the dark opacity of the Piano Concerto, Carter's new-found orchestral brilliance and command of musical space is most impressive. This arises partly from the reappearance in the total chromatic of a diatonic or at least polytonal element, for instance in the tangy block progressions of the fourth-movement concertino (muted trumpets, oboes, and violas), and partly from the accession of an atmospheric quality, particularly in the swirling and soaring second-movement scherzo music.

6. LATER WORKS.

(i) 1960–81. If the slowly appearing pieces of the 1950s and 1960s constitute almost paradigmatic studies in relating the boldest formal concepts to the most individualized exploitation

of the various chosen ensembles, Carter's productivity since 1970 suggests an increasing spontaneity in his mastery of the musical language he has elaborated for himself, enabling him to recover textural simplicity as a compositional resource and to resume vocal composition for the first time since 1947. Among the nonvocal works, the String Quartet no.3 (1971) is conceived as a continuous interplay between two duos, of which the first (violin I and cello) plays *quasi rubato* throughout against the *giusto sempre* of the second (violin II and viola). The first duo is allotted four complete movements to play against the six of the second, but all ten are segmented and shuffled in such a way that each is sooner or later heard in combination with each of the others. On paper the permutatory form-plan appears about the most schematic that Carter has elaborated. In performance the kaleidoscopic rapidity of the textural switches and the transcendental virtuosity of the instrumental part-writing create perhaps the most volatile and immediate impact of all his chamber works.

Despite its comparable instrumental demands and freer formal unfolding, the Duo for violin and piano (1973–4) makes a relatively contained, at times even intimate effect. The work dramatizes the contrast of bowed and struck strings, the violin's sustaining power and enormous variety of color and attack against the piano's greater range of pitch and volume. This contrast is presented in a long opening paragraph of passionate recitative for violin against a more regular, impersonal chiming for piano, after which the work evolves in a series of dialectical waves, each generated by aspects of the one before. Despite confrontations of considerable violence, the work achieves its most personal moments where the passing back and forth of common pitches between the instruments seems to set up fugitive pedal points of a poetic euphony; the conclusion in which violin and piano to some extent exchange the expressive characteristic of the opening also creates a formal symmetry reminiscent of the Cello Sonata.

The Brass Quintet (1974) reverts to the quasi-anthropomorphic approach of such pieces at the String Quartet no. 2, starting metaphorically from the intention of the trumpets and trombones to play slow, solemn music, which is instantly and continually interrupted by the aberrant, egotistical horn. Yet the series of duos, trios, and "quodlibets" into which the subsequent arguments are marshaled creates a more formalistic impression than either the segmentation of the String Quartet no. 3 or the symmetry of the Duo. The overall structure, however, is possibly the most boldly asymmetrical in Carter's output, a lengthy sequence of pungent, contentious sound blocks finally giving way to a balancing shorter section of striking simplicity and calm.

If the 15-minute span of A Symphony of Three Orchestras (1976) achieves at times an incandescent multiplicity beyond even that of the Concerto for Orchestra, its structure seems to derive rather from the chamber works: its extended central section is constructed, after the precedent of the String Quartet no. 3, from the permutational overlappings of 12 movements, four assigned to each of the three large chamber orchestras into which the standard symphonic line-up is divided, and the work is "framed" by a solo obbligato completed at the end, analogous with the String Quartet no. 1. But in this instance the obbligato adumbrates not a rise but a descent, the surpassingly lyrical opening trumpet solo wheeling and banking downwards through ethereal string chords (expressly inspired by Hart Crane's vision of seagulls at dawn over New York in his long poem *The Bridge*) and the final catastrophic piano obbligato plunging to the depths, after a series of brutal tutti chords have pulverized the central section into broken phrases and aimless ostinatos, perhaps symbolizing the suicide of the poet himself.

Night Fantasies (1980), Carter's first solo piano piece since 1946, relates more closely in structure and tone to the Duo, its contrasting materials (initially suggested by the characters of the

229

four well-known New York pianists who commissioned the work and, by analogy, the character suites of Schumann) being cross-cut in a continuous 20-minute sequence, a kind of fantastical nocturne "suggesting the fleeting thoughts and feelings that pass through the mind during a period of wakefulness at night." The piece begins with, and intermittently returns to, a remote "night music" comprising a static background of fixed pitches, out of which the "thoughts and feelings" erupt unpredictably as a contrasting series of figurations each dominated by a different interval plus its inversion – with the noninvertible tritone reserved for a stubborn "recitativo collerico" marking the center-point. The work's range of expression is epitomized when, after a final climax of grinding grandeur, the music "drops off" with almost ironic casualness.

Meanwhile, in returning to vocal writing (and the song cycle genre at that) with *A Mirror on which to Dwell* (1975), for soprano and nine players, Carter posed himself a double problem: how to rethink the possibilities of the voice in terms of his later style and how to interrelate a sequence of separate movements after a two-decade preoccupation with more or less continuous structures. His approach was to derive the contours and inflections of his vocal lines from reading Elizabeth Bishop's poems aloud, and to balance and clarify differently the accompaniment functions of picturesque illustration, emotional expression, and "objective" symbolism in each of the settings, so that the work as a whole would cohere as a sequence of bold contrasts. Thus, for instance, the opening setting, "Anaphora," inclines to the symbolic in the way its cyclical subject matter is mirrored in the permutations of a fixed scheme of registers and pitches; "A View of the Capitol from the Library of Congress" is more illustrative, with its almost Ivesian evocation of a distant military band; while, in function, the twittering oboe obbligato in "Sandpiper" falls somewhere between the two. A comparable approach can be discerned in the six Robert Lowell settings *In Sleep, in Thunder* (1981), for tenor and 14 players, in which, for example, the distant soprano who is overheard singing vocalises in the second poem, "Across the Yard: La Ignota," is evoked by a florid trumpet obbligato. But whereas *A Mirror* was unified by alternations of chosen poems on the general themes of nature, love, and isolation, *In Sleep, in Thunder*, which opens with a short, dedication-like setting of "Dolphin" accompanied by string quintet alone, is conceived as a "portrait" of the poet himself; and the wider range of the music, from the gently mocked New England pastoral simplicities of "Careless Night" to the jagged turbulence of "Dies irae," mirrors the greater emotional range of Lowell's poems, from human intimacy to religious wrath.

Between these works, however, Carter also sought to combine his new-found vocal style with the continuous structuring of his later instrumental music in *Syringa* (1978), an extended vocal duet with accompaniment for 11 players – difficult to classify but owing something in provenance both to opera and to the spiritual dialogues of the baroque. Here, a relatively conjunct setting for mezzo-soprano of John Ashbery's specially written eponymous text – a modern meditation upon the Orpheus myth – is counterpointed by an elaborate commentary for bass on Ancient Greek texts selected by Carter himself and set in the original, while a third continuity is sustained by a guitar obbligato suggestive of Orpheus's lute. *Syringa* is broadly cast in three wave-like sweeps of continuously evolving material, running to almost 20 minutes; the elaboration of this scheme is mitigated, out of consideration for the audibility of the texts, by the often exceptional delicacy of its scoring, but the piece remains among Carter's most demanding to grasp entire.

(ii) From 1981. Having rethought in his own terms each of the four standard voice-types in his trilogy of vocal works, Carter

231

has turned since 1981 to new challenges in the purely instrumental sphere. As its title suggests, the *Triple Duo* (1982–3) splits its instrumentation by family into three pairs. But the commission (from the Fires of London) also specified that the work be performable without conductor, thus compelling Carter for once to relate his cross-tempos to a common pulse. His solution was to couch the argument of his flute/clarinet duo in rhythmic threes as against the fours of the violin/cello duo and the fives of the piano and percussion. As if in defiance of this apparent compromise, the beginning and end of the piece sound deceptively the most random of any of his works, while much of the intervening dialectic is conducted with the high spirits of a divertimento.

Penthode (1984–5), commissioned for the Ensemble Intercontemporain, is by contrast not only Carter's longest large-ensemble score since the 1960s but also his most elaborate study in multiple structure: its 20 players are divided into five quartets of mixed family (one quartet consists of trumpet, trombone, harp, and violin, another of flute, horn, marimba, and double bass, and so on), and an ever evolving melodic line is passed continuously among the quartets. Yet the viola solo which gradually summons the five groups into being at the outset seems also to relate, in its improvisatory style, to four short pieces completed between the *Triple Duo* and *Penthode*. The shortness is material: Carter appears deliberately to have set himself the task of concentrating some of his procedures into tighter time-spans. Certainly the cross-cutting of material and mood in *Changes* (1983) for solo guitar creates the sense of a microcosm of his larger works, just as its harmonic structure of intervallic permutations around a sequence of nodes (suggested by change-ringing) is a distillation of his more elaborate pitch schemes – to all of which *Riconoscenza* for solo violin (1984) sounds like a still shorter, purer double. By contrast, the bubblings of the flute and clarinet duet, *Esprit rude/esprit doux* ("Rough breathing/smooth breathing," 1984), compound more the effect of a single layer of one of Carter's multiple structures, for once extracted and exhibited for itself, while the *Canon for 4* (1984) is a masterly re-animation in his current manner of a strict contrapuntal procedure – canon by simultaneous inversion, retrograde, and retrograde inversion – which he essayed long before in the second movement of the *Canonic Suite*. In 1986, Carter complemented these with a three-minute flourish, *A Celebration of some 100 × 150 Notes*, for full orchestra, commissioned by the Houston Symphony Orchestra for the 150th anniversary of the founding of the State of Texas in 1987. This evolves as a series of fanfares, each built round one of 11 possible intervals which are also combined in an all-interval chord that dominates the piece. In its volatile fluctuations between ensemble groupings – there is even a solo for celeste – and massive tuttis, *A Celebration* sounds like a distillation of the Concerto for Orchestra and A Symphony of Three Orchestras.

That these short pieces in no way imply a slackening of Carter's grasp has been confirmed not only by the scale of *Penthode* but also by that of the String Quartet no.4 (1985–6), which is some minutes longer than either no.2 or no.3. And while the four instrumental "characters" of the latest quartet resemble those of no.2 grown (a little) more compatible over the years, Carter has countered their potential garrulousness with a new interest in the possibilities of unexpected silences to articulate, heighten, and question process and mood. If some of the faster passages in the continuous four-movement structure take on an ironic neatness, almost suggesting an echo of the Classical divertimento origins of the quartet tradition itself, the epilogue, with its three-way dialectic of tranced and tumultuous textures with long silences, attains a real sense of mystery. And that Carter is likely to continue in fruitful dialectic with his own compositional past is suggested by the Piano Concerto-like format of his one-movement Oboe Concerto commissioned for Heinz Holliger by Paul Sacher and begun in 1986. The oboe is surrounded by a concertino group of violas and percussion against a ripieno chamber orchestra of flute, trumpet, trombone, and strings (without violas). But the composer typically adds, "I have been concerned with developing different characters for the oboe than the ones usually assigned to it in Romantic or Baroque music." Meanwhile he is contemplating a Violin Concerto for Ole Böhn and commissions from the New York PO and Chicago SO.

Carter's mature output reveals an enterprise somewhat at variance with most of his contemporaries, for the major achievements of Copland, Shostakovich, Dallapiccola, Lutosławski, Britten, and Tippett have been principally expressions of personal sensibility rather than attempts to expand the language. His aim to complement the innovations of the earlier modern masters in the handling of pitch (Schoenberg), rhythm (Stravinsky), and texture (Varèse) with parallel developments in the domain of timing, through the large-scale integration of tempo relationships and harmonic backgrounds, can be compared, in his own generation, only with that of Messiaen. But where Messiaen has amplified the static Debussian hierarchies, excelling in color and decoration, Carter is all dialectic and movement, displaying a grasp of dynamic form comparable, among 20th-century composers, only with Berg. The result is music of genuine difficulty, not only because of the complexities created, for instance, by cross-tempos, but also, as Rosen has pointed out, because of the way these banish coordinating strong beats. There was a period, in the 1950s and 1960s, when Carter's one arguable weakness – the packing of his scenarios with incident to the detriment of dramatic economy – seemed a real stumbling block for orchestras. But younger generations of virtuoso soloists and ensemble players have proved ever more eager to tackle, and quick to master, the unique challenges of each new Carter piece as it appears.

WORKS

STAGE

Philoctetes (incidental music, Sophocles), T, Bar, male chorus, ob, perc, 1931, unpubd; Cambridge, MA, 15 March 1933

Mostellaria (incidental music, Plautus), T, Bar, male chorus, chamber orch, 1936, unpubd; Cambridge, MA, 15 April 1936

Pocahontas (ballet legend, 1), pf, 1936, Keene, NH, 17 Aug 1936, withdrawn, orch version, 1938–9; New York, 24 May 1939, cond. F. Kitzinger

Much Ado about Nothing (incidental music, Shakespeare), 1937, withdrawn

The Minotaur (ballet), 1947; New York, 26 March 1947, cond. L. Barzin

ORCHESTRAL

Symphony, 1937, withdrawn

The Ball Room Guide (ballet suite), 1937, inc., withdrawn [Polka used in Prelude, Fanfare and Polka]

English Horn Concerto, 1937, inc., withdrawn

Prelude, Fanfare and Polka, small orch, 1938, unpubd

Suite, from Pocahontas, 1939, rev. 1960

Symphony no.1, 1942, rev. 1954; Rochester, NY, 27 April 1944, cond. H. Hanson

Holiday Overture, 1944, rev. 1961; Frankfurt am Main, Germany, 1946, cond. H. Blümer

Suite, from The Minotaur, 1947

Elegy, str, 1952 [arr. of Elegy, vc, pf]; New York, 1 March 1953, cond. D. Broekman

Variations for Orchestra, 1954–5; Louisville, 21 April 1956, cond. R. Whitney

Double Concerto, hpd, pf, 2 chamber orch, 1961; New York, 6 Sept 1961, cond. G. Meier

Piano Concerto, 1964–5; Boston, 6 Jan 1967, cond. Leinsdorf

Concerto for Orchestra, 1968–9; New York, 5 Feb 1970, cond. Bernstein

A Symphony of Three Orchestras, 1976; New York, 17 Feb 1977, cond. Boulez

Penthode, 5 inst qts, 1984–5; London, 26 July 1985, cond. Boulez

A Celebration of Some 100 × 150 Notes, 1986; Houston, 10 April 1987, cond. Commissiona

Oboe Concerto, 1986–7

CHORAL

Tom and Lily (comic opera, 1), 4 solo vv, mixed chorus, chamber orch, 1934, withdrawn

235

Tarantella (Ovid), male chorus, pf 4 hands/orch, 1936; orch version, unpubd [from incidental music to Mostellaria]

The Bridge (oratorio, H. Crane), 1937, inc.

Harvest Home (Herrick), unacc., 1937, unpubd; New York, spr. 1938

Let's be Gay (J. Gay), female chorus, 2 pf, 1937, unpubd; Wells College, spr. 1938

To Music (Herrick), unacc., 1937; New York, spr. 1938

12 madrigals, 3–8vv, 1937, most withdrawn [incl. To Music]

Heart not so heavy as mine (Dickinson), unacc., 1938; New York, 31 March 1939

The Defense of Corinth (Rabelais), speaker, male vv, pf 4 hands, 1941; Cambridge, MA, 12 March 1942

The Harmony of Morning (M. Van Doren), female vv, small orch, 1944; New York, 25 Feb 1945

Musicians Wrestle Everywhere (Dickinson), mixed vv, str ad lib, 1945; New York, 12 Feb 1946

Emblems (A. Tate), male vv, pf, 1947, perf. 1952

SOLO VOCAL

My Love is in a Light Attire (Joyce), 1v, pf, 1928, unpubd; other Joyce settings, late 1920s, lost

Tell me where is fancy bred? (Shakespeare), A, gui, 1938

Three Poems of Robert Frost, Mez/Bar, pf, 1943: Dust of Snow, The Rose Family, The Line Gang; arr. S/T, chamber orch, 1975

Warble for Lilac-Time (Whitman), S/T, pf/small orch, 1943, rev. 1954; Saratoga Springs, NY, 14 Sept 1946

Voyage (H. Crane), Mez/Bar, pf, 1943; New York, 16 March 1947; arr. with small orch, 1975, rev. 1979

The Difference (Van Doren), S, Bar, pf, 1944, unpubd

A Mirror on which to Dwell (E. Bishop), S, fl + pic + a fl, ob + eng hn, cl + E♭ cl + b cl, perc, pf, vn, va, vc, db, 1975: Anaphora, Argument, Sandpiper, Insomnia, A View of the Capitol, O Breath; New York, 24 Feb 1976

Syringa (J. Ashbery, Ancient Gk.), Mez, B, 11 players, 1978; New York, 10 Dec 1978

In Sleep, in Thunder (R. Lowell), T, 14 players, 1981: Dolphin, Across the Yard: La Ignota, Harriet, Dies irae, Careless Night, In Genesis; London, 27 Oct 1982

Work-list

Piano Sonata, late 1920s, withdrawn

3 string quartets, ?c1928, 1935, 1937, withdrawn

Sonata, fl, pf, 1934, withdrawn

Musical Studies, c1938; nos.1–3 rev. as Canonic Suite; no.4, Andante espressivo, withdrawn

Canonic Suite, 4 a sax, 1939; rev. for 4 cl, 1955–6; rev. for 4 sax, 1981

Pastoral, eng hn/va/cl, pf, 1940

Elegy, vc, pf, 1943; arr. str qt, 1946, arr. str orch, 1952, arr. va, pf, 1961

Piano Sonata, 1945–6; New York, broadcast 16 Feb 1947

Woodwind Quintet, 1948; New York, 21 Feb 1949

Sonata, vc, pf, 1948; New York, 27 Feb 1950

Eight Etudes and a Fantasy, fl, ob, cl, bn, 1949–50; New York, 28 Oct 1952

Eight Pieces for Four Timpani, 1 player, 1950–66

String Quartet no.1, 1950–51; New York, 26 Feb 1953

Sonata, fl, ob, vc, hpd, 1952; New York, 19 Nov 1953

String Quartet no.2, 1959; New York, 25 March 1960

String Quartet no.3, 1971; New York, 23 Jan 1973

Canon for 3: in memoriam Igor Stravinsky, 3 equal insts, 1971; New York, 23 Jan 1972

Duo, vn, pf, 1973–4; New York, 21 March 1975

Brass Quintet, 2 tpt, hn, 2 trbn, 1974; London, broadcast 20 Oct 1974

A Fantasy about Purcell's "Fantasia Upon One Note," 2 tpt, hn, 2 trbn, 1974; New York, 13 Jan 1975

Birthday Fanfare for Sir William Glock's 70th, 3 tpt, vib, glock, 1978, unpubd; London, 3 May 1978

Night Fantasies, pf, 1980; Bath, England, 2 June 1980

Triple Duo, vn, vc, fl, cl, pf, perc, 1982–3; New York, 23 April 1983

Changes, gui, 1983; New York, 11 Dec 1983

Canon for 4, Homage to William [Glock], fl, b cl, vn, vc, 1984; Bath, England, 8 June 1984

Esprit rude/esprit doux, fl, cl, 1984, ded. Boulez; Baden-Baden, Germany, 31 March 1985

Riconoscenza per Goffredo Petrassi, vn, 1984; Pontino, nr Rome, 15 June 1984

String Quartet no.4, 1985–6; Miami, 17 Sept 1986

Principal publishers: Associated, Boosey & Hawkes

BIBLIOGRAPHY

P. Rosenfeld: "The Newest American Composers," *MM*, xv (1937–8), 157

R. F. Goldman: "Current Chronicle," *MQ*, xxxvii (1951), 83

A. Skulsky: "Elliott Carter (Study of his works)," *ACAB*, iii/2 (1953), 2

W. Glock: "A Note on Elliott Carter," *Score* (1955), no. 12, p.47

R. F. Goldman: "The Music of Elliott Carter," *MQ*, xliii (1957), 151

Compositores de América/Composers of the Americas, ed. Pan American Union, v (Washington, DC, 1959)

H. Koegler: "Begegnungen mit Elliott Carter," *Melos*, xxvi (1959), 256

A. Copland: "America's Young Men of Music," *Music and Musicians*, ix/4 (1960), 11

O. Daniel: "Carter and Shapero," *Saturday Review*, xliii (17 Dec 1960), 11

R. F. Goldman: "Current Chronicle: New York," *MQ*, xlvi (1960), 361

"Carter, Elliott (Cook)," *CBY 1960*

M. Steinberg: "Elliott Carters 2. Streichquartett," *Melos*, xxviii (1961), 35

K. Stone: "Problems and Methods of Notation," *PNM*, i/2 (1963), 9

I. Stravinsky and R. Craft: *Dialogues and a Diary* (New York, 1963), 47ff

C. Wuorinen: "The Outlook of Young Composers," *PNM*, i/2 (1963), 58

M. Boykan: "Elliott Carter and Postwar Composers," *PNM*, ii/2 (1964), 125

R. Henderson: "Elliot Carter," *Music and Musicians*, xiv/5 (1966), 20

D. Hamilton: "New Craft of the Contemporary Concerto: Carter and Sessions," *HiFi*, xviii/5 (1968), 67

R. Kostelanetz: "The Astounding Success of Elliott Carter," *HiFi*, xviii/5 (1968), 41

——: *Master Minds: Portraits of Contemporary American Artists and Intellectuals* (New York, 1969), 289ff

K. Stone: "Current Chronicle: New York," *MQ*, lv (1969), 559

B. Boretz: "Conversation with Elliott Carter," *PNM*, viii/2 (1970), 1

A. Edwards: *Flawed Words and Stubborn Sounds: a Conversation with Elliott Carter* (New York, 1971)

R. Hurwitz: "Elliott Carter: the Communication of Time," *Changes in the Arts*, no.78 (1972), 10

B. Northcott: "Elliott Carter: Continuity and Coherence," *Music and Musicians*, xx/12 (1972), 28

N. Rorem: "Elliott Carter," *New Republic*, clxvi (26 Feb 1972), 22

R. Jackson, ed.: *Elliott Carter: Sketches and Scores in Manuscript* (New York, 1973)

A. Porter: "Mutual Ordering," *New Yorker*, xlviii (3 Feb 1973), 82 [on String Quartet no.3]

C. Rosen: "One Easy Piece," *New York Review of Books*, xx/2 (1973), 25; repr. in Rosen, 1984 [on Double Conc.]

Bibliography

R. Morgan: "Elliott Carter's String Quartets," *Musical Newsletter*, iv/3 (1974), 3

A. Whittall: "Elliott Carter," *1st American Music Conference: Keele 1975*, ed. P. Dickinson (Keele, England, n.d. [?1977]), 82

A. Clements: "Elliott Carter Views American Music," *Music and Musicians*, xxvi/7 (1978), 32 [review of *The Writings of Elliott Carter*]

Elliott Carter: a 70th Birthday Tribute (London, 1978) [incl. contributions by P. Boulez, P. Fromm, W. Glock, B. Northcott, R. Ponsonby]

M. Mayer: "Elliott Carter: Out of the Desert and into the Concert Hall," *New York Times* (10 Dec 1978)

B. Northcott: "America's Magna Carter," *Sunday Telegraph* (London, 17 Dec 1978)

———: "Carter in Perspective," *MT*, cxix (1978), 1039

M. Steinberg: "Elliott Carter: an American Original at Seventy," *Keynote*, ii/10 (1978), 8

J. F. Weber: *Carter and Schuman*, Discography Series, xix (Utica, NY, 1978)

A. Whittall: "The Writings of Elliott Carter," *Tempo*, no.124 (1978), 40

B. Northcott: "Carter's 'Syringa', " *Tempo*, no.128 (1979), 31

A. Porter: "Famous Orpheus," *New Yorker*, liv (8 Jan 1979), 56 [on Syringa]

D. Schiff: "Carter in the Seventies," *Tempo*, no.130 (1979), 2

L. Kerner: "Creators on Creating: Elliott Carter," *Saturday Review*, vii/12 (1980), 38

H. Gleason and W. Becker: "Elliott Carter," *20th-century American Composers*, Music Literature Outlines, ser. iv (Bloomington, IN, rev. 2/1981), 20 [incl. further bibliography]

A. Porter: "Music in the Silence of the Night," *New Yorker*, lvii (30 Nov 1981), 184

C. Gagne and T. Caras: "Elliott Carter," *Soundpieces: Interviews with American Composers* (Metuchen, NJ, 1982), 87 [on Night Fantasies]

D. Schiff: " 'In Sleep, in Thunder': Elliott Carter's Portrait of Robert Lowell," *Tempo*, no.142 (1982), 2

J. Bernard: "Spacial Sets in Recent Music of Elliott Carter," *Music Analysis*, ii/1 (1983), 5

W. Crutchfield: "Paul Jacobs Talks about Carter and Messiaen," *Keynote*, vii/10 (1983), 18

J. Rockwell: "American Intellectual Composers & the 'Ideal Public', " *All American Music: Composition in the Late Twentieth Century* (New York, 1983), 37

D. Schiff: *The Music of Elliott Carter* (New York, 1983)

A. W. Mead: "Pitch Structure in Elliott Carter's String Quartet no.3," *PNM*, xxii/1–2 (1983–4), 31

239

M. M. Coonrod: *Aspects of Form in Selected String Quartets of the Twentieth-century* (diss., Peabody Conservatory, 1984) [on String Quartet no.3]

C. R. Kies: *A Discussion of the Harmonic Organization in the First Movement of Elliott Carter's "Sonata for Violoncello and Piano" in the Light of Certain Developments in 19th and Early 20th Century Music* (diss., Brandeis U., 1984)

R. M. Meckna: *The Rise of the American Composer-Critic: Aaron Copland, Roger Sessions, Virgil Thomson, and Elliott Carter in the Periodical "Modern Music," 1924–1946* (diss., U. of California, Santa Barbara, 1984)

B. Northcott: "Fascinatin' Modulation," *New York Review of Books*, xxxi/9 (1984), 18

W. C. Pflugradt: *Elliott Carter and the Variation Process* (diss., Indiana U., 1984)

C. Rosen: *The Musical Languages of Elliott Carter* (Washington, DC, 1984) [incl. interview and M. Cundiff: "A Guide to Elliott Carter Research Materials at the Library of Congress Music Division"]

G. J. Detweiler: *The Choral Music of Elliott Carter* (diss., U. of Illinois, Urbana, 1985)

R. Johnston: "Elliott Carter's Imagery Drawn from Modern Life," *Music Magazine*, viii/5 (1985), 12

D. Harvey: *The Later Music of Elliott Carter: a Study in Music Theory and Analysis* (diss., U. of Oxford, 1986)

A. Porter: "Quaternion," *New Yorker*, lxiii (24 Nov 1986), 114 [On String Quartet no.4]

L. Schwartz: "Four Quartets; Elliott Carter and the Individual Voice," *Boston Phoenix* (18 Nov 1986), §III, 9

SAMUEL BARBER

Richard Jackson
Barbara Heyman

CHAPTER EIGHT

Samuel Barber

1. CAREER. Samuel Barber was born in West Chester, Pennsylvania, on 9 March 1910; he had his first piano lessons at six and began composing when he was seven; he also had cello lessons briefly. Among his juvenile pieces was a short opera, *The Rose Tree*, which was performed by him and his sister Sara. This early attempt could be seen as the beginning of an inclination towards vocal music, an important area of his work as a mature composer. He was supported and encouraged in his respect by his mother's sister, the contralto Louise Homer, and her husband Sidney Homer, a composer who concentrated almost exclusively on song. (Barber edited an anthology of Homer's songs as a tribute to his uncle in 1943.) As a teenager Barber was organist at Westminster Presbyterian Church and attended the West Chester High School, graduating in 1926. His academic musical training began at the age of 14 when he entered the Curtis Institute as a member of its first class in 1924. (Its founder, Mary Louise Curtis Bok, was to become one of Barber's devoted benefactors.) There he was exposed to a group of talented musicians; he studied piano with Boyle and later with Vengerova, composition with Scalero, and conducting with Reiner. He was also interested in developing his baritone voice and studied singing with Emilio Edoardo de Gogorza. His vocal progress was encouraging enough for him to entertain the notion for a time of pursuing a singing career. He gave vocal recitals at the Curtis Institute and, after graduation, studied with John Braun in Vienna and sang publicly there. In

1935 he was heard in recitals on NBC radio and recorded his *Dover Beach*.

During his eight years at the Curtis Institute, Barber's skill as a composer was firmly established. A number of the works composed during these years – such as the first two songs of op.2, the Serenade for string quartet, *Dover Beach*, and the Cello Sonata – are not those of a merely talented student: they are the products of an assured composer. These works, along with many later ones, became standards in the American repertory. Furthermore, elements of Barber's style that emerged during the student years – the long lyric lines, the felicitous text-setting, and the knowing exploitation of instrumental color and technique – were not radically changed in later years.

The first of Barber's numerous awards was the Bearns Prize of Columbia University in 1928 for his Violin Sonata. This enabled him to travel abroad (to Italy) for the first time. He won the Bearns Prize a second time in 1933, for the overture to *The School for Scandal*, his first work to be performed by a major orchestra. In 1935 and again in 1936 he traveled in Europe and composed at the American Academy in Rome as the result of Pulitzer Traveling Scholarships and the Rome Prize. The compositions produced during these years – the *Music for a Scene from Shelley*, the First Symphony, and the String Quartet – were performed immediately in New York and Rome. The symphony was played in the USA for the first time by Rodzinski and the Cleveland Orchestra in January 1937. Rodzinski conducted it again in July at the Salzburg Festival – the first time an American work was performed there. In 1935 Barber met Toscanini in Italy and showed him some of his work. Three years later Toscanini conducted the NBC SO in premières of two works by Barber on the same program, the *First Essay* for orchestra and the Adagio for Strings; the latter is an orchestral transcription of the second movement of the String Quartet. Toscanini also

18. Samuel Barber, c1972

recorded the Adagio, and it became Barber's most popular and most frequently performed piece.

Barber returned to the Curtis Institute in 1939 as a teacher of composition and remained there until 1942, though he had no great liking for this kind of work and never again accepted a teaching position. He was elected to the National Institute of Arts and Letters in 1941 and in 1958 to the American Academy of Arts and Letters. In 1943 he purchased a house in Mount Kisco, New York, with Menotti, who had been a fellow student at the Curtis Institute and his traveling companion in Europe. Barber was to do most of his composing there until 1974, when he and Menotti sold the house. In April 1943 he was conscripted into the US Army and assigned to the Army Air Force. During the first year of his military service, spent largely in Fort Worth, he composed two works, the *Commando March* for band and the Second Symphony (dedicated to the Army Air Force), on commission from the Air Force. The latter work was performed by Koussevitzky and the Boston SO in Boston and New York, but it did not find wide acceptance. Barber revised the symphony in 1947 but apparently was never very satisfied with it; 24 years after its composition he withdrew it and destroyed the manuscript score and performance materials. The second movement, however, exists in a revised version as *Night Flight*.

Barber was released from military service at the end of World War II, and he returned to Europe almost immediately on a Guggenheim Fellowship. He was made a consultant to the American Academy in Rome in 1948. During the later 1940s and throughout the 1950s he composed a number of large works as the result of important commissions. The Cello Concerto (which won the 1947 New York Music Critics' Circle Award) was commissioned by John Nicholas Brown for Garbousova, and the ballet *Medea* (*The Cave of the Heart*) by the Ditson Fund for Martha Graham. Another dance score, *Souvenirs*, was commissioned by

246

Lincoln Kirstein for the Ballet Society of New York. Three vocal works – *Knoxville: Summer of 1915*, *Hermit Songs*, and *Prayers of Kierkegaard* – were commissioned respectively by Eleanor Steber, the Coolidge Foundation of the Library of Congress, and the Koussevitzky Foundation. The Piano Sonata was written on a League of Composers commission.

The most ambitious work produced by Barber in the 1950s was the four-act opera *Vanessa*, completed in 1957, with a libretto by Menotti. After its première season the Metropolitan Opera staged the work during two other seasons, 1958–9 and 1964–5. It was also performed at the Salzburg Festival in 1958. Sargeant described the score as "both complex and highly charged with emotional meaning"; he also considered that Barber demonstrated "that an American composer with sufficient knowledge of and feeling for the great international operatic tradition can turn out a near masterpiece in the genre." *Vanessa* won the 1958 Pulitzer Prize for music.

A second Pulitzer Prize was awarded to Barber for his 1962 Piano Concerto, commissioned by his publisher, G. Schirmer, on its centenary. At its première Schonberg drew parallels between the concerto and Prokofiev's piano writing and found in the piece "a sense of confidence in the entire conception – the confidence that comes only from an experienced composer engaged in a work that interests him." Barber's biggest work of the decade, however, was again a full-scale opera, *Antony and Cleopatra*, with a libretto by Zeffirelli after Shakespeare. It was commissioned by the Metropolitan Opera for the opening of its new house at Lincoln Center in September 1966. *Antony and Cleopatra* was largely a failure with the critics and with the public; the score was considered generally weak, but it was by no means condemned out of hand. While Peter Heyworth considered its "late romantic style" devoid of originality, "it clearly came from the workshop of a composer who knew what he was about, had

pondered the problems of opera, of combining action and movement with the need for lyrical expansion, and who had a welcome
feeling for the human voice." There was widespread agreement
that the most prominent factor in the opera's failure was the
production, designed and directed by Zeffirelli. Desmond Shawe-
Taylor wrote that "throughout the evening there was a recurrent
impression that Barber's music, rich in substance and sometimes
very engaging, was being submerged beneath the glitter and
complexity of the spectacle." With highly elaborate sets and
costumes, a large chorus, dancers, hundreds of supernumeraries,
and live animals, the production was decidedly old fashioned,
clumsy, and often confused. Barber recalled the failure later with
equanimity, but he left New York immediately after the première
and remained in virtual seclusion for about five years in the Italian
Alps. It was announced in April 1974 that *Antony and Cleopatra*
would be revised and the libretto reshaped by Menotti. The
première of this revised version was presented by the Opera
Theater of the Juilliard School in New York on 6 February 1975;
it was far more successful with critics and audiences than the
original version.

Barber produced one distinct oddity in the late 1960s: a third
version of his most famous piece, the Adagio for Strings, set as
a choral work to the text of the *Agnus Dei*. He returned to the
concert scene in 1971 with two commissioned works, *The Lovers*
and *Fadograph of a Yestern Scene*. Barber composed little in his
last years; he died in New York of cancer on 23 January 1981,
at the age of 70.

2. STYLE. In his notice of the revised version of the First Symphony, Thomson commented that Barber's chief problem seemed
to be "laying the ghost of romanticism without resorting to
violence." This idea proved to be off the mark, however, for not
only did Barber not lay the Romantic ghost (with or without

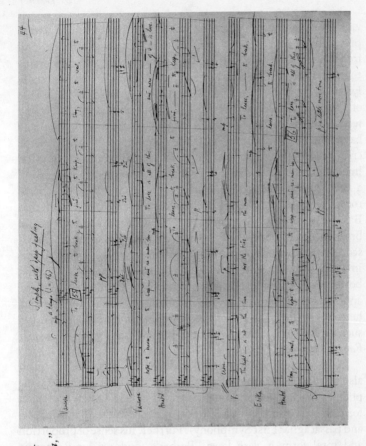

19. *Excerpt from the autograph vocal score of Barber's opera "Vanessa," completed in 1957*

249

violence), he apparently never wanted to: his music is always primarily an expression of personal emotion. He could be (and frequently has been) classified as a neoromantic, if indeed this too general term has much meaning. Barber's art is essentially lyric and dramatic, and his harmonic language is basically that of the late 19th century. Much of his music is based on key relationships. In the 1940s he began to incorporate elements having more in common with the contemporary idiom. Some critics have pointed to the Violin Concerto, which has angular lines and diatonic dissonance in the last movement, as signaling a new stylistic "period" in Barber's music, but this is perhaps too strong an interpretation. The concerto demonstrated that Barber had simply (and importantly) added to his resources and broadened the scope of his artistic choices. His later orchestral scores have fairly dense harmonic textures but are always rooted in a key or tonal center. At least two movements of the flamboyant Piano Sonata, however, incorporate 12-tone rows (these appearances seem to be unique in his music). On the other hand he could produce a work of great simplicity, skirting triviality, such as *Souvenirs*, which recalls the elegant café style of Walton's *Façade*.

In his discipline and use of traditional forms, Barber could also be considered something of a classicist. The concertos, symphonies, and other instrumental works adhere loosely to sonata form; he has also used fugue (most notably in the Piano Sonata) and passacaglia (First Symphony). Further, his sense of proportion and total form is very keen. Barber's fondness for Romantic fullness and lyricism, combined with Classical procedures, places him in a position within his era somewhat similar to that of Brahms in his. Also, neither Barber nor Brahms was known as an innovator and both produced works of substance and beauty with a distinct personal stamp. If the entrepreneur and knowledgeable contemporary-music enthusiast Ashley Pettis could write in a letter to the *New York Times* in 1938 that he found Barber's music "utterly anachronistic as the utterance of a young man of 28, A.D. 1938," Hans Heinsheimer could write of it in 1980 that "it speaks its own language, [and] shows a very personal, recognizable handwriting which is the trademark of any important composer." Barber himself made a statement in 1971 that could serve as his credo as a composer:

[When] I'm writing music for words, then I immerse myself in those words, and I let the music flow out of them. When I write an abstract piano sonata or a concerto, I write what I feel. I'm not a self-conscious composer . . . it is said that I have no style at all but that doesn't matter. I just go on doing, as they say, my thing. I believe this takes a certain courage.

WORKS
(all published unless otherwise stated)

op.

STAGE

–	The Rose Tree (opera, A. S. Brosius), 1920, inc., unpubd; West Chester, PA
–	One Day of Spring (incidental music, M. Kennedy), 1v, str, 1935, lost, unpubd; Winter Park, FL, 24 Jan 1935
23	Medea (Serpent Heart) (ballet, M. Graham), 1946, New York, 10 May 1946; rev. as The Cave of the Heart, New York, 27 Feb 1947; arr. as orch suite, 1947, Philadelphia, 5 Dec 1947, Philadelphia Orchestra, cond. Ormandy; Medea's Meditation and Dance of Vengeance, op.23a, 1953, New York, 2 Feb 1956, New York PO, cond. Mitropoulos
28	Souvenirs (ballet, T. Bolender), 1952, New York, 15 Nov 1955; arr. as suite, pf 4 hands, 1952, NBC television, July 1952; suite, orch, 1952, Chicago, 12 Nov 1953, Chicago SO, cond. Reiner
32	Vanessa (opera, 4, Menotti), 1956–7, New York, 15 Jan 1958, Metropolitan Opera, cond. Mitropoulos; rev. 1964
35	A Hand of Bridge (opera, 1, Menotti), 4 solo vv, chamber orch, 1953; Spoleto, Italy, 17 June 1959
40	Antony and Cleopatra (opera, 3, Zeffirelli, after Shakespeare), 1966, New York, 16 Sept 1966, Metropolitan Opera, cond. Schippers; rev. 1974, New York, 6 Feb 1975, cond. Conlon

ORCHESTRAL

5   The School for Scandal, ov., 1931–3; Philadelphia, 30 Aug 1933, Philadelphia Orchestra, cond. Smallens

7   Music for a Scene from Shelley, 1933; New York, 24 March 1935, Philharmonic Symphony Society, cond. W. Janssen

9   Symphony in One Movement [no.1], 1936, Rome, 13 Dec 1936, Augusteo Orchestra, cond. B. Molinari; rev. 1942

11   Adagio for Strings, 1936 [arr. of 2nd movt of Str Qt]; New York, 5 Nov 1938, NBC SO, cond. Toscanini; arr. org, W. Strickland, 1949

12   [First] Essay for Orchestra, 1937; New York, 5 Nov 1938, NBC SO, cond. Toscanini

14   Violin Concerto, 1939; Philadelphia, 7 Feb 1941, A. Spalding, Philadelphia Orchestra, cond. Ormandy

17   Second Essay, 1942; New York, 16 April 1942, Philharmonic Symphony Society, cond. Walter

–   Funeral March [based on Army Air Corps Song], 1943, unpubd

–   Commando March, band, 1943; Atlantic City, NJ, sum. 1943, Army Air Force Band, cond. Barber

19   Symphony no.2, 1944, Boston, 3 March 1944, Boston SO, cond. Koussevitzky; rev. 1947, Philadelphia, 21 Jan 1948; 2nd movt rev. as Night Flight, orch, op.19a, 1964, Cleveland, 8 Oct 1964, Cleveland SO, cond. Szell

21   Capricorn Concerto, fl, ob, tpt, str, 1944; New York, 8 Oct 1944, Saidenberg Little SO, cond. D. Saidenberg

22   Cello Concerto, 1945; Boston, 5 April 1946, R. Garbousova, Boston SO, cond. Koussevitzky

–   Horizon, *c*1945, unpubd; Merrick, NY, 19 Jan 1985, Merrick SO, cond. C. Gouse

–   Adventure, fl, cl, hn, harp, "exotic" insts, 1954, unpubd; New York, CBS television, 25 Nov 1954, cond. Barber

36   Toccata festiva, org, orch, 1960; Philadelphia, 30 Sept 1960, P. Callaway, Philadelphia Orchestra, cond. Ormandy

37   Die natali, chorale preludes for Christmas, 1960; Boston, 22 Dec 1960, Boston SO, cond. Munch

38   Piano Concerto, 1962, New York, 24 Sept 1962, J. Browning, Boston SO, cond. Leinsdorf; 2nd movt transcr. fl, pf, 1961

–   Mutations from Bach, brass choir, timp, 1967; New York, 7 Oct 1968

–	Variations on Happy Birthday [to Eugene Ormandy], 1970; Philadelphia, 24 Jan 1970
44	Fadograph of a Yestern Scene (after Joyce: Finnegans Wake), 2 solo vv, orch, 1971; Pittsburgh, 11 Sept 1971, B. Valente, J. Simon, Pittsburgh SO, cond. Steinberg
47	Third Essay, 1978; New York, 14 Sept 1978, New York PO, cond. Mehta
48 posth.	Canzonetta, ob, str, orchd C. Turner, 1977–8; New York, 17 Dec 1981, H. Gomberg, New York PO, cond. Mehta

CHORAL

XIII	Christmas Eve: a Trio with Solos, 2 solo vv, SAA, org, *c*1924, unpubd
–	Motetto (Job), 4vv, 8vv, 1930, unpubd
8/1–2	The Virgin Martyrs (Siegebert of Gembloux, trans. H. Waddell), SSAA, 1935, Philadelphia, CBS radio, 1 May 1939; Let Down the Bars, O Death (E. Dickinson), SATB, 1936
–	Mary Ruane (J. Stephens), 4vv, *c*1936, unpubd
–	Peggy Mitchell (Stephens), 4vv, *c*1936, unpubd
–	God's Grandeur (G. M. Hopkins), double chorus, 1938, unpubd; Shippensburg, PA, 31 Jan 1938, Westminster Choir, cond. J. F. Williamson
15	A Stopwatch and an Ordnance Map (S. Spender), male vv, 3 kettledrums, 1940; Philadelphia, 23 April 1940
–	Ave Maria (after Josquin Desprez), 4vv, *c*1940, unpubd
16	Reincarnations (Stephens): Mary Hynes, Anthony O'Daly, The Coolin', 4vv, 1937–40
–	Ad "bibinem" cum me regaret ad cenam (V. Fortunatus), 4vv unacc., 1943
–	Long Live Louise and Sidney Homer, canon, 1944, unpubd; Winter Park, FL, 9 Jan 1945
30	Prayers of Kierkegaard (Kierkegaard), S, A ad lib, T ad lib, chorus, orch, 1954; Boston, 3 Dec 1954, L. Price, St. Cecilia Chorus, Boston SO, cond. Munch
–	Chorale for Ascension Day (Easter Chorale) (P. Browning), chorus, brass, timp, org ad lib, 1964; Washington, DC, 7 May 1964
11	Agnus Dei, chorus, org/pf, 1967 [arr. of 2nd movt of Str Qt]
42	Twelfth Night (L. Lee), To be Sung on the Water (L. Bogan), 4vv unacc., 1968

43	The Lovers (P. Neruda), Bar, chorus, orch, 1971; Philadelphia, 22 Sept 1971, T. Kraus, Temple University Choirs, Philadelphia Orchestra, cond. Ormandy

CHAMBER

–	Fantasie, 2 pf, 1924, unpubd; Philadelphia, 29 April 1924, Barber, Daisy Barber
XVI	Sonata in Modern Form, 2 pf, *c*1925, unpubd
1	Serenade, str qt/str orch, 1928; Philadelphia, 5 May 1930, Swastika Quartet
4	Violin Sonata, f, 1928, lost, unpubd; Philadelphia, 10 Dec 1928, G. Gilbert, Barber
6	Cello Sonata, 1932; New York, 5 March 1933, O. Cole
11	String Quartet, 1936; Rome, 14 Dec 1936, Pro Arte Quartet [arrs. for str and chorus, org, see op.11, ORCHESTRAL and CHORAL]
–	Wedding March, vn, vc, pf, 1940, unpubd
31	Summer Music, wind qnt, 1955; Detroit, 20 March 1956
38a	Canzone (Elegy) fl, pf, 1961 [transcr. of 2nd movt of Pf Conc.]

SOLO INSTRUMENTAL

I/3	Melody in F, pf, 1917, unpubd
–	Sadness, pf, 1917, unpubd
I/4	Largo, pf, 1918, unpubd
I/5	War Song, pf, 1918, unpubd
III/1	At Twilight, pf, 1919, unpubd
III/2	Lullaby, pf, 1919, unpubd
X/2	Themes, pf, *c*1923, movts 2–3 unpubd [movt 1 = Three Sketches no.3]
–	Three Sketches, pf: Love Song (to Mother), To my Steinway (to Number 220601), Minuet (to Sara) [= Themes: movt 1], 1923–4
–	[Untitled work] ("Laughingly and briskly"), pf, *c*1924, unpubd
–	Petite berceuse (to Jean), pf, *c*1924, unpubd
–	Prelude to a Tragic Drama, pf, 1925, unpubd
–	To Longwood Gardens, org, 1925, unpubd
–	Main Street, pf, *c*1925, unpubd
–	Fresh from West Chester (Some Jazzings): Poison Ivy, a Country Dance, 1925; Let's Sit it out, I'd Rather Watch (I Sam Barber did it with my little hatchet, a walls [sic]), 1926; unpubd
–	Three Essays, pf, 1926, unpubd

–	Four Chorale Preludes, kbd, 1927, unpubd
–	Four Partitas, kbd, 1927, unpubd
–	Prelude and Fugue, b, org, 1927, unpubd; Philadelphia, 10 Dec 1928, C. Weinrich
–	Pieces for Carillon: Round, Allegro, Legend, 1930–31, unpubd; Mountain Lake, FL
–	Suite for Carillon, 4 pieces, 1932
–	Two Interludes (Intermezzi), pf, 1931–2, unpubd; New York, 1 March 1939, J. Behrend
20	Excursions, pf, 1942–4; New York, 1945, Horowitz
26	Sonata, pf, 1949; Havana, 9 Dec 1949, Horowitz
–	Wondrous Love, variations on a shape-note hymn, org, 1958
33	Nocturne (Homage to John Field), pf, 1959; New York, 1959, Browning
37	Stille Nacht [arr. of Silent Night from Die natali], org, 1960
–	After the Concert, pf, *c*1973, unpubd
46	Ballade, pf, 1977; Fort Worth, Sept 1977, S. De Groote

SONGS
(1v, pf, unless otherwise stated)

–	Sometime (to Mother), Mez, 1917, unpubd; West Chester, PA, 25 April 1926
–	Why Not (K. Parsons), 1917, unpubd
II/3	In the Firelight, 1918, unpubd
II/4	Isabel (J. G. Whittier), 1919, unpubd
–	An Old Song (C. Kingsley), 1921, unpubd
–	Hunting Song (J. Bennett), Bar, pf, cornet, *c*1921, unpubd
V/2	Thy Will be Done (3 verses from The Wanderer), *c*1922, unpubd
VII	Seven Nursery Songs (to Sara), S, 1920–23, unpubd; West Chester, PA, 25 April 1926
–	October Weather (Barber), S, *c*1923, unpubd; West Chester, PA, 25 April 1926
–	Dere Two Fella Joe, high v, 1924, unpubd; West Chester, PA, 25 April 1926
–	Minuet, S, A, pf, *c*1924, unpubd
XIV	My Fairyland (R. T. Kerlin), 1924, unpubd; West Chester, PA, 25 April 1926
–	Summer is Coming (after A. Tennyson), 2 solo vv, pf, *c*1924, unpubd; West Chester, PA, 4 June 1927

255

–	Two Poems of the Wind (F. MacCleod): Little Children of the World, Longing, 1924, unpubd; West Chester, PA, 25 April 1926
–	A Slumber Song of the Madonna (A. Noyes), 1v, org, 1925, unpubd; West Chester, PA, 25 April 1926
–	Fantasy in Purple (L. Hughes), 1925, unpubd; West Chester, PA, 25 April 1926
–	Lady when I Behold the Roses (anon.), 1925, unpubd; West Chester, PA, 25 April 1926
–	La nuit (A. Meurath), 1925, unpubd; West Chester, PA, 25 April 1926
–	Two Songs of Youth: I Never Thought that Youth would Go (J. B. Rittenhouse), Invocation to Youth (L. Binyon), 1925, unpubd; West Chester, PA, 25 April 1926
–	Addio di Orfeo (C. Monteverdi), 1926, arr. 1v, str, hpd, unpubd
–	An Earnest Suit to his Unkind Mistress not to Forsake him (Sir T. Wyatt), 1926, unpubd
–	Ask me to Rest (E. H. S. Terry), 1926, unpubd
–	Au clair de la lune, 1926, unpubd; West Chester, PA, 25 April 1926
–	Hey Nonny No (Christ Church MS), 1926, unpubd
–	Man (H. Wolfe), 1926, unpubd; West Chester, PA, 25 April 1926
–	Music when Soft Voices Die (P. B. Shelley), *c*1926, unpubd; West Chester, PA, 25 April 1926
–	Thy Love (E. Browning), 1926, unpubd; West Chester, PA, 25 April 1926
–	Watchers (D. Cornwell), 1926, unpubd; West Chester, PA, 25 April 1926
–	Dance (J. Stephens), 1927, lost, unpubd; London, 25 June 1935
–	Mother I cannot Mind my Wheel (W. S. Landor), 1927, unpubd
–	Only of Thee and Me (L. Untermeyer), *c*1927, lost, unpubd; West Chester, PA, 4 June 1927
–	Rounds: A Lament (Shelley); To Electra (R. Herrick); Dirge: Weep for the World's Wrong; Farewell; Not I (R. L. Stevenson); Of a Rose is al myn Song (anon., 1350); Sunset (Stevenson); The Moon (Shelley); Sun of the Sleepless (G. G. Byron); The Throstle (Tennyson); When Day is Gone (R. Burns); Late, Late, so Late (Tennyson: Guinevere); 3 vv, pf, 1927, unpubd
–	There's Nae Lark (A. Swinburne), 1927, unpubd
2	Three Songs: The Daisies (Stephens), 1927, With Rue my Heart is

	Laden (A. E. Houseman), 1928, Bessie Bobtail (Stephens), 1934; Philadelphia, 23 Oct 1934
–	The Shepherd to his Love and the Nymph's Reply, 1928, unpubd
3	Dover Beach (M. Arnold), Mez/Bar, str qt, 1931; New York, 5 March 1933
–	Love at the Door (from Meleager, trans. J. A. Symonds), 1934, unpubd
–	Serenades (G. Dillon), 1934, unpubd
–	Love's Caution (W. H. Davies), 1935, unpubd
–	Night Wanderers (Davies), 1935, unpubd
–	Of that so Sweet Imprisonment (J. Joyce), 1935, unpubd
–	Peace (from Bhartrihari, trans. P. E. More), 1935, unpubd
–	Stopping by Woods on a Sunny Evening (R. Frost), 1935, unpubd
–	Strings in the Earth and Air (Joyce), 1935, unpubd
10	Three Songs (Joyce: Chamber Music): Rain has Fallen, Sleep Now, 1935, Rome, 22 April 1936; I Hear an Army, 1936, Philadelphia, 7 March 1937, arr. 1v, orch
–	The Beggar's Song (Davies), 1936, unpubd; Rome, 22 April 1936
–	In the Dark Pinewood (Joyce), 1937, unpubd
13	Four Songs: A Nun Takes the Veil (G. M. Hopkins), 1937; The Secrets of the Old (W. B. Yeats), 1938, New York, 12 Feb 1939; Sure on this Shining Night (J. Agee), 1938, arr. 1v, orch, and chorus, pf; Nocturne (F. Prokosch), 1940, arr. 1v, orch; perf. complete, Philadelphia, 4 April 1941
–	Song for a New House, 1v, fl, pf, 1940, unpubd
–	Between Dark and Dark (K. Chapin), 1942, lost, unpubd
18	Two Songs: The Queen's Face on a Summery Coin (R. Horan), 1942; Monks and Raisins (J. G. Villa), 1943; New York, 22 Feb 1944
24	Knoxville: Summer of 1915 (Agee), high v, orch, 1947, unpubd, Boston, 9 April 1948, E. Steber, Boston SO, cond. Koussevitzky; rev. 1v, chamber orch, 1950, Washington, DC, Dumbarton Oaks, 1 April 1950
25	Nuvoletta (from Joyce: Finnegans Wake), 1947
27	Melodies passagères (R. M. Rilke): Puisque tout passe, Un cygne, Tombeau dans un parc, Le clocher chante, Départ, 1950–51; nos. 1, 4, and 5 perf. Washington, DC, 1 April 1950; perf. complete, Washington, DC, 21 Jan 1952
29	Hermit Songs (Irish texts of 8th–13th centuries): At Saint Patrick's Purgatory (trans. S. O'Faolain), Church Bells at Night (trans. H. Mumford Jones), Saint Ita's Vision (trans. C. Kallman), The

257

Heavenly Banquet (trans. O'Faolain), The Crucifixion (anon., from The Speckled Book, trans. Mumford Jones), Sea-snatch (trans. W. H. Auden), Promiscuity (trans. Auden), The Monk and the Cat (trans. Auden), The Praises of God (trans. Auden), The Desire for Hermitage (trans. O'Faolain), 1952–3; Washington, DC, 30 Oct 1953, L. Price, Barber

39   Andromache's Farewell (from Euripides: The Trojan Women, trans. J. P. Creagh), S, orch, 1962; New York, 4 April 1963, M. Arroyo, New York PO, cond. Schippers

41   Despite and Still: A Last Song (R. Graves), My Lizard (T. Rilke), In the Wilderness (Graves), Solitary Hotel (from Joyce: Ulysses), Despite and Still (Graves), 1968–9; New York, 27 April 1969

45   Three Songs: Now I have Fed and Eaten Up the Rose (G. Keller, trans. Joyce), A Green Lowland of Pianos (J. Harasymowicz, trans. C. Milosz), O Boundless, Boundless Evening (G. Heym, trans. C. Middleton), 1972; New York, 30 April 1974

MSS in *DLC*
Principal publisher: G. Schirmer

BIBLIOGRAPHY

A. Copland: "From the '20's to the '40's and Beyond," *MM*, xx (1942–3), 80

R. Horan: "Samuel Barber," *MM*, xx (1943), 161

"Barber, Samuel," *CBY 1944*

N. Broder: "The Music of Samuel Barber," *MQ*, xxxiv (1948), 325

H. Dexter: "Samuel Barber and his Music," *MO*, lxxii (1949), 284

N. Broder: "Current Chronicle: New York," *MQ*, xxxvi (1950), 276

H. Tischler: "Barber's Piano Sonata Opus 26," *ML*, xxxiii (1952), 352

N. Broder: *Samuel Barber* (New York, 1954)

R. Friedewald: *A Formal and Stylistic Analysis of the Published Music of Samuel Barber* (diss., U. of Iowa, 1957)

C. Turner: "The Music of Samuel Barber," *Opera News*, xxii/13 (1958), 7

"Classified Chronological Catalog of Works by the United States Composer Samuel Barber," *Inter-American Music Bulletin*, no.13 (1959), 22

"Samuel Barber," *Compositores de América/Composers of the Americas*, ed. Pan American Union, v (Washington, DC, 1959), 14

L. S. Wathen: *Dissonance Treatment in the Instrumental Music of Samuel Barber* (diss., Northwestern U., 1960)

J. Briggs: "Samuel Barber," *International Musician*, lx/6 (1961), 20

Bibliography

B. Rands: "Samuel Barber: a Belief in Tradition," *MO*, lxxxiv (1961), 353

"Barber, Samuel," *CBY 1963*

W. A. Dailey: *Techniques of Composition Used in Contemporary Works for Chorus and Orchestra on Religious Texts as Important Representative Works of the Period from 1952 through 1962* (diss., Catholic U., 1965)

E. Salzman and J. Goodfriend: "Samuel Barber: a Selective Discography," *HiFi/ Stereo Review*, xvii/4 (1966), 88

E. Salzman: "Samuel Barber," *HiFi/Stereo Review*, xvii/4 (1966), 77

J. E. Albertson: *A Study of Stylistic Elements of Samuel Barber's 'Hermit Songs' and Franz Schubert's 'Die Winterreise'* (diss., U. of Missouri, Kansas City, 1969)

R. L. Larsen: *A Study and Comparison of Samuel Barber's 'Vanessa,' Robert Ward's 'The Crucible,' and Gunther Schuller's 'The Visitation'* (diss., Indiana U., 1971)

L. L. Rhoades: *Theme and Variation in Twentieth-century Organ Literature: Analyses of Variations by Alain, Barber, Distler, Dupré, Duruflé, and Sowerby* (diss., Ohio State U., 1973)

S. L. Carter: *The Piano Music of Samuel Barber* (diss., Texas Tech U., 1980)

H. Heinsheimer: "Samuel Barber: Maverick Composer," *Keynote*, iv/1 (1980), 7

H. Gleason and W. Becker: "Samuel Barber," *20th-century American Composers*, Music Literature Outlines, ser. iv (Bloomington, IN, rev. 2/1981), 1 [incl. further bibliography]

D. A. Hennessee: *Samuel Barber: a Bio-bibliography* (Westport, CT, 1985)

B. Heyman: *Samuel Barber: a Documentary Study of his Works* (diss., CUNY, in progress)

J. Sifferman: *The Solo Piano Works of Samuel Barber* (diss., U. of Texas, in progress)

259

JOHN CAGE

Charles Hamm

CHAPTER NINE

John Cage

1. CHROMATICS. John Milton Cage, Jr., was born in Los Angeles on 5 September 1912. The son of an inventor, he excelled in Latin and oratory at Los Angeles High School, and on graduating in 1928 was elected one of 13 "Ephebians" by faculty vote, on the basis of his "scholarship, leadership, and character." After attending Pomona College in Claremont for two years, he went in the spring of 1930 to Europe, traveling to Paris, Berlin, Madrid, and other cities and devoting himself to the study of music, art, and architecture. On his return to California he continued to write poetry and music and to paint, holding a series of jobs and studying with the pianist Richard Buhlig. In 1933 he went to New York for a year to study theory and composition with Weiss. He also attended Cowell's classes in non-Western, folk, and contemporary music at the New School for Social Research. Back in California in the autumn of 1934 he studied counterpoint with Schoenberg and also took courses in theory at UCLA. There he became involved for the first time with a dance group, as accompanist and composer. In 1938 he moved to Seattle as composer-accompanist for Bonnie Bird's dance classes at the Cornish School; there he met Merce Cunningham, with whom he was to collaborate thenceforth.

His earliest compositions are based on a schematic organization of the 12 pitches of the chromatic scale. Such works as the Six Short Inventions (1934) and the *Composition for Three Voices* (1934) deal with the problem of keeping repetitions of notes among the different voices as far apart as possible, even though each voice uses the same 25-pitch range and must itself state all 25 pitches before repeating any one of them. *Music for Wind Instruments* (1938) and *Metamorphosis* (1938) use fragments of 12-tone series transposed to various pitches determined by the intervallic structure of the series itself. These works are all for small combinations of instruments and show the influence of the theories and compositions of his teachers.

2. DANCE, PERCUSSION, PREPARED PIANO. Cage organized a percussion orchestra in Seattle in 1938. In 1940 he moved to San Francisco, where he and Lou Harrison gave concerts of percussion music, and in 1941 he went to Chicago to give a course in new music at the Chicago Institute of Design. He accompanied for the dance classes of Katherine Manning and organized several percussion concerts. In the spring of 1943 he went to New York, which has remained his base. A program of percussion music under his direction presented by the League of Composers at the Museum of Modern Art on 7 February 1943, including three of his own works, brought him major public attention for the first time, being reviewed and reported even in such popular channels as *Life* magazine. He wrote music for Cunningham and toured with Cunningham's company as accompanist, eventually becoming its music director.

Almost all of Cage's music during this period was written for percussion or for prepared piano (a piano transformed into a percussion instrument of diverse timbres by the insertion of various objects between the strings at certain points). Among his first compositions for prepared piano was *Bacchanale*, written for the dancer Syvilla Fort in Seattle in 1940, when he had wanted to accompany a dance with percussion music but without using a number of instruments. By the late 1940s Cage had established a reputation as a talented and innovative composer. A performance at Carnegie Hall of his major work for prepared piano, *Sonatas and Interludes*, by Maro Ajemian in January 1949 was an important event of the New York music season, and Cage received awards that year from the Guggenheim Foundation and the National Institute of Arts and Letters, which cited him for "having thus extended the boundaries of musical art."

The prepared piano gave a wide range of percussive sounds; each note could have a distinctive timbre, determined by what objects were inserted in the strings and at what point (see fig. 21). And in his music for percussion ensembles Cage used a large variety of usual and unusual instruments. His *First Construction (in Metal)* of 1939 has the six percussionists play orchestral bells, thundersheets, piano, sleigh bells, oxen bells, brake drums, cowbells, Japanese temple gongs, Turkish cymbals, anvils, water gongs, and tam-tams. While in Chicago Cage had access to the sound-effects collection of a local radio station, and afterwards he began to use electrically produced sounds. For example, *Imaginary Landscape no.3* (1942) employs audio-frequency oscillators, variable-speed turntables for the playing of frequency recordings and generator whine, an electric buzzer, an amplified coil of wire, and an amplified marimba.

Many of the sounds produced by the prepared piano and some percussion instruments are of indeterminate or extremely complex pitch, and Cage quite logically turned from structures based on pitch organization to ones built on rhythmic patterns. The first 16 bars of *First Construction* are broken into the pattern $4 + 3 + 2 + 3 + 4$, which is repeated 16 times. The String Quartet (1949–50) has a rhythmic structure of $2\frac{1}{2} + 1\frac{1}{2} + 2 + 3 + 6 + 5 + 1\frac{1}{2} + 1\frac{1}{2}$; the pattern of *Music for Marcel Duchamp* (1947) is $11 \times 11 \ (2 + 1 + 1 + 3 + 1 + 2 + 1)$.

Patterns built on additive groups provide the basis for rhythmic structures in some Eastern music; as used by Cage, they give his music a static quality quite different from the linear, goal-

265

20. *John Cage, 1971*

oriented thrust of most western European and American art music, and he has explained that the expressive intent of certain of these pieces reflects Eastern attitudes. The ballet *The Seasons* (1947) attempts to express the traditional Indian view of the seasons as quiescence (winter), creation (spring), preservation (summer), and destruction (autumn); the Sonatas and Interludes (1946–8) express the "permanent emotions" of Indian tradition: the heroic, the erotic, the wondrous, the mirthful, sorrow, fear, anger, and the odious, and their common tendency towards tranquillity.

3. ZEN, I CHING, CHANCE. The external events of Cage's career in the late 1940s and early 1950s resembled those of the previous years, with continued activity in composition and work with the Cunningham Dance Company. He spent several summers teaching at Black Mountain College in North Carolina, he gave occasional classes at the New School for Social Research, and he went twice to Europe: in late 1949 with Cunningham and in 1954 with the pianist-composer David Tudor. The important events of these years were internal; it was at this time that the most dramatic changes in his thinking about music occurred.

In the late 1940s Cage had begun a study of Eastern philosophies with Gita Sarabhai and of Zen Buddhism with Daisetz T. Suzuki of Columbia University. By 1950 he was studying the I Ching, the Chinese book of changes; and in 1951 he began a series of pieces using various methods of composition in which elements of chance were introduced into the process of creation or performance, works in which Cage as the composer relinquished at least some control over what the final sounds of the piece would be. In *Music of Changes* (1951) – a lengthy piano work in four volumes – pitches, durations, and timbres were determined not by a conscious decision on the part of the composer but by the use of charts derived from the I Ching and the tossing of three coins. *Music for Piano I* (1952) is notated completely in whole notes, with the performer determining durations; pitches were chosen by ruling staves on pages of paper and then making notes where imperfections were observed on the page. *Imaginary Landscape no. 4* (1951) is performed with 12 radios with two performers at each, one manipulating the knob that changes stations and the other the volume control; the notation is precise, but of course the sounds for any given performance vary according to what is on the air.

Cage's aim in these works was "to make a musical composition the continuity of which is free of individual taste and memory (psychology) and also of the literature and 'traditions' of the art." Later he explained his philosophical basis for creating chance or random music. He came to believe that it should not be man's role to shape the world around him to his own desires and habits, but rather to adapt himself to the objects and people surrounding him. In music, as in life, one should make the best of the world oneself, should find for oneself what is beautiful and meaningful. "Now structure is not put into a work, but comes up in the person who perceives it himself. There is therefore no problem of understanding but the possibility of awareness." His *4'33"* (1952), which may be performed by any instrument or combination of instruments, epitomizes this attitude. The performer(s) sit silently on stage for the duration of the piece; the music consists of whatever noises are made by the audience and whatever sounds come from outside the auditorium during this time.

Until he moved into chance operations Cage had been slowly yet steadily building a reputation as a talented and serious innovator. But performances of such pieces as *Music of Changes*, consisting of a string of unrelated notes often separated by long silences and timed by a stopwatch held by the performer, or of the piece for 12 radios, were met with amusement, amazement, or hostility. Few musicians or critics understood what he was trying to do. A handful of men – Morton Feldman, David Tudor,

Christian Wolff, Earle Brown – worked with him and exchanged ideas during these years; together they founded the Project of Music for Magnetic Tape. Otherwise he found stimulation and encouragement from people in other arts: the visual artists Robert Motherwell, Robert Rauschenberg, and Jasper Johns, the poet Mary Caroline Richards, and the dancer Merce Cunningham.

4. TAPE, THEATER, INDETERMINACY. Cage had used electronic sounds in earlier pieces, but *Imaginary Landscape no. 5* (1952) was his first piece prepared on magnetic tape. Made as an accompaniment for a dance by Jean Erdman, it was put together by transferring the sounds from 42 phonograph records to tape, chopping these into fragments of varying lengths and reassembling them according to chance operations. *Williams Mix* (1952) was a much more complex piece. About 600 tapes of various sounds, musical and nonmusical, were assembled, fragmented, and then combined on eight tracks according to precise measurements and combinations arrived at by chance operations derived from the I Ching. The collecting, measuring, and splicing of these occupied Cage and Brown for many months.

In the summer of 1952, at Black Mountain College, Cage conceived and brought about an event that was an important precursor of the "happenings" of the following decade. This piece of "concerted action" involved simultaneous, uncoordinated music for piano and phonograph, poetry reading, dancing, lecturing, films, and slides. Other pieces of this time were planned to have visual as well as aural interest: *Water Music* (1952) is written for a pianist who must pour water from pots, blow whistles under water, use a radio and a pack of cards, and perform other actions to engage the eye.

Cage's chance music of the early 1950s had been constructed by one of several methods that ensured a random collection of notes, but once such a process had taken place the piece was fixed, was notated precisely, and would be just the same in each performance. A next step was to make pieces that would not be fixed, that would change from performance to performance. *Music for Piano 4–19* (1953) consists of 16 pages, the notes derived by chance operations; these pages "may be played as separate pieces or continuously as one piece or:" (sic). *Music for Piano 21–36* and *37–52* (1955) are two groups of pieces to be played alone or together or with *Music for Piano 4–19*. *Music for Piano 53–68* (1956) and *Music for Piano 69–84* (1956) complete the set of pieces, all of which may be performed, in whole or in part, by any number of pianists. *26' 1.1499"* for a string player (1955), with notes selected partly by chance and partly by observation of imperfections in the paper on which it was written, may be played as a solo, or several different sections may be played simultaneously by various instruments to make duets, trios, quar-

21. Detail of a piano "prepared" by Cage, 1940

270

tets, etc. The most ambitious piece of this sort is the Concert for Piano and Orchestra (1957–8). There is no master score; parts for each instrument of the orchestra were written using chance methods. The piece may be peformed by any number of players as a solo, ensemble piece, symphony, aria, or concert for piano and orchestra. Each player selects from his part any number of pages to play, in any sequence, and coordination is by elapsed time, with the conductor's arms functioning as the hands of a clock.

5. FAME AND NOTORIETY. Attitudes towards Cage and his work, always strong, became even more intense during this most radical period. Vigorously and violently attacked for what he was saying and doing, he was at the same time increasingly in demand as a lecturer, teacher, and performer. He and Tudor made a concert tour of Europe in 1954, performing in Cologne, Paris, Brussels, Stockholm, Zurich, Milan, and London and at the Donaueschingen Festival in Germany. Reaction was largely hostile, but soon afterwards such European composers as Stockhausen began discussing and experimenting with chance music. Back in the USA, Cage spent much of his time touring with the Cunningham Dance Company, which was performing more and more frequently. When in New York, he sometimes taught classes at the New School, attracting as students Dick Higgins, Allan Kaprow, George Brecht, Al Hansen, and Jackson MacLow, each of whom was to make a mark on the avant-garde scene. A retrospective concert of Cage's music, with a selection of pieces covering a span of 25 years, was given at New York's Town Hall in May 1958. The reception was mixed; audience response to the newly composed Concert for Piano and Orchestra was as violent as that which had greeted the first performance of *The Rite of Spring*, but a three-disc album of the concert, put out by George Avakian, made it possible for critics to evaluate Cage's

development in a more informed way than before.

Cage was in Europe again that summer (1958), giving concerts and lectures and teaching a class in experimental music at Darmstadt. Luciano Berio invited him to Milan, where he spent four months working in the tape studio operated by the Milan radio station, making the tape piece *Fontana Mix*. During this stay he appeared on the Italian television quiz show "Lascia o raddoppia," successfully answering questions on mushrooms over a five-week period, winning a large prize, and creating and performing several compositions (*Water Walk* and *Sounds of Venice*) as a prelude to the competition sessions. Back in New York in 1959 he taught courses in experimental music and mushroom identification at the New School, was commissioned to write a large orchestral work by the Montreal Festivals Society, was a co-founder of the New York Mycological Society, and accepted his first appointment at a degree-granting academic institution: he was a Fellow at the Center for Advanced Studies at Wesleyan University, Middletown, Connecticut, for the academic year 1960–61.

Bernstein undertook a performance of *Atlas eclipticalis* with the New York PO at Lincoln Center in February 1964. Contact microphones attached to each instrument fed sound into an elaborate electronic system, whence it was distributed to six loudspeakers in various parts of the auditorium. Most of the audience walked out during the first presentation, and in succeeding performances members of the orchestra hissed the composer and attempted to sabotage the piece. More positive events of these years were a six-week concert tour of Japan in 1962 with Tudor, appointments as composer-in-residence at the University of Cincinnati (1967), associate of the Center for Advanced Study at the University of Illinois (1967–9), and artist-in-residence at the University of California, Davis (1969), and election to the National Institute of Arts and Letters in 1968.

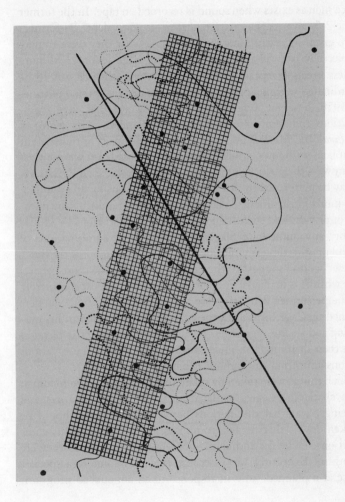

22. Graphic notation from Cage's "Fontana Mix" (1958)

6. "EVERYTHING WE DO IS MUSIC." Beginning with such works as *Music of Changes* (1951) and *Imaginary Landscape no.4*, Cage had employed notation expressing a relation between time and space such as exists when sound is recorded on tape. In the former piece 2.5 cm equals a quarter-note or its equivalent. Performers were given increasing freedom to choose what they were to play in pieces written in the later 1950s, but Cage's scores had more or less precisely notated pitches, and a performance was to be coordinated within a precisely notated or decided period of time. In 1958, however, Cage began creating works that were "compositions indeterminate of their performances." The scores of *Fontana Mix, Music Walk*, and Variations I consist of transparent templates with lines or dots, to be superimposed over one another in any way, the performer making his own part (fig. 22). Variations I may be performed by any number of players using any number and kind of instruments; Variations II (1961) requires "any number of players, and sound-producing means"; Variations IV (1963) is for "any number of players, any sounds or combinations of sound produced by any means, with or without other activities." These "scores" suggest to the performer only in the most general way what he is to play or do: sounds and actions almost completely of the performers' choosing are the result. *0'0"* (1962), as performed by Cage himself in the mid-1960s, consisted in his preparing and slicing vegetables, putting them in an electric blender, and then drinking the juice, with the sounds of these various actions amplified throughout the hall.

Such things were taken by many to be the actions of a madman or a charlatan. Cage's explanation, given in his lectures and writings, was that distinctions between life and art should be broken down, that he as a composer should, through his compositions, make his audiences more aware of the world they are living in. Expecting "art" because they had come to a specific place at a planned time in response to an announced program, they would be offered a collection of sounds and sights such as they might encounter elsewhere at other times. If they could learn to respond to these, they could do the same when they were not in the concert hall. As Cage wrote in *Silence* (1961):

Our intention is to affirm this life, not to bring order out of chaos or to suggest improvements in creation, but simply to wake up to the very life we're living, which is so excellent once one gets one's mind and one's desires out of the way and lets it act of its own accord.

And in his lecture "Where are we going? And what are we doing?" he wrote: "Here we are. Let us say Yes to our presence together in Chaos."

Musicircus (1967) was an "environmental extravaganza" consisting of simultaneous performances of rock, jazz, electronic, piano, and vocal music, pantomime and dance, together with films and slide shows. Cage's role consisted "simply in inviting those who were willing to perform at once (in the same place and time)." Such anarchistic, convention-defying affairs were very much in tune with the mood of the USA at that time, and Cage enjoyed unprecedented popularity, particularly among the young and radical and on college campuses. *HPSCHD* (1967–9), made with Lejaren Hiller, was an immense complex of sight and sound. Seven harpsichordists played computer-realized mixtures of the music of Mozart, Beethoven, Chopin, Schoenberg, Hiller, and Cage, 51 tapes planned and realized by computers were played through 51 amplifiers, and films, slides, and colored lights bathed the performance area. The composers had spent many months in preparing the scores and tapes; each individual event of sound or sight had been carefully planned and executed, though the relation of any event to any other was indeterminate.

7. REUNIONS AND CELEBRATIONS. From the late 1960s Cage has been willing to draw on any ideas and techniques of his earlier periods, or to mix these with new interests and procedures. Scores

may be precisely and intricately notated, or they may give only the most general guide to the shape and content of the piece. He writes for conventional instruments, for electronic sounds, and for amplified and distorted sound materials drawn from the natural world, or he draws on previously recorded material. Pieces may be designed for performance in conventional concert halls, in dance theaters, at home, or outdoors. One thing may become another: a chess game played on an amplified board becomes a musical composition in *Reunion* (1968); tiny drawings retrieved from Thoreau's *Journals* are used as a musical score in *Score* (1974); poetry is transformed into part of a musical piece in *62 Mesostics re Merce Cunningham* (1971). Yet however disparate their methods or media, all these pieces are unmistakably Cageian, having in common his continuing desire to utilize various chance procedures and improvisations to create sound patterns divorced from self-expression.

Typical is *Etudes australes* (1974–5), a virtuoso piece for piano that has a precisely notated score derived from tracing astronomical charts onto music staves. *Cheap Imitation*, written for piano in 1969 and orchestrated in 1972, is based on a piece by Satie; the original rhythmic patterns are kept but pitches are replaced with notes selected through chance procedures. *Child of Tree* (1975) and *Branches* (1976) make use of amplified plant sounds; *Roaratorio, an Irish Circus on Finnegans Wake* (1979) is an electronic piece built of thousands of sounds mentioned in Joyce's novel, many of them recorded in places mentioned in the book. *A Dip in the Lake* (1978), written for performance in Chicago and its surrounding area, is scored for "two places, three places and four places"; participants are instructed to "go to the places and either listen to, perform at and/or make a recording of" a number of quicksteps, waltzes, and marches. Thoreau and Joyce have joined Satie and Duchamp as persons of unusual interest to Cage. He often uses a computer to perform chance operations more efficiently and dispassionately than any human. His first major graphic work, *Not Wanting to Say Anything about Marcel* (1969), has been followed by a series of others. And his long-time interests in mycology and games (bridge, cribbage, poker, Scrabble, backgammon) continue unabated.

Honors have come his way increasingly. His 60th birthday was marked by a concert at the New School in July 1972 and another at Lincoln Center the following January. Commissions for major compositions have come from the Canadian Broadcasting Corporation (*Lecture on the Weather*, 1975), the Boston SO for the American Bicentennial celebration (*Renga*, 1976), IRCAM (*Roaratorio*, 1979), and the Cabrillo Music Festival (*Dance Four Orchestras*, 1981). He was elected to the American Academy of Arts and Sciences in 1978, he was one of eight New Yorkers (and the only musician) to be given the Mayor's Award of Honor for Arts and Culture in 1981, and in 1982 the French government awarded him its highest honor for distinguished contribution to cultural life, Commandeur de l'Ordre des Arts et des Lettres. His 70th birthday brought a festival in his honor in Chicago (New Music America) and a major exhibition at New York's Whitney Museum of American Art, "John Cage: Scores and Prints," coordinated with three concerts of his music at the museum.

WORKS

Cage created various nonnotated collaborative works that he does not claim as his own; for the most part these works are excluded from this list. All works are published unless otherwise stated.

Three Songs (G. Stein), 1v, pf, 1932

Sonata, cl, 1933

Sonata for Two Voices, 2 or more insts, 1933

Solo with Obbligato Accompaniment of Two Voices in Canon, and Six Short Inventions on the Subject of the Solo, 3 or more insts, 1933–4

Composition for Three Voices, 3 or more insts, 1934

Music for Xenia (A Valentine out of Season), prepared pf, 1934

277

Six Short Inventions, a fl, cl, tpt, vn, 2 va, vc, 1934
Quartet, 4 perc, 1935
Quest, 2nd movt, pf, 1935
Three Pieces, 2 fl, 1935
Two Pieces, pf, *c*1935, rev. 1974
Trio, suite, 3 perc, 1936
Five Songs (Cummings), A, pf, 1938
Metamorphosis, pf, 1938
Music for Wind Instruments, wind qnt, 1938
First Construction (in Metal), 6 perc, 1939
Ho to AA (C. Tracy), 1v, pf, 1939, unpubd
Imaginary Landscape no.1, 2 variable-speed turntables, frequency recordings, muted pf, cymbal, 1939
Bacchanale, prepared pf, 1940
Living Room Music, perc and speech qt, 1940
Second Construction, 4 perc, 1940
Double Music, 4 perc, 1941, collab. L. Harrison
Third Construction, 4 perc, 1941
And the Earth shall Bear Again, prepared pf, 1942
The City Wears a Slouch Hat (K. Patchen), radio play, perc, 1942, unpubd
Credo in Us, 4 perc, 1942
Forever and Sunsmell (Cummings), 1v, 2 perc, 1942
Imaginary Landscape no.2 (March no.1), 5 perc, 1942
Imaginary Landscape no.3, audio-frequency oscillators, variable-speed turntables, elec buzzer, amp wire, amp mar, 1942
In the Name of the Holocaust, prepared pf, 1942
Primitive, prepared ("string") pf, 1942
Totem Ancestor, prepared pf, 1942
The Wonderful Widow of Eighteen Springs (Joyce), 1v, closed pf, 1942
Amores, 2 prepared pf solos, 2 perc trios, 1943
A Room, pf/prepared pf, 1943
Our Spring will Come, pf, 1943
She is Asleep, qt for 12 tomtoms, duet for 1v, prepared pf, 1943
Tossed as it is Untroubled (Meditation), prepared pf, 1943
A Book of Music, 2 prepared pf, 1944
Four Walls (M. Cunningham), pf, vocal interlude, 1944
The Perilous Night, prepared pf, 1944
Prelude for Meditation, prepared pf, 1944
Root of an Unfocus, prepared pf, 1944
Spontaneous Earth, prepared pf, 1944

The Unavailable Memory of, prepared pf, 1944
Three Dances, 2 amp prepared pf, 1944–5
Daughters of the Lonesome Isle, prepared pf, 1945
Mysterious Adventure, prepared pf, 1945
Party Pieces (Sonorous and Exquisite Corpses), *c*1945, 20 pieces by Cage, Cowell,
    Harrison, Thomson [arr. fl, cl, bn, hn, pf, by R. Hughes]
Experiences, duo for 2 pf, solo for 1v (Cummings), 1945–8
Ophelia, pf, 1946
Two Pieces, pf, 1946
Sonatas and Interludes, prepared pf, 1946–8
Dreams that Money can Buy, film score, 1947, unpubd
Music for Marcel Duchamp, prepared pf, 1947
Nocturne, vn, pf, 1947
The Seasons (ballet, 1), orch/pf, 1947
Dream, pf, 1948
In a Landscape, harp/pf, 1948
Suite, toy pf/pf, 1948
String Quartet, 1949–50
A Flower, 1v, closed pf, 1950
Six Melodies, vn, kbd, 1950
Concerto, prepared pf, chamber orch, 1950–51
Imaginary Landscape no.4 (March no.2), 12 radios, 1951
Music of Changes, pf, 1951
Sixteen Dances, fl, tpt, 4 perc, vn, vc, 1951
Two Pastorales, prepared pf, 1951
For M.C. and D.T., pf, 1952
4′33″, tacet for any inst/insts, 1952
Imaginary Landscape no.5, tape, 1952
Music for Carillon no.1, 1952
Music for Piano 1, 1952
Seven Haiku, pf, 1952
Waiting, pf, 1952
Water Music, pianist, 1952
Williams Mix, 8 1-track/4 2-track tapes, 1952
$59\frac{1}{2}″$, any 4-string inst, 1953
Music for Piano 2, 1953
Music for Piano 3, 1953
Music for Piano 4–19, 1953
Music for Piano 20, 1953
26′ 1.1499″, str player, 1953–5

Music for Carillon nos.2–3, 1954
34′ 46.776″, prepared pf, 1954
31′ 57.9864″, prepared pf, 1954
Music for Piano 21–36, 1955
Music for Piano 37–52, 1955
Speech, 5 radios, newsreader, 1955
26′ 1.1499″, str player, 1955
Music for Piano 53–68, 1956
Music for Piano 69–84, 1956
Radio Music, 1–8 radios, 1956
27′ 10.554″, perc, 1956
For Paul Taylor and Anita Dencks, pf, 1957
Winter Music, 1–20 pf, 1957
Concert for Piano and Orchestra, 1957–8
Aria, 1v, 1958
Fontana Mix, tape, 1958
Music Walk, pf (1 or more players), 1958
Solo for Voice 1, 1958
TV Koeln, pf, 1958
Variations I, any number of players, any insts, 1958
Sounds of Venice, TV piece, 1959
Water Walk, TV piece, 1959
Cartridge Music, amp sounds, 1960
Music for Amplified Toy Pianos, 1960
Music for The Marrying Maiden (J. MacLow), tape, 1960
Solo for Voice 2, 1960
Theatre Piece, 1–8 pfmrs, 1960
WBAI, auxiliary score for perf. with other works, 1960
Where are we going? And what are we doing?, lecture on 4 1-track tapes, 1960
Atlas eclipticalis, any ens from 86 insts, 1961
Music for Carillon no.4, 1961, rev. 1966
Variations II, any number of players, any means, 1961
4′ 33″ (no.2) (0′ 0″), solo for any player, 1962
Variations III, any number of people performing any actions, 1962–3
Variations IV, any number of players, any means, 1963
Electronic Music for Piano, pf + elec, 1964
Rozart Mix, tape, 1965
Variations V, audio-visual perf., 1965
Variations VI, plurality of sound systems, 1966
Variations VII, any number of players, any means, 1966, unpubd

Music for Carillon no.5, 1967

Musicircus, mixed-media event, 1967

Newport Mix, tape loops, 1967, unpubd

HPSCHD, 1–7 amp hpd, 1–51 tapes, 1967–9, collab. L. Hiller

Reunion, diverse pfmrs, 1968, unpubd, collab. D. Behrman, L. Cross, Mumma, Tudor

Cheap Imitation, pf, 1969, orchd 1972, vn version 1977

Sound Anonymously Received, any insts, 1969, unpubd

33⅓, any recordings, audience, 1969, unpubd

Song Books (Solos for Voice 3–92), 1970

Les chants de Maldoror pulvérisés par l'assistance même, French-speaking audience of not more than 200, 1971

62 Mesostics re Merce Cunningham, amp 1v, 1971

WGBH-TV, composers and technicians, 1971

Bird Cage, 12 tapes, 1972

Mureau, mix from Thoreau's writings, 1972

Etcetera, small orch, tape, 1973

Score (40 Drawings by Thoreau) and 23 Parts, any insts/vv, 1974

2 Pieces, pf, 1974

Etudes australes, 32 pieces, pf, 1974–5

Child of Tree, perc using amp plant materials, 1975

Lecture on the Weather, 12 insts/vv, tapes, film, 1975

Apartment House 1776, mixed media, 1976

Branches, perc solo/ens, amp plant materials, 1976

Quartets I–VIII, 24/41/93 insts, 1976

Renga, 78 insts/vv, 1976

Quartet, 12 amp vv, concert band, 1976–8

49 Waltzes for the Five Boroughs, any number of players, any means, 1977

Inlets, conch shells, tape, 1977

Primitive: Music for Dance, pf, 1977

Telephones and Birds, 3 pfmrs, 1977

The Unavailable Memory of:, prepared insts, 1977

Freeman Etudes, vn, 1977–80

A Dip in the Lake: Ten Quicksteps, 62 Waltzes, and 56 Marches for Chicago and Vicinity, listener, pfmr and/or recorder, 1978

Chorals, vn, 1978

Etudes borealis, pf and/or vc, 1978

Letters to Erik Satie, 1v, tape, 1978, unpubd

Someday, radio event, 1978, unpubd

Some of the Harmony of Maine, org, 3/6 assistants, 1978

Il treno, prepared trains, 1978, unpubd

Variations VIII, poster, 1978

Hymns and Variations, 12 amp vv, 1979

Roaratorio, an Irish Circus on Finnegans Wake, elec, 1979

Sonata for Two Voices, any 2 or more insts, 1979

Improvisations III, duets, 1980, unpubd

Litany for the Whale, 2 solo vv, 1980

Composition in Retrospect, computer, 1981

Dance Four Orchestras, 1981

30 Pieces for 5 Orchestras, 1981

A House Full of Music, 1982

Atlas borealis, orch, vv, 1982

Improvisations IV, 1982

Instances of Silence, installation, tapes, 1982, unpubd

Postcard from Heaven, 1–20 harps, 1982

Ear for Ear, vv, 1983

Souvenir, org, 1983

30 Pieces for String Quartet, 1983

A Collection of Rocks, orch without cond., 1984

Eight Whiskus (C. Mann), 1v, 1984, arr. vn, M. Goldstein, 1985

Mirakus^2 (M. Duchamp), 1v, 1984

Nowth upon Nacht, 1v, pf, 1984

Perpetual Tango, pf, 1984

Selkus^2 (Duchamp), 1v, 1984

Music for ———, fl, cl, vn, vc, 3 perc, pf, trbn, 1984–5

Ryoanji, vv, fl, ob, db, perc, small orch, 1984–5

Aslsp, pf, 1985

Essay, tape, 1985

Etcetera, 2/4 orch, 1985

Sonnekus^2 (Genesis), 1v, 1985

Europera I/II (opera, Cage), solo vv, orch, 1985–7

Haikai, gamelan, 1986

Hymnkus, 13 insts, 1v, 1986

Principal publisher: Peters

GRAPHIC WORKS

with C. Sumsion: Not Wanting to Say Anything about Marcel (1969)

with L. Long and A. Smith: Mushroom Book (1972)

Series re Morris Graves (1974)

Score without Parts (40 Drawings by Thoreau), (1978)

Seven-day Diary (Not Knowing) (1978)
17 Drawings by Thoreau (1978)
Signals (1978)
Changes and Disappearances (1979–82)
On the Surface (1980–82)

WRITINGS

with K. Hoover: *Virgil Thomson: his Life and Music* (New York, 1959)
Silence (Middletown, CT, 1961) [essays and lectures]
A Year from Monday (Middletown, 1967) [essays and lectures]
To Describe the Process of Composition Used in Not Wanting to Say Anything about Marcel (Cincinnati, OH, 1969)
with A. Knowles: *Notations* (New York, 1969)
M (Middletown, CT, 1973) [writings, 1967–72]
Writings through Finnegans Wake (Tulsa, OK, and New York, 1978)
Empty Words (Middletown, CT, 1979) [writings, 1973–8]
with S. Barron: *Another Song* (New York, 1981)
Mud Book (New York, 1982) [with illustrations by L. Long]
Themes and Variations (New York, 1982)

BIBLIOGRAPHY

CATALOGUE
R. Dunn, ed.: *John Cage* (New York, 1962) [annotated]

GENERAL STUDIES
(1945–65)
K. List: "Rhythm, Sound and Sane," *New Republic*, cxiii (1945), 870
S. Goldstein: "John Cage," *Music Business* (1946), April
P. Glanville-Hicks: "John Cage," *MusAm*, lxviii/10 (1948), 5, 20
R. Maren: "The Musical Numbers Game," *Reporter*, xviii (6 March 1958), 37
H. G. Helms: "John Cage's Lecture 'Indeterminacy'," *Die Reihe*, v (1959), 83–121
L. A. Hiller and L. M. Isaacson: *Experimental Music* (New York, 1959)
K. G. Roy: "The Strange and Wonderful Sonic World of John Cage," *HiFi/Stereo Review*, v/5 (1960), 62
V. Thomson: "John Cage Late and Early," *Saturday Review*, xliii (30 Jan 1960), 38
M. Wilson: "John Cage," *Canadian Music Journal*, iv/4 (1960), 54
"Cage, John (Milton, Jr.)," *CBY 1961*
T. Ichiyanagi: "John Cage," *Ongaku geijutsu*, xix/2 (1961)

N. Slonimsky: "If Anyone is Sleepy, Let him Go to Sleep," *Christian Science Monitor* (14 Dec 1961), 11

J. Johnston: "There is No Silence Now," *Village Voice* (8 Nov 1962)

K. McGary: "I have Nothing," *Antioch Review*, xxii (1962), 248

B. Markgraf: "John Cage: Ideas and Practices of a Contemporary Speaker," *Quarterly Journal of Speech*, xlviii (1962), 128

W. Mellers: "The Avant-garde in America," *PRMA*, xc (1963–4), 1

D. Heckman: "The Sounds and Silences of John Cage," *Down Beat*, xxxi/11 (1964), 20

G. Steinem: "Music, Music, Music, Music," *Show* (1964), Jan, 59

C. Tomkins: "Figure in an Imaginary Landscape," *New Yorker* (28 Nov 1964), 64, 68

D. Charles: "Entr'acte: 'Formal' or 'Informal' Music?," *MQ*, li (1965), 144

W. Mellers: *Music in a New Found Land* (New York, 1965), 177

C. Tomkins: *The Bride and the Bachelors: the Heretical Courtship in Modern Art* (New York, 1965)

(1966–75)

E. Morris: "Three Thousand Seven Hundred Forty-seven Words about John Cage," *Notes*, xxiii (1966–7), 468

L. B. Meyer: "The End of the Renaissance?," *Music, the Arts and Ideas* (Chicago, 1967), 68

U. Dibelius: "John Cage oder gibt es kritische Musik?," *Melos*, xxxv (1968), 377

S. Kubota: *Marcel Duchamp and John Cage* (New York, 1968)

C. Tomkins: *Ahead of the Game: Four Versions of the Avant-garde* (Harmondsworth, England, 1968)

W. Bartsch and others: *Die unvermeidliche Musik des John Cage* (Kolb, Switzerland, 1969)

R. Kostelanetz: "The American Avant-garde, Part II: John Cage," *Stereo Review*, xxii/5 (1969), 61; repr. in *Master Minds* (New York, 1969)

W. E. Lewinski: "Where do we Go from Here?: a European View," *MQ*, lv (1969), 193

E. Salzman: "Milton Babbitt and John Cage, Parallels and Paradoxes," *Stereo Review*, xxii/4 (1969), 60

S. Sontag: "The Esthetics of Silence," *Styles of Radical Will* (New York, 1969), 3

R. C. Clark: "Total Control and Chance in Musics: a Philosophical Analysis," *Journal of Aesthetics and Art Criticism*, xxviii (1970), 355; xxix (1970), 53

P. Gaboury: "Electronic Music: the Rift between Artist and Public," *Journal of Aesthetics and Art Criticism*, xxviii (1970), 345

Bibliography

R. Kostelanetz, ed.: *John Cage* (New York, 1970)

M. Siegel: "Come in, Earth, are you There?," *Arts in Society*, vii (1970), 70

E. J. Snyder: *John Cage and Music since World War II: a Study in Applied Aesthetics* (diss., U. of Wisconsin, 1970)

D. Charles: "Cage et l'expérience du non-vouloir," *ReM*, nos. 276–7 (1971), 19

Chou Wen-Chung: "Asian Concepts and Twentieth-century Western Composers," *MQ*, lvii (1971), 211

M. Nyman: "Cage and Satie," *MT*, cxiv (1973), 1227

C. Cardew: *Stockhausen Serves Imperialism and Other Articles* (London, 1974)

M. Nyman: *Experimental Music: Cage and Beyond* (New York, 1974)

V. Toncitch: "Kants Denkkategorien verpflichet: zur Ästhetik und Musik von John Cage," *Melos/NZM*, i (1975), 7

(from 1976)

B. E. Johnson: "John Cage," *Nutida Musik*, xxi (1977–8), 8

D. Charles: *Gloses sur John Cage* (Paris, 1978)

S. Emmerson: "John Cage," *Music and Musicians*, xxvii/3 (1978), 74

H. K. Metzger and R. Riehn: *John Cage* (Munich, 1978)

H. Åstrand: "Glosor om John Cage," *Nutida Musik*, xxii (1978–9), 54

J. Bell: "John Cage," *Art News*, lxxiii/3 (1979), 61

E. Lo Bue: "Nothing to say: John Cage come letterato," *Italia musicale*, xiv/1 (1979), 155

D. Bither: "John Cage: a Grand Old Radical," *Horizon*, xxiii/12 (1980), 48

S. Buettner: "Cage," *IRASM*, xii (1981), 141

P. Griffiths: *Cage* (New York, 1981)

T. J. O'Grady: "Aesthetic Value in Indeterminate Music," *MQ*, lxvii (1981), 306

P. Gena and J. Brent, eds.: *A John Cage Reader: in Celebration of his 70th Birthday* (New York, 1982)

S. Montague: "Significant Silences of a Musical Anarchist," *Classical Music* (London, 22 May 1982), 11

R. Stevenson: "John Cage on his 70th Birthday: West Coast Background," *Inter-American Music Review*, v/1 (1982), 3

C. Hamm: "The American Avant-garde," *Music in the New World* (New York, 1983), 580–617

J. Rockwell: "The American Experimental Tradition & its Godfather," *All American Music: Composition in the Late Twentieth Century* (New York, 1983), 47

D. Vaughan: "Duet: the Forty-year Collaboration of Avant-gardists Merce Cunningham and John Cage," *Ballet News*, iv/9 (1983), 21

T. DeLio: *Circumscribing the Open Universe: Essays on Cage, Feldman, Wolff, Ashley and Lucier* (Lanham, MD, 1984)

J. Rockwell: "The Impact and Influence of John Cage," *New York Times* (8 Feb 1987), §II, TK

WORKS

J. Pence: "People call it Noise – but he calls it Music," *Chicago Daily News* (19 March 1942), 4

"Percussion Concert," *Life*, xiv/11 (1943), 42, 44

L. Harrison: "The Rich and Varied New York Scene," *MM*, xxi (1945), 181

D. M. Hering: "John Cage and the 'Prepared Piano'," *Dance Magazine*, xx/3 (1946), 21, 52

S. Finkelstein: "John Cage's Music," *New Masses*, lxii (7 Jan 1947), 30

V. Thomson: "Expressive Percussion," *The Art of Judging Music* (New York, 1948), 164

P. Yates: "Music for Prepared Piano," *Arts and Architecture*, lxvi/4 (1949), 21

H. Cowell: "Current Chronicle," *MQ*, xxxviii (1952), 123

H. Curjel: "Cage oder das wohlpräparierte Klavier," *Melos*, xxii (1955), 97

G. Avakian: "About the Concert," *The 25-year Retrospective Concert of the Music of John Cage* (matrix no. KOBY 1499–1504, 1959) [liner notes]

A. Frankenstein: "In Retrospect – the Music of John Cage," *HiFi*, x/4 (1960), 63

J. Hollander: Review of *Silence*, *PNM*, i/2 (1963), 137

P. Dickinson: "Way Out with John Cage," *Music and Musicians*, xiv/3 (1965), 32

L. Austin: "HPSCHD," *Source*, ii/2 (1968), 10

R. Filliou: *Lehren und Lernen als Aufführungskünste* (New York, 1970)

S. Kisielewski: "Awangarda czy bezsilnosc," *Ruch muzyczny*, no.13 (1970), 10

W. E. Duckworth: *Expanding Notational Parameters in the Music of John Cage* (diss., U. of Illinois, 1972)

D. Charles: *Pour les oiseaux* (Paris, 1977; Eng. trans. as *For the Birds*, Salem, NH, 1981)

M. Fürst-Heidtmann: "Det preparerade Pianots Idé och Teknik," *Nutida Musik*, xxi (1977–8), 9

M. Fürst-Heidtmann: *Das präparierte Klavier des John Cage* (Regensburg, Germany, 1979)

V. Thomson: "Cage and the Collage of Noises," *A Virgil Thomson Reader* (Boston, 1981)

S. Husarik: "John Cage and Lejaren Hiller: HPSCHD, 1969," *American Music*, i/2 (1983), 1

Bibliography

D. A. Campana: *Form and Structure in the Music of John Cage* (diss., Northwestern U., 1985)

B. Hambraeus: "John Cage, Aria con Fontana Mix," *Nutida Musik*, xxix (1985–6), 9

INTERVIEWS

M. Kirby and R. Schechner: "An Interview," *Tulane Drama Review*, x/2 (1965), 50

L. G. Bodin and B. E. Johnson: "Semikolon: Musical Pleasure (interview with John Cage)," *Dansk musiktidskrift*, xli (1966), 36

D. Charles: "Soixante réponses à trente questions," *Revue d'esthétique*, xxi/2–4 (1968), 9

W. Zimmermann: "John Cage," *Desert Plants: Conversations with 23 American Musicians* (Vancouver, BC, 1976)

A. Gillmor: "Intervju med John Cage," *Nutida Musik*, xxi (1977–8), 13

R. Reynolds: "John Cage and Roger Reynolds: a Conversation," *MQ*, lxv (1979), 573

T. Everett: "10 Questions: 270 Answers," *Composer*, x–xi (1980), 57–103

R. Kostelanetz: "John Cage," *The Old Poetries and the New* (Ann Arbor, 1981), 247

C. Gagne and T. Caras: "John Cage," *Soundpieces: Interviews with American Composers* (Metuchen, NJ, 1982)

S. Montague: "John Cage at Seventy: an Interview," *American Music*, iii (1985), 205

R. Kostelanetz: "John Cage and Richard Kostelanetz: a Conversation about Radio," *MQ*, lxxii (1986), 216

LEONARD BERNSTEIN

Joan Peyser

CHAPTER TEN

Leonard Bernstein

1. CHILDHOOD AND STUDENT YEARS: 1918–43. Bernstein is a first-generation American whose artistic temperament derives as much from his Russian-Jewish roots as from his American experience. His father, Samuel, the oldest child of a scholar-rabbi, was 16 when he left the Ukraine for New York, where he took a job in the Fulton fish market; his mother, Jennie Resnick, was seven when she arrived in Lawrence, Massachusetts, where she worked in the mills from the age of 12. The eldest of three children, Leonard was born in Lawrence on 25 August 1918; he attended the highly competitive Boston Latin School. His introduction to music came late for one who was to become a professional musician; he was ten when the family acquired an upright piano. Immediately he was drawn to it, but his father bitterly opposed this interest, expecting him to join his beauty supply business. Bernstein began lessons, however, with a neighbor, Frieda Karp, and went on to study with Susan Williams, a faculty member of the New England Conservatory; Helen Coates, an assistant to Heinrich Gebhard, Boston's foremost piano teacher; and finally with Gebhard himself.

In 1935 Bernstein entered Harvard University, where he studied with Edward Ballantine, Edward Burlingame Hill, A. Tillman Merritt, and Walter Piston. While an undergraduate he wrote incidental music for a production of The Birds (Aristophanes), directed and played the piano for Blitzstein's left-wing musical The Cradle will Rock, and met Dimitri Mitropoulos, who exerted a profound influence on his musical life. After graduating in 1939 (BA), Bernstein studied at the Curtis Institute: piano with Isabella Vengerova, score reading with Renée Longy, orchestration with Randall Thompson, and conducting with Fritz Reiner (winters of 1939–40 and 1940–41). He also studied conducting with Koussevitzky at the Berkshire Music Center (summers of 1940 and 1941), where in 1942 Koussevitzky appointed him his assistant. Meanwhile, he had become involved with the Revuers (a group of popular entertainers that included Adolph Green and Betty Comden), who composed and sang sophisticated songs at the Village Vanguard, New York, where Bernstein often spent the evening and occasionally played the piano (without pay). In the autumn of 1942 he began working at Harms-Remick, arranging popular songs for piano, transcribing band pieces, and notating improvisations by such jazz artists as Coleman Hawkins and Earl Hines; these were published under the pseudonym Lenny Amber (Amber being an English translation of the German Bernstein).

In August 1943 Artur Rodzinski, the newly appointed music director of the New York PO, named Bernstein his assistant conductor. On 14 November 1943 Bruno Walter, who was scheduled to conduct the orchestra, fell ill, and Bernstein substituted for him in a concert that was broadcast throughout the USA. His performance was reviewed on the front page of the *New York Times* and in other newspapers across the country; the widespread publicity not only launched his conducting career, it made him instantly recognizable to millions.

2. EARLY CAREER: 1944–50. After serving in 1944–5 as guest conductor of seven major orchestras, including the Pittsburgh SO and the Boston SO, Bernstein was appointed music director of the New York City SO, replacing Stokowski. During his tenure with the orchestra (1945–8), he conducted mostly 20th-century

compositions, concentrating on works by Stravinsky, Bartók, Chávez, Hindemith, Prokofiev, and Shostakovich; although he did present excerpts from Berg's *Wozzeck* (with Rose Bampton), he felt little affinity for the music of the Second Viennese School. In the summer of 1946 he conducted the American première of Britten's *Peter Grimes* at the Berkshire Music Center. That year he also led the Czech PO in two programs devoted to American music including pieces by Copland, Barber, Roy Harris, Schuman, Gershwin, and himself. He proved to be an effective ambassador for American music; not only did he look the role, with his wide smile and informal manner, but he captured American music, with its special inflections and particular rhythms, more successfully than anyone else. In Tel Aviv in 1947 he conducted the first of a series of concerts with the Palestine PO (later Israel PO), to which he was music adviser during 1948–9. Also in 1948 he conducted a concert given by concentration camp survivors in a refugee camp near Munich, appeared with orchestras in Milan, Vienna, Budapest, Paris, Munich, and Scheveningen (the Netherlands), and in the USA was appointed to the faculty at the Berkshire Music Center. He was not yet 30.

The Clarinet Sonata (1941–2) was Bernstein's first published composition. His works of this period possess both the vitality of popular genres and the restraint normally associated with art music. The first such work for orchestra was the Symphony no. 1 "Jeremiah," which he conducted with the Pittsburgh SO in January 1944; it won the New York Music Critics' Circle Award as the best American work of the year. In April, at the Metropolitan Opera, Hurok presented *Fancy Free*, a ballet choreographed by Jerome Robbins; it became the basis for the musical *On the Town* (with book and lyrics by Comden and Green), which opened on Broadway in December of that year and enjoyed great popularity as well as considerable critical acclaim. During these years Bernstein also continued his activities as a pianist and in

293

1949 appeared as soloist under Koussevitzky in his Symphony no.2 "The Age of Anxiety."

3. YEARS OF PATH-BREAKING ACTIVITY: 1951–63. After Koussevitzky died in June 1951, Bernstein became head of the orchestra and conducting departments at the Berkshire Music Center. In the same year he married Felicia Montealegre Cohn, a Chilean actress, and was appointed professor of music at Brandeis University, where he served until 1955. He continued to compose works for the stage: *Trouble in Tahiti*, his first opera (one act), was produced at Brandeis in 1952; *Wonderful Town* opened on Broadway in 1953; and *Candide*, a comic operetta based on Voltaire's novel, was completed in 1956. The musical theater work *West Side Story*, conceived and choreographed by Robbins, was finished in 1957. The last, widely acclaimed as a musical of unprecedented dramatic, choreographic, and musical integrity, was to become extraordinarily successful in the USA and abroad in both stage and film versions. Other works of this period include the *Serenade*, commissioned by the Koussevitzky Foundation, and music for the film *On the Waterfront* (starring Marlon Brando), which was released in 1954.

In 1953 Bernstein became the first American to conduct at La Scala when he directed Callas in Cherubini's *Medea*. And, after serving in 1957 as co-director (with Mitropoulos) of the New York PO, he became in 1958 the first American-born music director of that orchestra, organizing its seasons around themes such as "Keys to the 20th Century," "The Middle European Tradition," "Spring Festival of Theater Music," and "The Gallic Approach." In 1960 he conducted the orchestra in a Mahler festival (Bernstein has since come to be identified with the anguished composer-conductor, and he claims that, while Copland was his musical father, Beethoven and Mahler were his forefathers), and in September 1962 he conducted it at the opening concert of

Philharmonic Hall at Lincoln Center. At the inaugural gala for John F. Kennedy, he presented his *Fanfare I* written specially for the occasion.

During the 1950s and early 1960s Bernstein's international reputation flourished. He was the first to take the New York PO to South America, Israel, Japan, New Zealand, the USSR, Turkey, and several European countries; his first book, *The Joy of Music*, was published in 1959; *West Side Story* was performed widely in the USA and abroad; and he made his début at the Metropolitan Opera conducting Verdi's *Falstaff* (1963). Especially important to Bernstein's career at this time was his recognition of the potential of television for reaching a large audience. After his remarkable success as a lecturer on the television series "Omnibus" in 1954, he began other series in 1958 – the "Young People's Concerts," which ran for 15 years, and two programs for adults, "Lincoln Presents" and "Ford Presents," all with the New York PO. These televised lectures appealed to the musically literate but were also accessible to people with no knowledge of music, and in them Bernstein set the standard for those who would follow him. He has said that his efforts to teach music to his own children (born in 1952, 1955, and 1962) lay behind his success with his television programs.

From the beginning of his career, Bernstein had profited from exposure in the mass media. It was fortunate for him that the concert in which he substituted for Walter was broadcast nationally: others were not. Radio brought him initial recognition, and then print, recordings, and television increased his popularity. He played a central role in the burgeoning of performing arts and the building of cultural centers in the USA, and he transformed the image of the American musician from a somewhat forlorn figure to a remarkable and exciting one.

4. LATER YEARS: FROM 1963. Partly because he was welcome

23. *Excerpt from the autograph vocal score of Bernstein's "Tonight" from "West Side Story," completed 1957*

at the White House and partly because he thought the youthful President shared many of his liberal political views, Bernstein exulted in the brief period of Kennedy's tenure. On 22 November 1963 the President was assassinated. In many public statements made since, Bernstein has returned obsessively to that event, and it marked a turning point in his career. Although negative criticism of his conducting style had begun as early as 1947, it escalated in the early 1960s; in the *New York Times*, the music critic Harold Schonberg consistently ridiculed his gestures, once saying "Bernstein rose vertically, à la Nijinsky, and hovered there a good 15 seconds by the clock." This was also a difficult period for Bernstein as a composer. The widespread use of 12-tone techniques among his contemporaries, including his friend and mentor Aaron Copland, as well as criticisms leveled against him for adhering to tonality undoubtedly undermined his confidence.

In November 1963 Bernstein completed his Symphony no. 3 "Kaddish"; in it he uses serial techniques in the first part and tonal writing in the second, a lullaby. Bernstein explains this alternation of language thus: "the agony expressed with 12-tone music has to give way . . . to tonality and diatonicism." In order to confront 12-tone music, Bernstein arranged for a sabbatical from the orchestra in 1964. He claims that during this period he threw away more 12-tone pieces and bits of pieces than he had written otherwise. At the end of the sabbatical he confirmed his commitment to tonality with the *Chichester Psalms*.

It was not as a composer, however, that Bernstein enjoyed international renown throughout the 1960s and 1970s but as a conductor, and he was invited to conduct on many notable occasions. The Viennese in particular held him in high regard. In 1966 he conducted *Falstaff* at the Staatsoper; in 1969, to celebrate the Staatsoper's centennial, he conducted Beethoven's *Missa solemnis*; and in 1970 (in honor of Beethoven's 200th anniversary) he conducted *Fidelio*. In Berlin Bernstein began filming a series of concerts of Mahler's music with the Vienna PO (1971), and he also led the Vienna Staatsoper and the Vienna PO in performances at La Scala to celebrate the latter's 200th anniversary (1978).

Bernstein remained as music director of the New York PO until 1969, when he retired as conductor laureate. His concerts had attracted capacity audiences, and during his tenure the orchestra made more recordings than ever before. Additional income from television programs brought about unprecedented financial stability. On 15 December 1971 Bernstein returned to conduct his 1000th concert with the New York PO, and he has continued to tour with the orchestra. Despite his reputation as a conservative, Bernstein has conducted numerous nontonal works including more than 40 world premières, among them Carter's Concerto for Orchestra, Babbitt's *Relata II*, Schuller's *Triplum*, and Cage's *Atlas eclipticalis*. In the late 1970s, however, he began to devote himself primarily to the standard repertory, and he has emerged as America's most overtly Romantic conductor; he has refined his approach to Brahms and Schumann, continued to explore Mahler, and in 1983 recorded Wagner's *Tristan und Isolde*.

Bernstein was also in demand as a public speaker, and as Charles Eliot Norton Professor of Poetry at Harvard University (1973), he gave a series of lectures in which he discussed music ranging from Hindu ragas through Mozart to Copland; these were later published as *The Unanswered Question* (1976). All music, Bernstein believes, is rooted in a universal language comparable to Noam Chomsky's universal grammar of speech, and this conviction underlies these lectures (as well as his earlier television series and even his undergraduate thesis); it also illuminates his belief that good music can be found in jazz and popular song as well as in the symphony. His own compositions are an eloquent testimony to this belief. Bernstein's works from the early 1970s include *Mass*, composed for the opening of the Kennedy Center (8 September 1971). He wrote relatively little during the remain-

298

24. *Bernstein conducting the Symphony Orchestra of the Curtis Institute, in a performance of his Symphony no. 2 "The Age of Anxiety" at a concert celebrating the institute's 60th anniversary, 22 April 1984*

der of the decade, perhaps due to his wife's long illness and her death (1978), but in 1980 he began the opera *A Quiet Place* (commissioned by the Houston Opera, La Scala, and the Kennedy Center), which he considers his most important work. Conceived as a sequel to *Trouble in Tahiti*, it was first performed on a program with that opera; later *Trouble in Tahiti* was incorporated into *A Quiet Place* as a flashback. Despite problems of structure and text, the work is bold and ambitious, and contains some of Bernstein's most complex and beautiful music. In 1984 *A Quiet Place* became the first American opera ever to be performed at La Scala. Bernstein was elected to the Academy of the American Academy and Institute of Arts and Letters in 1981 and in 1985 received the Academy's Gold Medal for Music, in recognition of him as a composer. In 1986 he was awarded the *Legion d'honneur* in Paris and in 1987 received the Siemens Prize, the most distinguished music award in Germany.

Bernstein has not, in his music, expanded the boundaries of musical thought; nor has he crystallized a style associated with a past era. What he has done above all is proclaim that an American can be a remarkable and exciting musician. No musician of the 20th century has ranged so wide. As a composer, he has written symphonies, chamber and vocal music, and opera, as well as music for dance, film, and Broadway. As a public personality, he has conducted, written books, appeared on television, lectured at universities, and remained a thoroughly professional pianist. As a conductor, he has not only shown himself a searching interpreter but has also introduced American works around the world. He has in sum achieved an unparalleled renown.

WORKS
(all published unless otherwise stated)

DRAMATIC

The Birds (incidental music, Aristophanes), vv, chamber orch, 1938, unpubd; Cambridge, MA, 21 April 1939

The Peace (incidental music, Aristophanes), chorus, inst ens, 1940, unpubd; Cambridge, MA, 23 May 1941

Fancy Free (ballet, J. Robbins), 1944; New York, 18 April 1944

On the Town (musical, B. Comden, A. Green, Bernstein), orchd H. Kay, Bernstein, 1944; Boston, 13 Dec 1944

Facsimile (ballet, Robbins), 1946; New York, 24 Oct 1946, cond. Bernstein

Peter Pan (incidental music, Bernstein, after J. M. Barrie), orchd Kay, 1950; New York, 24 April 1950, cond. B. Steinberg

Trouble in Tahiti (opera, 1, Bernstein), 1951; Waltham, MA, 12 June 1952, cond. Bernstein

Wonderful Town (musical, Comden, Green, after J. A. Fields, J. Chodorov: My Sister Eileen), orchd D. Walker, 1953; New Haven, 19 Jan 1953

On the Waterfront (film score), 1954; film, dir. E. Kazan, released 28 July

The Lark (incidental music, L. Hellman, after J. Anouilh), 7 solo vv, 1955; Boston, 28 Oct 1955

Salome (incidental music, Wilde), vv, orch, 1955, unpubd

Candide (comic operetta, Hellman, R. Wilþur, J. La Touche, D. Parker, Bernstein, after Voltaire), orchd Kay, Bernstein, 1956, Boston, 29 Oct 1956; rev. 1973 (Wilbur, La Touche, Sondheim, Bernstein, after H. Wheeler, after Voltaire), Brooklyn, NY, 20 Dec 1973, cond. J. Mauceri

West Side Story (musical, Sondheim, after A. Laurents), orchd S. Ramin, I. Kostal, Bernstein, choreographed Robbins, 1957; Washington, DC, 19 Aug 1957

The Firstborn (incidental music, C. Fry), 1958, unpubd; New York, 20 April 1958

Mass (theater piece, S. Schwartz, Bernstein), orchd J. Tunick, Kay, Bernstein, 1971, Washington, DC, 8 Sept 1971, cond. M. Peress; arr. S. Ramin for chamber orch, Los Angeles, 26 Dec 1972, cond. Peress

Dybbuk (ballet), 1974; New York, 16 May 1974, cond. Bernstein

By Bernstein (revue) [based on unpubd and withdrawn theater songs], 1975, withdrawn; New York, 23 Nov 1975

1600 Pennsylvania Avenue (musical, A. J. Lerner), orchd Ramin, Kay, 1976; Philadelphia, 24 Feb 1976

A Quiet Place (opera, 1, S. Wadsworth), 1983, Houston, 17 June 1983, cond. J. De Main; rev. 1984 in 3 acts, incl. Trouble in Tahiti

ORCHESTRAL

Fancy Free, suite [based on ballet], 1944; Pittsburgh, 14 Jan 1945, Pittsburgh SO, cond. Bernstein

On the Town, 3 dance episodes [based on musical], 1945, San Francisco, 13 Feb 1946, San Francisco SO, cond. Bernstein; transcr. concert band

Facsimile, choreographic essay [based on ballet], 1946; Poughkeepsie, NY, 5 March 1947, Rochester PO, cond. Bernstein

Symphony no.2 "The Age of Anxiety," after Auden, pf, orch, 1949, Boston, 8 April 1949, Boston SO, cond. Koussevitzky; rev. 1965

Prelude, Fugue and Riffs, cl, jazz ens, 1949, ABC television, 16 Oct 1955, cond. B. Goodman; choreographed J. Clifford, New York, 15 May 1969

Serenade [after Plato: Symposium], vn, str, harp, perc, 1954; Venice, Italy, 12 Sept 1954, I. Stern, Israel PO, cond. Bernstein

On the Waterfront, sym. suite [based on film score], 1955; Lenox, MA, 11 Aug 1955, Boston SO, cond. Bernstein

West Side Story, sym. dances [based on musical], 1960; New York, 13 Feb 1961, New York PO, cond. Foss

Fanfare I [for inauguration of J. F. Kennedy], 1961; Washington, DC, 19 Jan 1961, cond. Bernstein

Fanfare II [for 25th anniversary of the High School of Music and Art], 1961; New York, 24 March 1961, cond. Richter

Two Meditations from Mass, 1971; Austin, TX, 31 Oct 1971, cond. Peress

Meditation III from Mass, 1972, withdrawn; Jerusalem, 21 May 1972, Israel PO, cond. Bernstein

Dybbuk Suite nos.1–2 (Dybbuk Variations) [based on ballet], 1974; no.1, Auckland, New Zealand, 16 Aug 1974, cond. Bernstein; no.2, New York, 17 April 1977, cond. Bernstein

Three Meditations from Mass, vc, orch, 1977, arr. vc, pf, 1978; Washington, DC, 11 Oct 1977, Rostropovich, National SO, cond. Bernstein

Slava!, ov., 1977; Washington, DC, 11 Oct 1977, National SO, cond. Rostropovich

CBS Music, 1977; pts.1 and 5, CBS television, 1 April 1978

Divertimento, 1980; Boston, 25 Sept 1980, cond. S. Ozawa

A Musical Toast, 1980; New York, 11 Oct 1980, cond. Z. Mehta

Halil, nocturne, fl, str, perc, 1981; Jerusalem, 23 May 1981, cond. Bernstein

CHORAL AND VOCAL

Symphony no.1 "Jeremiah" (Bible), Mez, orch, 1942; Pittsburgh, 28 Jan 1944, Pittsburgh SO, cond. Bernstein

302

Hashkivenu (Heb. liturgy), T, chorus, org, 1945; New York, 11 May 1954, cond. M. Helfman

Yidgal (Heb. liturgy), chorus, pf, 1950

Harvard Choruses (Lerner): Dedication, Lonely Men of Harvard, 1957; New York, 7 March 1957, cond. G. W. Woodworth

Symphony no.3 "Kaddish" (Heb. liturgy, Bernstein), S, speaker, chorus, boys' chorus, orch, 1963, Tel Aviv, 10 Dec 1963, Israel PO, cond. Bernstein; rev. 1977, Mainz, Germany, 25 Aug 1977, cond. Bernstein

Chichester Psalms (Bible), Tr, chorus, orch, 1965; New York, 15 July 1965, J. Bogart, Camerata Singers, New York PO, cond. Bernstein

Warm-up, mixed chorus, 1970 [incorporated into Mass]

A Little Norton Lecture (Cummings), male vv, 1973, unpubd, arr. as no.8 in Songfest; Cambridge, MA, 1973

Songfest: To the Poem (F. O'Hara), The Pennycandy Store beyond the El (L. Ferlinghetti), A Julia de Burgos (J. de Burgos), To What you Said (Whitman), I, too, Sing America (L. Hughes), Okay "Negroes" (J. Jordan), To my Dear and Loving Husband (A. Bradstreet), Storyette H. M. (G. Stein), If you can't eat you got to (Cummings), Music I Heard with You (C. Aiken), Zizi's Lament (G. Corso), What Lips my Lips have Kissed (Millay), Israfel (Poe), 6 solo vv, orch, 1977; Washington, DC, 11 Oct 1977, National SO, cond. Bernstein

Olympic Hymn (G. Kunert), chorus, orch, 1981; Baden-Baden, Germany, 23 Sept 1981

Arrs.: Simchu Na (Heb. folksong), SATB, pf, 1947; Reena (Heb. folksong), chorus, orch, 1947, unpubd

CHAMBER

Piano Trio, 1937, unpubd

Music for Two Pianos, 1937, unpubd [incl. in On the Town]; Brookline, MA, 12 June 1938

Piano Sonata, 1938, unpubd

Music for the Dance, nos.1 and 2, 1938, unpubd [incl. in On the Town]; Brookline, 12 June 1938

Scenes from the City of Sin, pf 4 hands, 1939, unpubd

Violin Sonata, 1940, unpubd

Four Studies, 2 cl, 2 bn, pf, c1940, unpubd; radio broadcast, Philadelphia, 1940

Clarinet Sonata, 1941–2; Boston, 21 April 1942

Seven Anniversaries, pf, 1943; Boston, 14 May 1944

Four Anniversaries, pf, 1948; Cleveland, 1 Oct 1948
Brass Music, tpt, hn, trbn, tuba, pf, 1948; New York, 8 April 1959
Five Anniversaries, pf, 1954
Shivaree, brass, perc, 1969 [incorporated into Mass]; New York, 28 Sept 1970
Touches, pf, 1981
Arr. Copland: El salón México, pf/2 pf; Boston, 18 Nov 1941

SOLO VOCAL
(all with pf acc.)

Psalm cxlviii, 1932
I Hate Music (Bernstein), song cycle: My Name is Barbara, Jupiter Has Seven
    Moons, I Hate Music, A Big Indian and a Little Indian, I'm a Person Too,
    1943; Lenox, MA, 24 Aug 1943
Lamentation, 1943 [arr. of 3rd movt of Sym. no.1 "Jeremiah"]
Afterthought (Bernstein), 1945, withdrawn; New York, 24 Oct 1948
La bonne cuisine (4 recipes, Bernstein), 1947; New York, 10 Oct 1948
Two Love Songs (Rilke): Extinguish my eyes, When my soul touches yours,
    1949; New York, 13 March 1963
Silhouette (Galilee) (Bernstein), 1951; Washington, DC, 13 Feb 1955
On the Waterfront (La Touche), 1954, withdrawn
Get Hep! (Bernstein), 1955, withdrawn
So Pretty (Comden, Green), 1968; New York, 21 Jan 1968
Mad Woman of Central Park West, My New Friends, Up! Up! Up!, 1979;
    Buffalo, NY, 6 April 1979
Piccola serenata, 1979; Salzburg, Austria, 27 Aug 1979

Principal publishers: Amberson, Harms, Jalni

WRITINGS
The Joy of Music (New York, 1959)
Young People's Concerts for Reading and Listening (New York, 1962, rev. and
    enlarged 2/1970)
The Infinite Variety of Music (New York, 1966)
The Unanswered Question (Cambridge, MA, 1976)
Findings (New York, 1982)

BIBLIOGRAPHY

EwenD

P. Gradenwitz: "Leonard Bernstein," *MR*, x (1949), 191

W. Hamilton: "On the Waterfront," *Film Music*, xiv/1 (1954), 3

D. Drew: "Leonard Bernstein: *Wonderful Town*," *Score*, no.12 (1955), 77

H. Keller: "On the Waterfront," *Score*, no.12 (1955), 81

H. C. Schonberg: "New Job for the Protean Mr. Bernstein," *New York Times Magazine* (22 Dec 1957), 14, 31

H. Stoddard: *Symphony Conductors of the U.S.A.* (New York, 1957), 26

D. Gow: "Leonard Bernstein, Musician of Many Talents," *MT*, ci (1960), 427

J. Briggs: *Leonard Bernstein, the Man, his Work, and his World* (Cleveland, 1961)

A. Holde: *Leonard Bernstein* (Berlin, 1961)

J. Gottlieb: *The Music of Leonard Bernstein: a Study of Melodic Manipulations* (diss., U. of Illinois, 1964)

——: "The Choral Music of Leonard Bernstein, Reflections of Theater and Liturgy," *American Choral Review*, x (1968), 156

J. Gruen: *The Private World of Leonard Bernstein* (New York, 1968)

W. W. Tromble: *The American Intellectual and Music: an Analysis of the Writings of Suzanne K. Langer, Paul Henry Lang, Jacques Barzun, John Dewey, and Leonard Bernstein – with Implications for Music Education* (diss., U. of Michigan, 1968)

E. Ames: *A Wind from the West: Bernstein and the New York Philharmonic Abroad* (Boston, 1970)

M. Cone: *Leonard Bernstein* (New York, 1970)

G. Jackson: "*West Side Story*: Thema, Grundhaltung und Aussage," *Maske und Kothurn*, xvi (1970), 97

D. Wooldridge: *Conductor's World* (New York, 1970), 310

H. Berlinski: "Bernstein's Mass," *Sacred Music*, xcix/1 (1972), 3

J. Gruen: "In Love with the Stage," *Opera News*, xxxvii/3 (1972), 16

E. Salzman: "Quo vadis Leonard Bernstein?," *Stereo Review*, xxviii/5 (1972) 56

N. Goemanne: "Open Forum: the Controversial Bernstein Mass: Another Point of View," *Sacred Music*, c/1 (1973), 33

A. Pearlmutter: "Bernstein's Mass Revisited: a Guide to Using a Contemporary Work to Teach Music Concepts," *MEJ*, lxi/1 (1974), 34

J. W. Weber: *Leonard Bernstein* (Utica, NY, 1975) [discography]

R. Chesterman: "Leonard Bernstein in Conversation with Robert Chesterman," *Conversations with Conductors* (Totowa, NJ, 1976), 53, 69

G. Gottwald: "Leonard Bernsteins Messe oder der Konstruktion der Blasphemie," *Melos/NZM*, ii (1976) 281

J. Ardoin: "Leonard Bernstein at Sixty," *HiFi/MusAm*, xxviii/8 (1978), 53

P. Davis: "Bernstein as Symphonist," *New York Times* (26 Nov 1978), §II, 17

J. Gottlieb: *Leonard Bernstein: a Complete Catalogue of his Works* (New York, 1978)

A. Keiler: "Bernstein's *The Unanswered Question* and Problems of Musical Competence," *MQ*, lxiv (1978), 195

J. Gottlieb: "Symbols of Faith in the Music of Leonard Bernstein," *MQ*, lxvi (1980), 287

J. Hiemenz: "Bernstein on Television: Pros and Cons," *HiFi/MusAm*, xxx/4 (1980), 14

B. Bernstein: "Personal History: Family Matters," *New Yorker*, lviii (22 March 1982), 53, (29 March 1982), 58; repr. as *Family Matters* (New York, 1982)

H. Matheopoulos: *Maestro: Encounters with Conductors of Today* (London, 1982), 3

P. Robinson: *Bernstein* (New York, 1982)

U. Schneider: "Die Wiedergeburt der Musik aus dem Geist des Dreiklangs – Leonard Bernstein als verbaler Musikdeuter," *HiFi Stereophonie*, xxi/1 (1982), 56

P. Gradenwitz: *Leonard Bernstein* (Zurich, 1984)

J. W. Moore: *A Study of Tonality in Selected Works by Leonard Bernstein* (diss., Florida State U., 1984)

G. De Sesa: *A Comparison between Descriptive Analysis of Leonard Bernstein's "Mass" and the Musical Implications of the Critical Evaluation Thereof* (diss., New York U., 1985)

S. Lipman: "Lenny on our Minds," *New Criterion*, iii/10 (1985), 1

A. J. Pearlmutter: *Leonard Bernstein's "Dybbuk": an Analysis including Historical, Religious, and Literary Perspectives of Hasidic Life and Lore* (diss., Peabody Conservatory, 1985)

J. Rockwell: "Bernstein Triumphant," *New York Times Magazine* (31 Aug 1986), 14

D. Ewen: *American Songwriters* (New York, 1987)

J. Peyser: *Bernstein: a Biography* (New York, 1987)

Index